Two Drifters
OFF TO SEE THE WORLD

To Dick & Nancy:
Happy trails wherever you may go.

Helen H. Rogers

Two Drifters
OFF TO SEE THE WORLD

Herb Keyser

SUNBELT EAKIN   Austin, Texas

PREVIOUS BOOKS BY THE AUTHOR:
Women Under the Knife
Prescription for Disaster: Healthcare in America

For CIP
information,
please access:
www.loc.gov

FIRST EDITION
Copyright © 2002
By Herb Keyser
Published in the U.S.A.
By Sunbelt Eakin Press
A Division of Sunbelt Media, Inc.
P.O. Drawer 90159
Austin, Texas 78709-0159
email: sales@eakinpress.com
website: www.eakinpress.com
ALL RIGHTS RESERVED.
1 2 3 4 5 6 7 8 9
1-57168-660-6

*To all the wonderful friends
who shared so many of our experiences during this year
and brought such great joy and laughter,
which I hope will be transmitted to our readers.
No one could have had better traveling buddies.*

Acknowledgments

In *Two Drifters* I have taken a sharp turn away from all my previous literary efforts. The change could never have been accomplished without the gracious help of so many others.

I wish to thank with deep gratitude:

My dear, bright, and beautiful wife Barbara, who was my stalwart companion throughout the marvelous year covered in this book. She also functioned as a continuous reviewer and advisor in my daily writing of our adventures.

Two special friends and tough editors, Sondra Sugerman and Judy Palans, who took my words and moved them around to make some sense of my meager effort. Without them *Two Drifters* would have drifted forever.

David Meltzer and Bernard Lifschutz, who provided the photographic talent to produce the pictures on the front and back covers.

Virginia Messer, who supervised all the production of the book including the design of the cover.

Angela Buckley, my editor at Eakin, who made certain that the final product was free of errors—especially the spelling of words from other languages.

Amber Stanfield, who designed and typeset the book.

The huge number of literary agents and publishers, many of whom ... some of whom ... a few of whom gave me a great deal of encouragement in their perpetual rejection of my manuscript.

And finally to Ed and Charlene Eakin, who believed enough in me to publish *Two Drifters, Off to See the World*. I can never thank them sufficiently.

Preface

I'm not exactly certain how it all happened, but it unquestionably was not a grand plan that had been developing over many years of fantasies.

Frankly, I'd like to blame Barbara for it. You see, it was she who frequently would say, "Wouldn't it be nice to stay in one place for a longer period of time, and get to feel more like residents than tourists?"

Then again, Barbara would definitely blame me, based on a totally different interpretation of the origin of this trip. She claims that all she has to do is say, "wouldn't something be nice," in an off-the-cuff manner, and I will take it to mean she absolutely craves it. That might apply to something for our house or a piece of jewelry, either of which might suddenly appear after her innocuous statement. In this case it was a trip.

Travel was hardly a new experience for us, and the same could be said for writing. Over a number of years I had written prodigiously whenever we went abroad. It provided a method of telling others about our trips and a memory of them for us as well.

Taking her comment to be the gospel, I immediately began planning an adventure which would last almost a year.

In order to finance this adventure, on three occasions we returned to the United States for me to work for about three weeks and earn some money. The result is that the book is divided into four chapters, each describing approximately seven weeks of travel in between the trips back home.

From the moment the decision was made to write about our travels, it occurred to me that in every person's life, traveling or at home in New York, San Antonio, or in the smallest towns in rural America, there are funny incidents that happen to us almost every day. We experience them and laugh. Sometimes we laugh our heads off, and forget them until the next funny incident the next day, or even the same day.

The commitment was a simple one. Every night, when all the day's activities were done, regardless of how late it might be, I would sit down at my computer and write. I knew that by the next day everything would be forgotten. It would be more of a travelogue than a travel guide.

Over a period of just a few months the entire itinerary was planned. We decided to base ourselves in France and take trips all over Europe from there. It would be the adventure of a lifetime. We ended up visiting seven countries and driving 15,000 miles, as well as using planes, trains, and boats. We even kept within our budget. Well, it was almost within our budget.

In the process my novel was completed and this book as well. It is a compilation of all the wonderful experiences I shared with my darling wife Barbara. I hope, as they are shared with you, they bring the same smiles and laughter to you that they brought to us at the time.

Though it was in no way meant to be a guide book there are numerous tips about places to go, things to see, and wonderful food to eat. Mainly you will read of the funny adventures of two not-so-young Americans in love, and their meetings with their friends, as they go traveling through Europe for eight months.

It was a year that Barbara and I would not trade for anything, so we're not giving it to you. We're just sharing it.

Bon voyage!

Part One

DRIFTING THROUGH
France, Greece, and Turkey

Having left at 11:30 A.M. yesterday, we arrived in Marseille's airport shortly after noon. That would be a little after 5:00 A.M., San Antonio time. In her state of utter fatigue, Barbara wasn't thrilled with my plan. I informed her it was important to go into Marseille to exchange traveler's checks for francs in order to pay our French landlord. Barbara can't sleep on planes, so in a stupor, and annoyed, she told me about Marseille.

"I saw the movies in the Fifties. Yes, I did! The streets will be lined with muscular men in tight-fitting, black-and-white striped knit shirts. Yes! And there will be dark streets where they're dancing roughly with scantily clad women. And berets will be on their heads, and stumps of cigarettes will hang out of the sides of their mouths. Even now I can hear the slow, seductive French music in the background."

With her eyes glazed over I was not about to cross her.

"I agree completely! After all, it's just like home in San Antonio where everyone rides the streets on horseback, having just come into town to get supplies for their ranches, preparing for the next battle with the Comanche Indians."

We drove into the *vieux village* (the old town), where hundreds of beautiful private sailing boats were moored. On the quai we saw that last thing we wanted to experience here in France, a restaurant serving Tex-Mex food.

Unfortunately, the banks were closed for lunch. But I noted that the exchange rate was 4.9 francs to the dollar. Before heading for our rented home in Entrechaux we stopped in Vaison-la-Romaine, the largest town near Entrechaux, to resolve our cash problem, and again we were unsuccessful. The bank didn't change money in the afternoon. Nevertheless, we received a significant piece of information. The exchange rate there was 4.8 francs per dollar. How lucky can you get? I had driven ninety miles, and already we had lost 2 percent of our money!

A driving rainstorm had accompanied us during the entire trip. Our host was graciously waiting for us at the house, and we all got thoroughly soaked carrying in our eleven pieces of luggage. That might seem excessive, but to be fair, four of them were small carry-on pieces, three of which were specifically for writing, not clothing. Barbara couldn't be blamed. Anyway, we were going to be gone for a long while.

Philippe, our host, had lunch waiting for us. God bless Barbara, though her figure is superb, and her weight just right, she's never been too tired to eat. We had prosciutto, lasagna, French bread, cheese, wine, and figs. Barbara ate her share ... and some of mine.

By the end of the meal Barbara was getting awfully woozy. She staggered up to the bedroom, which was littered with suitcases, and collapsed on the bed. Five hours later, at 10:00 in the evening, she hadn't been heard from.

Philippe, having decided to spend the night in the second bedroom before returning to Paris in the morning, made dinner at about 8:30. I had decided to wait for Barbara, but it wasn't working out. I wanted to lie down, but wasn't certain what I'd do when the inevitable occurred. There was no doubt in my mind that sometime, around 4:00 in the morning, she was going to roll over and say, "I'm starving." The problem was that Entrechaux is only about three city blocks long, with no all-night restaurants.

Meanwhile, getting organized for an eight-month period of writing, I hit the usual snags one finds in another country. The phone was an old pulse ringer, not a tone phone. Every electronic device I hooked into, from France to back home in the U.S., required a tone phone. Fortunately, Philippe found one for me. Having fussed with the phones for a while, I began getting quite tired. Jet lag was hitting me, like it had earlier hit Barbara.

I decided, *I'll get more organized tomorrow.*

* * *

My prediction for Barbara to wake up hungry was not exactly accurate. As I quietly tiptoed into our bedroom, shortly after 11:00 A.M., Barbara turned over and mumbled, "I'm hungry." Luckily, Philippe had left some food for us. An omelet made with vegetables and prosciutto was still in the kitchen. I warmed the omelet, and Barbara devoured it with bread. The next thing I knew, she was sound asleep again.

Her circadian clock remained out of order, and she later told me she awoke again around 3:00 and couldn't get back to sleep.

My first project in the morning was the telephone. Telephone access to the United States was an important matter, since we were facing months away from home. I had arranged with a company in the United States to utilize a service which significantly decreased the cost of intercontinental calls. That was one of the functions that could only be handled by a tone phone. I knew the system wouldn't be functioning for another day, so I decided I would temporarily utilize one of the major long-distance companies to call my answering machine back home for messages. I called the company and asked for the charges.

"That will be $4.35 for the first minute and $1.25 for each minute after that!"

A funny thought occurred to me. *My answering machine doesn't say that many interesting things. I can listen to a great CD and it will cost me a lot less money.*

I opted to wait until the new system was in operation.

I still had to resolve the problem of obtaining francs to pay Philippe. I told him of my dismay in finding such a bad exchange rate locally. He gave me the typical French look, which means "no problem," and we went to the bank. Over the next eight months I would often hear Europeans say lyrically, "No problem," even if there might be one.

When we arrived at the bank Philippe said to the clerk, *"Je suis un client."* He was a customer, possibly of major proportions. They gave me a rate even better than what was available in Marseille. Once again I learned a cardinal rule. No matter where you are, it pays to know the right people. In my next life I'm going to know somebody connected with everything. Then I'll get great seats at the tennis matches, instead of on the top row.

As an initial decision, Barbara and I agreed to spend the first two weeks leisurely finding our way in the area, scouting out restaurants and making plans for the upcoming months, pressure free. There was much time to be spent in Provence over the year, and so many exciting places to see, it seemed a good idea to pace ourselves.

I spent the morning learning everything about the house, from the heating system to the locks, the alarm system, the housekeeper, the plumber, and even the secret hidden safe. Philippe and I went off to the baker, the laundry, the shoemaker, the *tabac* (the tobacconist's shop, where newspapers could be purchased), and the garage for bottled gas for the stove, and got the general lay of the land in the local community.

Barbara and I then made our first find of the trip. On the advice of Philippe we took a back country road to another, even smaller, road. It led to a charming little inn and restaurant called Auberge d'Anaïs. The restaurant's official address is Entrechaux, but it's on the way to St. Marcellin, an adjacent town just five minutes away. The restaurant was in the middle of vineyards where men were busily cutting grapes. We had arrived at harvest time in Provence. For about $10 each, we had a green salad with sliced tomatoes and onions and olives and a lovely dressing. That was followed by what our grandmothers would call a pot roast with potatoes in a rich brown sauce, typical of country French, and of course a glass of wine. For dessert they served lemon tarts, which in France are usually something special and not to be missed. We began to realize that we could, if we chose our restaurants wisely, eat not only better but more cheaply than back home.

The afternoon was spent in the market buying food and staples and trying our best to make ourselves understood as we asked questions in French.

* * *

Philippe had told us about the tennis court, but we were thrilled to find it so close to the house. This municipal court was almost always empty, except on weekends.

Over the course of the upcoming months Barbara and I would play tennis or take long walks every day the weather was not inclement. I did fine with the walking, but when it came to tennis, Barbara would win most of the time. Her will to win is fierce.

From the tennis court, we could see a medieval French castle, sitting immediately above the house we were renting. Some of the walls appeared to be completely gone. We planned at some later time to climb up and have a closer look.

Every morning, as part of my normal daily routine, I was up early, taking the ten-minute car ride to Vaison to pick up the *International Herald Tribune*. It was our only source for news. There was no English-language television, and trying to understand the newscasters on French television was impossible for us, as they spoke so rapidly.

My first day in town I picked up a baguette at the bakery, wandered over to the tourist office to get information about local concerts, and purchased some tennis balls. Then, arming myself with all the courage I could muster, I made my way to the last stop, an electronics shop. There I would face a major challenge to my language skills.

I had been hoping to keep in touch with friends and working responsibilities through e-mail. Before leaving home I had a modem installed, which in itself took great motivation, since I had always believed my computer was nothing more than a word processor. I had no interest in the Internet, e-mail, or computer games. But Barbara kept encouraging me. She wanted us to get involved in this exciting new world. I knew she was wrong. We were definitely too old for all this modern stuff with disclaimers on them. "Not for Herb Keyser's generation!" Nevertheless, I took the plunge.

In our temporary home in Entrechaux I found a remarkable thing. The French and Americans were not speaking to each other. They had separately decided on the type of wall jacks they would use for telephones ... and they were not the same. Now I had all the equipment. I just couldn't plug it in. That's what led me to the electronics store.

I attempted in my very poor French to explain my problem. I had already made many language mistakes on this trip. The previous day at the lovely small country restaurant where we had lunch, a pitcher of water had been left on the table, but no glasses. When the waitress came over I forgot I wasn't in the U.S. and asked for a glass. She smiled, and returned with a bucket of ice. The French word for ice is *glace*. After a while I made myself clearer and obtained the *verre* I should have asked for in the first place.

The electronics clerk listened to my explanation of the problem. He nodded knowingly, and brought me an adapter which would enable me to insert my United States electric plug into a French electric socket. You see, they have different electric outlets as well. But I had known that before I came and already had those adapters. Unfortunately, I had great difficulty trying to clarify that my problem was the phone wire, not the electric cord. At last I made myself clear and he told me, *"Je n'ai pas une fiche comme ça."* He didn't have that type of equipment. But he did refer me to a shop in Orange.

We got to Orange the following day, but no one at that shop spoke English either. After my slowly spoken request in French, their first response was negative. But after prolonged explanations, wires and adapters were assembled, and *voilà*, they worked.

After our success we lunched in Vaison-la-Romaine, and disproved the old canard that good food in France is expensive. Including wine, tax, and tip, *l'addition*, "the bill" in French, was only $25 per person. It began with a *surprise*, usually a small hors d'oeuvre that isn't on the menu. It was a plate of baby clams that were a challenge to dig out of the shell. Mostly it was a little game to play while awaiting a great meal over a glass of wine.

As an appetizer Barbara had a country pâté marbled with *tapenade*. I had a warm salad of greens with a section of tomato in the center and a round of goat cheese. The tomato and goat cheese were baked together and scrumptious.

As our main course we had sliced breast of duckling on a bed of mashed potatoes with a delicious brown sauce. Then they served *fromage blanc* (a white cheese similar to thick yogurt) with honey. We've had it at other restaurants in France with a fruit *coulis* or with sugar sprinkled on the top.

For dessert they served a pear in caramel sauce and pear ice cream in a cookie-dough cup. This superb restaurant, Le Brin d'Olivier, is operated by a charming young couple with the wife working as the chef and her husband serving out front.

* * *

In this first week in October the odor of crushed grapes being harvested strongly permeated the air throughout Provence. The roads were filled with an army of motorized carts, going much slower than normal traffic, and overflowing with picked grapes. We decided to search out a winery where we could watch the crushing. At each request we were told no observers were allowed in for tours of the facilities. Finally, we drove to Châteauneuf-du-Pape, a town in Provence with many wineries. At the tourist office we were advised that only one winery, Beaurenard, would allow us in to watch them work. We walked the short distance from the tourist center to the winery, where we were graciously shown the process. It was very generous of them during their busiest time of the year.

Our next goal for the day was to go to Avignon to see a new movie, winner of the Cannes film festival, and complete a chore. We had heard from English-speaking friends, living in France, that going to the movies was an easy pastime. The era of English-language films dubbed in French had gone by the wayside. American films are primarily seen in the original English with French subtitles, enabling us to see anything we'd like.

Our chore on this day was to buy a compact-disc player in order to have music in the house. Barbara recalled seeing billboard ads for what the French call a *hypermarché*, or "superstore," Leclerc. In Avignon signs directed us to the store in a distant suburb. After a long drive beyond Avignon, we found the store and a CD player to our liking. Best of all it had a French plug. Then we returned to Avignon to see the film.

Driving back into Avignon there it was, in front of our eyes, another Leclerc store, right in the center of town.

We spent the next hour searching for the theatre, "Utopia." Misunderstood because of our language weakness, we were directed to two other theatres before finding the correct one. Unfortunately, the film had started five minutes before we arrived and the doors were locked. At least now we knew where the theatre was located, so we laughed off our minor misadventure and decided we would see the picture another day.

On our way home we passed through Carpentras. And, lo and behold, there was another Leclerc outlet, even closer to our house. That would have made it much too easy.

A dinner at home, listening to CDs on our new player, even having missed the movie, ended the day beautifully in Provence for two drifters.

* * *

One morning we drove to Gordes through dramatic hills, ravines, and valleys. The Provençal landscape is exquisite. On arriving at this hilltop village we followed a hike described in a travel guide, ending in the center of town where a fair was taking place. Visiting outdoor fairs and markets became one of our favorite pastimes.

Flashback

The story of our attachment to France is quite special. Barbara and I had been there twice before, once in Paris, and once in Provence. While in Provence we visited a couple who had moved there from the United States a number of years previously, Barbara and Frank Alweis. They had both been teachers, and Frank was an author, as well. In their new life in Provence, they shared music, painting, weaving, and writing. Barbara Alweis was the sister of an old friend of my wife, Barbara.

One afternoon in San Antonio I received a call from a gentleman speaking perfect English with a French accent. He had been given our name by the Alweises because he was in nearby Austin working on a book. I invited him to spend a few days with us.

Bruno, our new French friend, was a former industrialist, turned author. He lives in Fontainebleau and has an apartment in Paris, as well as a home in a small, charming town in Provence, Gigondas. It was the first of several visits Bruno made to San Antonio. As it turned out he came from quite a family. His father was a curator at the Louvre. A sister is an internationally known harpsichordist. And a brother is in the Paris Symphony.

Bruno invited us to stay at his home in Provence, which was the beginning of our adventures in the south of France. I recall very well our first visit. The arrangement was that we would arrive in Paris, pick up a rental car, and drive to Fontainebleau. There we would get a key for Bruno's house in Provence and be on our way to Lyon, staying overnight before heading for Gigondas. But when we arrived at Orly airport Bruno was waiting for us like a mother hen, concerned we might get lost. He led us to Fontainebleau, served lunch, and sent us on our way. His kindness was above and beyond the call of duty.

Shortly after arriving at our hotel in Lyon, Bruno's son, Dominique, and his girlfriend, both students in Lyon, came to meet us. We went out to dinner at a wonderful restaurant, Le Champier. I recall most vividly how when Dominique drove us to the restaurant he was fiddling under the dashboard before exiting the car. I asked what he was carrying.

"Oh! It's just the car radio. There's no way I would leave it in the car in Lyon."

The following afternoon we were on our way to Carpentras. As prearranged, the Alweises met us on the steps of a church and led us to our new temporary home. I remember they brought a picnic basket of pâté, cheese, fruit, and wine which the four of us shared for dinner. It was typical of the kindness we have so often found in our travels.

When we returned several years later we were intelligent enough to manage getting into the house all by ourselves without a guide— almost, that is. We had the key and entered easily enough, but had forgotten about the burglar alarm. That brought out the local policeman. He was a charming fellow in a sweatshirt and jeans.

I said, in order to avoid the expected incarceration for breaking and entering, "Amis de Monsieur et Madame Verlet."

We got a great big smile and a "Hello." That's what I call great police protection.

The house was a sixteenth-century, three-story stone building with wonderful gray-blue shutters on all the windows. Originally the *presbytère* (residence) of an ancient church, it was a French country home in feeling and furnishings, with heavy natural log beams on high plaster ceilings. The rooms were filled with pictures of ancestors and there were shelves of books wherever the eye could turn. A charming courtyard garden was where Barbara and I frequently had lunch. On the third floor a large room looked out for miles onto rolling hills of farms and vineyards. It was the perfect location for me to work on my novel.

One evening we heard a choir of fifty seniors in a church in Vaison. Between the French songs they sang "We Shall Overcome" in English. But the pièce de resistance brought down the house: they closed with "Home on the Range" in French.

During that trip we had our first exposure to the breathtaking markets held in different towns. Every Friday we went to the market in Carpentras. And, on more than one occasion, we traveled to L'Isle-sur-la-Sorgue on a Sunday. That town, which I will describe later, is built on canals. It remains one of the most charming in all of Provence.

The home of Bruno, and his wife Hélène, is near a small range of mountains, more properly described as hills, called the Dentelles of Montmirail. They could be seen clearly from the roadway every time we left the house. As their name indicates, they look like small, sharp teeth projecting into the sky, biting into the beautiful blue and nibbling on the clouds. During our two stays in Gigondas, on many days we walked up the sides of the Dentelles, where there were lovely terraced vineyards.

On one of our hikes to the Dentelles we noticed a small dirt road off the parking area. We would normally park there and begin walking. I suggested, on this occasion, we drive down the road to see where it would take us. It was narrow and curving and became more and more heavily covered with large rocks. Oh! Did I fail to mention at the beginning of this road there was a sign? But who understands French!

As we drove farther we found ourselves in the middle of a vineyard. Obviously we were on a road for trucks coming and going from the fields. Finally, after an exciting but treacherous drive, we came to the buildings of the vineyard. A few yards forward was a beautiful chateau, with flowers and fountains. A sign said "Hôtel Montmirail." We parked at the roadside and walked through iron gates and into the courtyard. Halfway up to the building someone called to us. We turned, and in French they asked us what we wanted.

"Information," we answered—with a French accent, of course.

He threw up his hands and asked what we wanted to know.

"Information about the hotel."

He led us back to the gate we had come through and pointed to a small, dilapidated building. "*C'est l'hôtel!*"

We quietly left. The sign we had originally passed apparently said, "No Entry."

Present

At the Vaison market there was barely a stand at which Barbara did not let out a guttural sound of amazement at the beauty of the displayed foods. There were tables of thirty different types of olives and tapenades, and traveling cheese shops with hundreds of varieties. We were told that an English statesman once said of France, "How can one trust the government of a country where they can't decide between three hundred cheeses?"

The produce stands, like works of art, exquisitely blossomed from the gardens.

There were traveling butcher shops and fish markets. Breads, pastries, candies, and everything that could tempt one's palate was there to behold.

Vendors sold chickens, geese, guinea hens, and pigeons cooked on rotating skewers in vehicles fitted with ovens. Each of ten skewers had eight of the fowl, and on a large track they passed over the flames continuously until they were cooked. There were potatoes beneath the skewers, and the fat and juices dripped off the birds onto them.

There were trucks with wood-burning pizza ovens and traveling Oriental-food merchants selling spring rolls and crab rolls which were tasty beyond words.

Even larger areas of the market were occupied by dealers of clothing, fabrics, table coverings, hardware, antiques, drug store items, soaps, and on and on and on.

We circled several times, and each time we saw something we had missed previously. Around noon the merchants were closing, and we took our purchases home for lunch. Later in the day we drove back through Vaison. There was not the slightest evidence a market had been there. No paper, trash, or garbage was on the streets.

* * *

In the house we were occupying there was a charming set of pottery. Barbara had seen some of it in shops in Avignon, where it was quite expensive. When we asked our host about it, he told us that his pottery was very inexpensive. They were made by a potter in a nearby town and were all seconds. Barbara and I had a destination to seek out.

The name of the town is Dieulefit. The literal translation is "God made it." We reached it by going through Nyons and following D538. The road signs were wonderfully clear. They provided directions by names of the towns and road numbers. The views on the one-hour ride to Dieulefit, like so many in Provence, were breathtaking.

Dieulefit is a pottery center with many shops. As directed, we went to the Milon factory. A large sign could not be missed when entering town from the south. But Barbara had decisions to make. The first was, "How does one carry this back?" Shipping costs would make the price prohibitive. The second question was, "What do I really need?" We bought some small items and the last of five soup bowls in a style Barbara really loved. She couldn't resist because the proprietor discounted the bowls, the last of that style.

* * *

One morning, with plans for a busy day, I heard no sounds from Barbara, so I went to see how she was doing in her preparations for leaving. I found her in the bathroom with her hand bleeding. She had dropped a mirror, broken it, and cut herself cleaning up the pieces. Not being superstitious, I disregarded the nonsense of seven years of bad luck. But I didn't discount the possibility that it could mess up at least one little day.

The first part of the plan involved a drive of more than one hour, to a town called Paradou. I was planning lunch at Bistro du Paradou, where we had once dined. It was a quirky sort of restaurant with no menu, where the owner brought the day's preparation. It was past 1:00 P.M. when we reached St. Rémy, about fifteen minutes shy of Paradou. Barbara was getting awfully hungry. Her hypoglycemia was beginning to rear its head. The one thing that can make her mean is hunger. She foresaw the possibility the restaurant would no longer be serving when we arrived, while I foresaw a bad day if we got there and couldn't eat. We decided to stay in St. Rémy for lunch and take no chances.

Checking the Michelin guide, we found three restaurants listed. The first was closed, serving dinner only. The second looked quite charming. But, although they did serve lunch, for some unknown reason it was closed that day. It was getting close to 1:30 P.M. when we arrived at the third choice. That one, as it turned out, was always closed on Wednesdays. Barbara's blood sugar was falling, and I was in deep trouble.

Across the street from the third restaurant stood a shabby little place that looked like half bar, half three-table restaurant. Having little choice, we wandered in. The name of the restaurant was Café du Lezard. The owner was serving one table and we filled the second. There were only a few choices of food and he recommended the daily special, which included a salad and wine. The dish was *brandade de morue*, a casserole of salt cod, mashed potatoes, olives, capers, onions, garlic, and a topping of cheese. It was more delicious than I can possibly describe and cost only $12 each.

The other reason I had made the drive was to stop at the factory shops of Soleiado and Olivades, the two premier decorative-fabric companies of Provence. Unfortunately, their prices were extremely high and we went away completely empty-handed.

* * *

We were invited to dinner by our dear friend Barbara Alweis, now widowed. My wife Barbara prepared an hors d'oeuvre of marinated roasted red peppers and a dish called white salad which she discovered at a restaurant in New York, composed of *frisée*, white radishes, fennel, and grated Parmesan cheese with a wonderful dressing. Our hostess made the main course, a delicious pasta-and-vegetable dish. For dessert there was a mouthwatering tart with apples, pears, and plums marinated in lemon juice, white wine, and sugar before cooking. It was a local Provençal specialty called *panade*. Our hostess also prepared a second hors d'oeuvre, besides the peppers we had brought, which consisted of a thin roll of pastry surrounding a filling of cheese, mustard, mayonnaise, and herbs.

We talked for hours about our families and her husband of forty-three years, Frank, whom with good reason she misses desperately, even though she goes on beautifully with her life. We looked at pictures of her family on this warm, fuzzy evening, not leaving until midnight. It was an evening in Provence filled with love and good feelings.

* * *

In our travels we tried to include varied activities. We wanted to be visually stimulated, hear good music, go to historical sites, and definitely eat great food.

At times we went to inexpensive restaurants. Pizzerias were a regular choice. In France the pizzas are wonderful. Cooking in with local ingredients was also always a joy. But then, on special days, we would splurge at a top-of-the-line restaurant. That was generally for lunch, as it could be accomplished at a much lower price than dinner. Those occasions could be weeks apart or close together depending on our itinerary. By the end of the year it averaged to about once every few weeks.

Doing that on rare occasions was great fun. The food and service were, without fail, quite special. Besides the food, we always enjoyed people-watching at the fancy restaurants. Barbara and I would fantasize something quite interesting about the lives of the people there, while, in truth, we didn't know the first thing about them.

We planned such a treat in Avignon one night after a movie. Leaving the theatre, we walked down a dark alley that was a thousand years old, not something we'd likely do in New York after dark. The walls surrounding us were part of the Palace of the Popes, where the Popes moved their residence for a century about six hundred years ago. That led into the Place d'Horloge with its giant two-level merry-go-round. It was in full activity with children riding the horses, up and down, as the merry-go-round made its turns. We turned down the rue de la République to Hiely-Lucullus, a restaurant with one Michelin star. Barbara and I had the first of our special food treats. It was wonderful.

* * *

On a bright, beautiful Sunday we decided to go to the market at L'Isle-sur-la-Sorgue, where canals pass through town. For aficionados of antique shops, the town is bursting with them. L'Isle-sur-la-Sorgue does for antiquities what Dieulefit does for pottery shops.

L'Isle-sur-la-Sorgue was a giant traffic jam. Like in a mall parking lot at home, we drove around looking for people carrying keys, getting ready to move their cars. After ten minutes, we hit the jackpot and found a great parking spot from which to begin our stroll.

We were seeking table coverings for our summer home. Barbara spotted a fabric that was perfect and a bargain at 50 francs/meter, $8.50 a yard. We bought two and a half meters and headed toward a particular restaurant we had enjoyed in the past.

On our way to the restaurant there was an open fabric shop which had a selection much larger than we had seen in the markets. And there it was. The shop was selling the same selection we had made at the market. What we had purchased for 50 francs/meter was selling for 49. We didn't overpay by much, but the lesson was simple. The prices in the market were no better than anyplace else. But shopping there was great fun.

We lunched at Le Jardin du Quai, not listed in Michelin, but always crowded, noisy, and delicious. It's opposite the train station and can be tricky to find. It's imperative to get a reservation before shopping. If not, it's impossible to have lunch there on market day.

Another restaurant, a short distance from L'Isle-sur-la-Sorgue and rated quite highly, is Mas de Cure Bourse. We've eaten there and enjoyed it very much. But it's much more formal, and more expensive. We generally have preferred going to the Jardin du Quai.

* * *

One day, as a wild and crazy thing to do, Barbara and I drove all the way to Lyon, about a two-hour trip, just to meet our dear friends Judy and Seymour for lunch. They traveled even farther, taking the train from Paris. We picked them up at the Part-Dieu station, and went straight to the restaurant, Fedora, which was wonderful. After the meal we dashed from the restaurant back to the station, where Judy and Seymour just made it in time for their train. Their stay was far too short, but we were thrilled to have seen them.

* * *

It was the beginning of a twenty-seven-day adventure from France to Italy, Greece, Turkey, and back through Italy to Entrechaux. The trip would be by ground transportation, two car ferries, and a brief airplane flight, seeing places we had never seen before.

Just like the day we arrived in France, there was a constant downpour. Every day since then had been beautiful. It seemed the rule for this trip was that unloading and loading the car had to be done in the rain. We drove on the autoroute in a rainstorm, dodging speeding eighteen-wheelers. At 1:00 P.M. we reached Moulin de Mougins, near Cannes, where we had one of our special meals. It was the great Michelin-starred restaurant of Roger Vergé. After lunch we toured the kitchen. One needn't be special to have the tour. It was only necessary to ask. One of the chefs was an American woman who was a student at Culinary Institute of America in Poughkeepsie, New York. She was working with Verge as an intern pastry chef. What a great experience for her! One of the most interesting things in that kitchen was a wall covered with the pieces of their own special dishes which had been broken over the years, plastered on the wall into a mosaic.

At a brief stop in Cannes we strolled the waterfront and stopped in at Hermès and bought the most inexpensive trinket we could find there. It's great fun, and always a wonderful memory to buy something small at a very famous place. That small expense will remind you of the trip every time you see or use the item.

The weather got worse and slowed us down. We didn't arrive at our next stop, Portofino, until after dark. It is a heavenly town that we always love to see.

We had reservations, but as so often happens when traveling, there was a slight mix-up. To keep a trip enchanting, it's necessary to take things like that in stride.

The hotel had us scheduled to arrive the next day, but fortunately still had one room available. Thank God, because the rain was coming down like cats and dogs. Our hotel, the Piccolo, was very near the Splendido, one of the grandest hotels in the world. They charge between $500 and $600 a night. We passed that up, leaving it to the athletes, movie stars, and investment bankers. As a special perk at the Piccolo, if you look out the window, you can see the Splendido. Sometimes you have to be satisfied with a look.

The Piccolo was reasonable and charming, but the funniest thing about it was the bathroom. Every place we've been to in Europe is very space conscious. As we looked into the small, square bathroom we saw a toilet, a bidet, and a sink. Strangely, on the ceiling above them was a showerhead. The desk clerk, a nice young man, explained its use. A curtain hanging from the ceiling could be pulled around in a small circle in the room, almost excluding all the fixtures. The commode projected slightly into the enclosed circle of the shower curtain. So in the center of this five-feet-square room, one took a shower and the water went down a drain in the floor. I tried it and it worked quite well.

With the ghastly weather, we left in the morning. Portofino, however, is one of the most enchanting Italian villages, so before leaving we strolled through the port in the rain.

Back on the road we knew it would be a long drive to our next stop, Ravenna, Italy. So in Santa Margherita we picked up sandwiches to avoid stopping in the rainstorm for lunch. Though our reservation was at the best hotel in Ravenna, Barbara laughed hysterically about the curtains on the windows. They were made of masonite.

After a lovely dinner at the recommended Belle Venezia the rain finally stopped. Inadvertently we left our umbrellas at the restaurant and didn't realize our faux pas until the morning when it began raining again. But, in a gesture so sweet, employees of the restaurant had returned the umbrellas to our hotel, which they knew from our reservation. It was typical of the kindness we experienced in our travels throughout Europe.

Ravenna, more than any other town we have seen in Europe, seemed tied to the bicycle. The town is small; distances to travel, short; and the streets are narrow. All of this made bicycles a perfect choice of transportation. Everyone there was riding them.

There were people, well into their seventies, riding on steep uphill roads that I'm certain I wouldn't be able to negotiate on my bike without severe breathlessness. It had no effect on them. Men and women dressed in the smartest of clothes, suits and jackets and ties, and long dresses with scarves waving from their necks, rode their bikes. On one occasion I saw an elderly man riding his bicycle while holding a second bicycle in one hand alongside. Obviously taking the second bike to someone else, he rode in perfect balance, rapidly, with no difficulty. The bicyclists of Ravenna were very impressive.

After visiting the sixteenth-century Byzantine churches and mausoleums decorated in beautiful mosaics, we drove to an even smaller town known for a restaurant the guidebooks say is the toast of Italy. The town is Imola and the restaurant is San Domenico. One of the wonderful things about France and Italy is that the towns post the names of hotels and restaurants on the road with directions to help you find your destination. If you keep your eyes peeled, you can find your way without too much difficulty. We loved our lunch.

I wanted to scout two other towns. One was San Marino, a separate country on the top of a mountain inside Italy. No matter how high we drove we came upon nothing.

"Do we have to keep driving up here? Let's go back," Barbara kept insisting.

But I persevered, and when I arrived at what appeared to be the top I found ... nothing. Basically Barbara felt that it was an idiotic drive with a driver that wasn't much better. The view from the top was quite impressive, but we won't make a return visit.

Then we stopped by a seaside resort, Rimini, where we had read that bikes could be rented to ride along the waterfront. Unable to find a rental shop, I stopped an auto driven by the local *polizia* (the police). In a typical friendly Italian manner they gave us a police escort. That's the biggest clue to having a great time. Be open to everything, ask questions even if you have difficulty with the language. The shop had no bikes left for that day and the owner wasn't certain he was going to open the next day. He was going to a family outing and might just close the shop for the day. What a great philosophy of life!

After such a special lunch, we decided on pizza in the evening. I believe no one else in the restaurant was American. The waiter took our order and asked if Barbara would like some *birra* (beer). She noted that the menu showed two brands, Piccolo and Media. She tried to ask of the waiter the difference. Finally a friendly Italian, who spoke English and saw we were suffering, interceded. Our English is reasonably good. Our French is fair. And Barbara's Spanish is quite good. But our Italian is almost worthless.

"There aren't two kinds. Piccolo is a small and Media is a medium like mine."

Feeling grateful, and a little foolish, Barbara ordered the piccolo.

Before leaving Ravenna Barbara had to do last-minute shopping. She bought stockings she needed, a scarf she didn't, and wonderful things from a darling man in a gourmet food shop. There she found dried porcini mushrooms, pasta made with porcini mushrooms, and arborio rice to make risotto. The owner gave us orange rinds covered in chocolate as a treat. While Barbara was having fun shopping, I was having fun trying to make myself understood to salespeople who laughed with me and at me. I made attempts to define the word *prego,* which apparently means many different things. I'm still not completely clear about the word. I could only be certain I was having a great time.

Once all that was accomplished we drove to Ancona to catch the ferry to Greece. Both Barbara and I had some concerns about what we would find, having never been on an extended trip on a car ferry. We arrived in Ancona at the prescribed time. After the paperwork and passport clearance we were on board the brand new "Superfast" car ferry from Ancona to Patras, Greece. The trip would take twenty hours, a much shorter time than older ships used to take for this same excursion.

As we stood on the deck, watching as the ship pulled away, a small boat traveled alongside, probably about fifteen yards off our port side. The boat kept inching closer to us, maintaining a distance of about fifteen feet. Then to my surprise it came closer. I was certain we would bump. Suddenly we realized what was happening. As it edged up to our large liner, a man jumped off our ship onto the powerboat. It was the pilot who had been guiding us out of the harbor. When we were clear, his boat took him back to the harbor.

The variations in accommodations ranged from economy, which provided a deck chair (probably only for warm weather) or a simple inside seat, as on an airplane, up through more expensive quarters. These included rooms with multiple bunk beds, and private rooms with a shower. We had the latter. Although the space was small, everything was new and modern. There were restaurants serving Greek food, cocktail lounges, and even a gambling casino. I saw people in the casino whenever I passed, so the ship must have been doing well financially in that portion of their enterprise. Barbara and I didn't use the casino. For us the boat was a way to save time while avoiding a very long drive.

Once on board, having missed lunch, we were famished by the time they opened their first food service in a cafeteria-style restaurant. The food was surprisingly good.

During the late afternoon we went out on the deck for a while and then relaxed in the lounge, where I reviewed our plans for the next few days and Barbara did handwork. She was making a ski sweater for me with a rather complicated pattern and it was taking her a bit longer than she had suspected. On occasion she had to rip back a significant portion of what she had done, and took it all in her stride. I must admit I don't believe I'd tolerate it so well if after so much work I had to start over again. But her attitude was grand. When she found a mistake, she would rip and go on as if nothing had happened.

After dinner Barbara was tired and went to our quarters. I remained in the lounge for a while watching table after table of men and women playing cards. It was fascinating. No tables were playing the same game and none I had ever seen. One seemed like rummy. The others I couldn't identify. Some used cards like those in the U.S. and others were completely dissimilar. Even the numbers of cards in the decks were different. Sometimes they played clockwise, as we do. But two of them were played counterclockwise. But even with my confusion, the conversations I had with the players about the rules were fun. Everyone was very nice to the American who repeatedly interrupted their games.

The weather was perfect, so I can't say the trip would be as nice in bad weather. The gentle rocking put us to sleep as if we were in a cradle. I remember dreaming we were in a storm with waves washing up against the portholes. But even that wasn't frightening.

After breakfast I asked to go to the captain's bridge. Two men were sitting in an ultramodern room, apparently doing nothing. I asked who was manning the ship. They laughed and said it was on automatic controls. A radar screen indicated our position and a multitude of small islands through which we had to navigate. We were on a dotted line weaving its way through the islands. The ship followed the line on its own. I hoped there was an alarm system to alert them should something come in the way of their dotted line.

Shortly after that, Barbara and I packed and got ready to drive our car out of the hold of the ship into Patras, where I had been told the street signs would appear in our alphabet, as well as Greek. Unfortunately, in Patras, that was not true. We were totally lost even with a map of Patras. Then I met the first of several Greeks who would make our day. I walked into an electronics shop where the owner spoke English and provided exact directions for driving to Athens. By that time we were both hungry, but decided that rather than linger in Patras, where the traffic was heavy, we would eat on the road.

At the first rest stop on the superhighway, which is not nearly as super as in France or Italy, we pulled in. I walked into the restaurant and saw a modification of McDonald's. I turned to Barbara and said, "I'd rather starve than eat hamburgers in Greece." She quickly agreed to leave, with the understanding that she felt that way only up to a point. I knew I'd have to find an acceptable place soon, before hypoglycemia set in.

With her craving for sustenance building, I soon found another stop. It wasn't gourmet, but it served Greek food. The toilets weren't nearly as clean as in France.

The drive along the highway was somewhat confusing. Sometimes one paid at tollbooths and sometimes the booths were unoccupied. The other cars seemed to know which were which, and zoomed past the booths where no payment was due. Barbara asked if I, like a fool, was going to continue to slow down at all of them.

"I have this terrible fear that I'll zip through one of them and have the police chasing me all the way to Athens."

No one chased me!

One of the funniest things on the drive related to keeping the car well gassed up. We wanted to be certain that we would never be short of gas and unable to find any. As a result, before we boarded the ferry, we filled up in Italy with gasoline at $4 a gallon (about the same price as France). Driving through Greece we now saw loads of stations. The difference was that the price was about $2.70 a gallon. I guess we fooled them.

Finally, by late afternoon we arrived in Athens, where the street signs were in both alphabets. Driving quite slowly, reading street signs and a map, we made the Athenian drivers crazy. But without too much difficulty we made our way to the Park Hotel, where we had reservations. The clerk looked at me and blithely said they had no listing for us.

"We'll send you someplace else," she casually told me.

After that long trip I was in no mood to look for a new hotel. I recalled a movie where the star got a room by speaking so loudly that everyone in the lobby could hear: "You mean you just gave our room away when we had a reservation, after we've traveled all this distance!"

Though the volume was way out of proportion to the anger I was feeling, and could be heard throughout the lobby, a remarkable thing happened. Nothing! They couldn't care less how many people knew they overbooked. But everything turns out for the best. They got us a reservation in a much more convenient part of town and sent us, with instructions, on our way. That's when we met the first of many wonderful Athenians.

This time we got lost looking for the second hotel. I stopped a passing cab and asked him how to get there. He insisted we follow him. When we arrived at the hotel, he went in to be certain that we had the reservation. We had to force him to accept a tip.

We were now at the Royal Olympic Hotel, not fancy, but satisfactory.

Barbara and I asked where to eat and were sent to an area called Kolonaki. With numerous restaurants, we were confused and stood on a street corner examining our map.

"Can we help you?" was the request from an Athenian couple. They lived nearby and were out strolling. We told them about our yearlong adventure and they mentioned that they ski in France. Before they recommended a restaurant, we exchanged phone numbers.

In the morning, with great weather, we went to the major historical site in Athens, the Acropolis. It was quite overwhelming. Built two and a half millennia in the past, it is a marvel of construction. Barbara and I couldn't help noting, sadly, that most of this must have been done by slave labor. Nevertheless, it was very impressive, towering there with the Parthenon and other temples and amphitheatres.

We had lunch in the Plaka at Diogenes Tavern. The Plaka is a neighborhood occupied by hundreds of restaurants and shops. The shops are back to back, selling everything from junk to expensive jewelry. Even if you just want to window-shop it can be great fun. People out on the street try to hustle you into their shop. Some of the personnel are so good at their trade, it's a joy just to listen to their pitch. We bought some folk art and made some initial inquiries about jewelry. The prices seemed quite good in Greece, where everything was less expensive than we had found in France or Italy.

We returned to our hotel to freshen up for a spectacular evening. A lesson we learned early as travelers was that the inability to speak the language does not limit great opportunities for pleasure through music. Shortly after arriving I obtained a magazine detailing the current events for Athens. Their symphony had a concert scheduled with three soloists doing selections from Borodin, Mussorgsky, Verdi, and Puccini. The opera house was very new and quite beautiful. By chance we got marvelous seats on the twelfth row of the center section of the orchestra for less than $30 per ticket. The hall was almost completely filled, and although a few people were dressed casually, most of the audience was extremely well dressed. It felt like an evening at Lincoln Center in New York.

Our treat didn't end there. The previous evening, while dining at Maritza's 47, we asked some Canadians seated next to us for a restaurant recommendation. They were in Greece with the Young Presidents Club, and without pause they suggested Daphne's.

The restaurant, located in Plaka, had no name on the door. Only two years old, it was the hit of Athens. It had been reserved by Hillary and Chelsea Clinton during their trip to Greece. On the day we were there, the Norwegian ambassador had been in for lunch, and it had been the choice of the president of Greece, celebrating his birthday.

The food was marvelous, but the setting even surpassed that. A roving guitarist who played and sang was outstanding. He sat with us for a few moments and told us about entertaining in Chicago, Toronto, and Montreal. The owner kept wandering into the dining area, joining his performer in song. When other employees tried to ask the owner questions that obviously dealt with managing the restaurant, he would get annoyed at being disturbed while singing and give a quick answer in order to get back to the duets he shared with his entertainer. It was very humorous to see this little slice of life. I couldn't help thinking that the owner really would have preferred to have a career as a singer.

Meals in Greece are eaten very late. Lunch is from 1:00 to 4:00 P.M. And almost no one can be found in restaurants at 8:00 in the evening. By 9:00 the customers begin to straggle in. At 10:00 it gets busy, but many don't arrive until 11:00 P.M. or later.

We enjoyed Athens, although the city is quite dirty with very bad air pollution. Smoking was pervasive, even where restrictions were posted. But we found the people to be absolutely wonderful, as opposed to the surroundings in which they live.

* * *

Our next stop, after a long drive into northern Greece, was Thessaloniki. It was nighttime when we arrived. Though it was dark, it was apparent we were in a different world than Athens. This modern

Aegean seaport was spotless. Trash receptacles were on every street. There was no pollution. As in the rest of Greece, the dollar was strong. So we decided to stay at their most luxurious hotel, the Macedonia Palace. It was grand!

As an example of prices, we left our car parked and used taxis for which the average cost was about $2.50 to $2.75. Even giving them a tip was somewhat difficult.

The hotel recommended we go for dinner to the best seafood restaurant in town. In Athens we had learned about the *meze* (assorted) plate of meat or fish dishes, as one chooses. We ate at the Archipelagos Restaurant, where the seafood was superb.

The Macedonia Palace was so lovely that we decided to stay an extra day in Thessaloniki just wandering around the town. From our hotel room we looked down on a wide concrete walkway along the sea wall. We immediately knew this would be a great place for riding bicycles as we saw others riding past our window. When we asked the desk clerk about renting bicycles, we were told that no one had ever made that request.

"The only bike riders are bike owners," he explained.

We were quite surprised that in such a sophisticated city it was impossible to rent bicycles. I decided in my next life I'm going open a bicycle-renting establishment right on Thessaloniki's concrete boardwalk. Along this seacoast I'm going to make my financial killing. Barbara made it quite clear, in very few words, she was not moving to Greece. So instead of opening a bicycle shop we went to dinner at the recommended Ta Nisia.

Out of Thessaloniki we were on our way to Turkey. I expected a six- or seven-hour ride, but didn't take into consideration a number of variables. We spent forty-five minutes at both the checkpoints on the Greek and Turkish sides of the border. The two-lane highways with slow trucks and buses for miles extended our traveling time considerably.

The ride between Thessaloniki and Kavala was breathtaking all along the seacoast. There were numerous goat and sheep herders, all older men, with their flocks. It gave the impression that the profession was not being undertaken by younger Greeks.

A less pleasant phenomenon was the constant smoke from fires intentionally started in fields where crops had already been picked. It was the local custom. I can't imagine such pollution being allowed in the United States. It was difficult to breathe driving through the area. I

. . . Off to See the World · 23

suppose this was a phenomenon just during that season of the year. On one occasion the fires were burning right up to the roadside on both sides. It was somewhat frightening, even though the fires were supposedly controlled.

There were some very funny road signs we passed along the highway. One sign read, "World's Best Jeans," on the side of a tiny shack; and on another, "Fast Food."

The stop at the control point was intimidating. Well-armed soldiers created the feeling that these two countries were at war. On the Greek side no one was there when we arrived. I got out of the car and inside found a man sitting and watching a television set. He asked some routine questions and sent us through the Greek military checkpoint. On the Turkish side I was sent from one desk to another, and asked the same questions. As the guidebooks indicated, we were required, for $20 U.S. per person, to purchase visas. One person told us to empty our trunk, and even opened one suitcase. Finding no weapons, he then said with a lilt and almost no accent, "Goodbye." It was rather cute because he spoke very little English, but that one word was learned perfectly.

During the ride of about two hours from there to Istanbul, night came upon us, bringing more difficulties. The first began forty miles outside Istanbul, when the road suddenly became superhighway quality. It was a toll road like those we were accustomed to using in France. But guess who had no Turkish lire for the toll. The exchange rate utilized rather huge numbers. One U.S. dollar was approximately 94,000 lire. Barbara was somewhat anxious about our lack of Turkish currency as we approached the toll gate.

It soon became apparent we would find the great majority of people did not speak any English. It was our problem and somehow I had to deal with it. When I told the young man in the booth I had no Turkish lire, I made absolutely no contact with him whatsoever.

Cars, however, were lining up behind us. I noted that the toll was 120,000 lire, which would be about a $1.30. I then said, "I have U.S. dollars."

He seemed uncertain as to what to do. The line kept getting longer. I gave him two dollars, and he examined them carefully. Then he rejected one and returned it. A tiny corner missing from the bill. Barbara was thoroughly annoyed with me, as confused by the rejection I handed it back to him, trying to explain to him it was perfectly fine.

Impatiently she said, "Give him another dollar."

"I don't have another dollar bill."

She looked in her wallet and gave me a replacement, which he accepted. Then I asked him about getting some change. Neither of us understood each other. Barbara, to put it mildly, was thoroughly exasperated with me. The line behind us kept getting longer.

"Let him keep the change," she castigated me.

Of course she was right. So I finally drove off, still with no Turkish lire.

We made our way in the dead of night into massive street crowding. Thousands of people, mostly young males, were dashing about the streets. Throngs of cars rushed about trying to avoid hitting other cars and people. I've never seen such a sight even on the busiest streets of New York. We wandered into what appeared to be a frightening neighborhood, but I felt certain there was no danger. Totally frustrated, it seemed to make more sense to get out of the car and ask for directions to the Pera Palace Hotel. I must admit Barbara was truly frightened. The crowds seemed like roving gangs, but they were only local young people participating in their own environment. When I got out, Barbara locked the car. Into a group of five men, none of whom spoke English, I went with my map and the one phrase they understood, the name of the hotel.

There was much shouting and pointing. But they were actually being quite nice, trying to provide directions to our destination. Disagreeing among themselves, they attempted to point me in the direction I should be taking. Suddenly, all the lights in the area, store lights and streetlights, went out. It was pitch dark outside. Obviously there was a power outage, but it didn't affect the local residents. I could only assume, from their reaction, it was something that occurred on a regular basis. Barbara and I were not feeling quite as unaffected by the episode. There we were in the middle of a Turkish ghetto and we could see absolutely nothing. Finally the electricity returned and we drove for a few blocks. Finding no way out of the crowds, I parked again in the middle of the street, where I saw some parked taxis. Five taxi drivers were standing outside of their vehicles as I approached to see if I could get some help. But the same language barriers existed. One finally said in broken English, "For five American dollars, you follow me." I jumped on the offer and away we went. The driving was nothing short of insane. But he kept his eye on me to make certain we didn't get separated. After all, the five dollars was not to be paid until arrival at the Pera Palace. It was the best five dollars I had spent in years.

The hotel appeared to be one that once was grand, a century ago. Now it looked rather shabby. Almost no one at the hotel spoke English. The only friendly employee was a young woman who was at a concierge desk. She was very helpful, but went off-duty shortly after we arrived. We were hoping we would find her again in the morning.

The luggage was shortly out of our car, but the car was nowhere to be seen.

"Where is my car? Do I get some sort of a ticket?"

"Don't worry."

"Do you have a schedule of what events are going on in Istanbul this week?"

"We have nothing."

"Do you have a suggestion as to where we can eat?"

"Anywhere."

The conversations got no better than that. We had dinner and returned to the hotel, hoping that the next day, with less fatigue, less anxiety, and more daylight, things would be better. Our friends Florence and Buddy Kost would be arriving to spend a week here with us. Barbara and I went to sleep trying to have only positive thoughts.

After a good night's sleep, things definitely did improve. We went walking around the streets of Istanbul to get the lay of the land. We found a bank, a place to purchase the *Herald Tribune*, telephone cards, and information about cultural events in Istanbul.

Barbara and I decided to go to the Grand Bazaar, where more than four thousand shops are bunched together, all selling the same jewelry and rugs. With high sales resistance, even the super salesmen had no success with us.

In the taxi, returning to see if our friends had arrived at the hotel, Barbara shouted, "There's Florence and Buddy!" They were walking down the street on which we were driving. We spent the next few hours primarily laughing with them about our rooms at the hotel. The subjects raised included the size of their room, the strange small size of the seat on their commode, off of which Buddy felt he might topple, and the relative absence of hot water. That is not to say that warm water couldn't be obtained, at least lukewarm.

Florence, unlike the rest of us, is the world's greatest sport. Well, at least she's the greatest among us four. She thought the hotel had a marvelously charming flavor.

A decision had to be made about dinner and I chose a restaurant in the most luxurious hotel in Istanbul, the Cirigan Palace Hotel, not a wise choice. Inevitably comparisons were made to our hotel. The dinner was wonderful in this palace-like structure exquisitely set on the Bosporus. We were cleverly able to rationalize our choice of a hotel. "Who wants to waste time in Istanbul in a hotel that is so lovely you don't want to leave? At least we have an incentive to get out of our rooms to see the city."

When we returned to our hotel we allowed ourselves one final big laugh. There were pictures on the wall of the hotel with menus and advertisements from one hundred years ago. One said, *"Eau courante, froide et chaude."* (Cold and hot running water)

I looked and said it's still almost the same, *"Eau courante, froide et froide."*

* * *

We met our guide, Honde, a lovely twenty-one-year-old student at the university. Having completed her undergraduate studies in tourism, she is studying Italian language and literature. She lives with her parents and a younger sister and loves Istanbul. Shelale, the niece of a friend in San Antonio, brought her to us. Shelale has been to San Antonio to visit her uncle and found she didn't like it in comparison to Istanbul. For her, life in the United States is much easier, in fact too easy, and she doesn't prefer it that way.

Our impression of life in Turkey was quite similar. Through our eyes as tourists, the crowding, wild traffic, and considerable disrepair and lack of cleanliness of the streets seemed very stressful for the permanent residents. But, as travelers, we found it to be a country where we had great fun. It provided the opportunity to see a life very different from ours, as we tried wonderful foods and learned of a totally different culture. But just as Shelale would prefer to live in her homeland, living there permanently would be not of my choosing. We learn to love the place we call home and prefer it to all other lifestyles.

Honde took us to wonderful places which were mind-boggling, eye-popping, and miraculous, especially in terms of the time in which they were built. We saw Topkapi Palace, the Great Church and Mosque, and the museum of St. Sofia. At midday we ate with the locals, while Honde proudly told us about the history and culture of her country.

In the afternoon we went to the underground Basilica Cisterna, where, in the distant past, water had been conserved. This place, where water flowed in from multiple sources centuries ago, now had a low enough water level for sightseers to walk on elevated platforms while classical music was played in the background. It's breathtaking.

As the day ended we went to the presently used and beautiful Blue Mosque, and made a brief stop for Honde to show the Grand Bazaar to Florence and Buddy. We planned to return there for an extended period of shopping. Everything there is purchased with a great deal of bargaining. Honde must have felt that we were some sort of silly fools, as we spent most of the day laughing and having a jolly good time.

Our sightseeing was tiring, but after a short rest we went for a walk around the area of our hotel. We wanted to find out about the famous Turkish baths. A brief search yielded the bathhouse, which actually looked quite nice. Time was flying, and we realized it was necessary to return so as not to be late for the dinner reservation arranged for us by the female concierge. There was a special seafood restaurant she was recommending.

The concierge put us into a taxi with instructions for the driver. He dropped us off, without any information, in an area with at least thirty seafood restaurants. We hadn't any idea where we had reservations. Each restaurant had a person in front, hawking for it.

"This is the finest restaurant in all of Istanbul."

"Here you will find the freshest fish. Don't go anyplace else."

"We will give you a dinner you will never forget."

They all spoke to us in English. Our status as tourists stuck out like a sore thumb. Maybe it was the camera around my neck. We were totally lost. I told Barbara, Florence, and Buddy to wait there and I would return. But Buddy decided to follow me. I mention that because when I finally returned, Barbara related that several men had approached them asking if Barbara and Florence were married. The women decided not to respond.

The next question asked was, "Will you marry me?" They were laughing about the incident hysterically over dinner, but I believe they were somewhat frightened at the time.

For my part, I was involved in an adventure. I tried calling the hotel to get the restaurant's name from the concierge. I found a phone where I could use my card, but I didn't have the language skills to call Information. So I asked a shopkeeper if he had a phone book. He responded negatively, but generously offered to call Information on his phone, if he could get them. I soon understood what he meant. He spent the next five minutes dialing Information and getting a busy signal. I thanked him and said I would go down the street, where I saw a hotel sign, and ask to look at their telephone book.

"Can I look up a number in your phone book?" I asked of a desk clerk who spoke enough English to let me know it was an item I wasn't likely to find anywhere in Istanbul.

Meanwhile the girls, and that was the proper terminology, as young men were still trying to pick them up, wondered if I was permanently lost on the streets of Istanbul.

I returned to the original store where I had tried to call Information. This time they were successful and called the hotel. I got the name of the restaurant and my telephone friends sent a young man to take me back to Buddy, who had rejoined Barbara and Florence, and then to the restaurant, Yengec, for the beginning of a wonderful evening.

The food was delicious, but the atmosphere was even better. Musicians serenaded us with Greek music. A belly dancer gyrated around the tables, cuddling up to the male customers. In a humorous rather than sensuous manner, she collected tips in her brassiere-type top, exposing her ample bosoms. The evening was all in great fun.

The morning brought an urgent mission. I had to have my underwear laundered before I left Istanbul or be in serious difficulty.

I began my search in a men's store where no one spoke English. No matter how I tried to demonstrate clothes-washing, my charades were deficient. After each attempt they brought out a different garment to sell, all the time patient with this American fool. Then a woman who understood English entered the shop and sent me to my destination. It was a dry cleaner, but the owner had a friend who could lead me to a laundry. It was another dry cleaner, but that shopkeeper knew where a laundry was located. Meanwhile, these wonderful people led me through heavy rains. They had no umbrellas, so I tried covering them with mine. But it wasn't easy. They were always dashing ahead to get me to the destination. Finally, at the laundry I was told everything would be done by 6:00 P.M. and they would close at 7:00. Since it was the weekend, and we were leaving town early Monday morning, it meant return by then or never see my underwear again.

When I returned to the hotel everyone was ready for our trip to the bazaar. Negotiating the price was to be the watchword, and Florence decided to start it off with a bang. She found a Turkish wall-hanging trinket and asked the price.

"It is three dollars," he said in broken English.

"Too much!" Florence responded.
"Three dollars is special price!"
"Too much!"
He picked up a smaller one and said, "Two dollars."
Florence responded, "No, I want this one," pointing to the original piece.
"How much do you want to pay?"
"One dollar."
Her suggestion that he sell it at one third of the price he was asking seemed to arouse some anger in him. But I was uncertain as to whether it was real or feigned.
"No ... three dollars!"
This bickering went on back and forth. Since Barbara and I could barely tolerate the verbal struggle, we walked away. In a few moments Florence and Buddy appeared. Florence had purchased three for three dollars, the dollar-a-piece she wanted. Florence, pleased with her negotiations, was certain as she walked away that the owner said, "Thank you!" Buddy disagreed, insisting she misunderstood him.

Buddy interpreted the dealer's comment as, "Son ova beech."

It was the beginning of another day of constant laughter. As we walked through the bazaar the hawkers were quite funny. One followed us trying to sell an aphrodisiac.

He kept saying, "All night long."

Another whispered in my ear, "Five times, at least."

The rest of the day went on like that, buying gifts for children and grandchildren. By the time it reached 5:30 the rain was teeming and, like everyone else there, we decided to get a cab and return to the hotel. It was almost impossible. Finally, Buddy waved down a cab; its driver stopped and said, instead of the meter, he would charge a flat rate of 500,000 lire, about twice the normal price. Buddy rejected it as the cab drove away.

Barbara, standing there soaking, shouted, "That's just five dollars, Buddy!"

But it was too late. The taxi was gone. However, we outsmarted them, because the next cab that came offered us a flat rate which we accepted. This time we negotiated a rate of 750,000. Smart move on our part. Big deal! So we aren't the best negotiators.

I rushed back in time to recapture my laundry, done nicely at a reasonable price.

* * *

    We decided to take the boat trip up the Bosporus. After breakfast we immediately went to the dock where the ferries leave, Eminonu. Arriving at 10:45 A.M. we found the boats leave at 10:30 A.M. and 1:30 P.M. We had just barely missed it. But it turned out to be our good fortune, as it brought us the opportunity to see a part of the city with a lifestyle totally foreign to us. We walked through an area of street vendors, which weren't for tourists. They were selling the necessities of life, new and used clothes, shoes, kitchen equipment, and so on and so forth. It was a remarkable market.

    Soon it was time to board the boat for the hour-and-forty-minute ride each way. The boat went up the Bosporus, crossing back and forth between the European and Asian sides, as we identified in our guidebook the special points to see. But the real treat came at the end of the outward-bound half of the ride. We docked on the Asian side, and the local economy was expecting us. There we found a plethora of seafood restaurants. Selecting one at random, we had a superlative lunch of fresh fish, grilled outdoors. Three of us had red mullet while Barbara tried the anchovies. She said it was among the best meals of the entire trip. After ice cream from a stand and shopping from dockside vendors, we were on our way back. Barbara and Florence each purchased lovely vests after some negotiating. The cost of the round trip was only $2 per person.

    In the evening we wandered on Istikal Caddesi, the main walking street near our hotel, to see if anything was open. What a joke! It was after 9:00 P.M. and thousands of people were on the street. Businesses, primarily eateries, were going full blast. The first night had overwhelmed us, but once accustomed to the lifestyle, each day was a treat.

    We decided to eat Turkish pizza, which is nothing like ours. It's a crisp pita with a sauce and pieces of lamb and lemon. There is no cheese or tomato. We ate five delicious ten-inch pizzas. Five pizzas, three salads, and five soft drinks cost $10. Not bad!

    Peeking into a candy shop, I requested a piece of Turkish candy and asked what I owed. He indicated nothing and waved us on. I felt so bad I asked for two more pieces and insisted that I pay. The people there had been exceptionally nice.

    It was getting late and was time to pack for our very early-morning departure to Cappadocia. The ride to the airport was wonderful because the driver spoke English very well and told us about his country, his family, and his philosophy of life.

When our flight arrived in Kayseri we ran into our first problem of this trip. No guide was there to meet us. In this extremely remote area of Turkey I was in a quandary about a course of action. It was of no great help that my phone card had expired and I had failed to replace it. A stranger in this primitive airport, hearing of my dilemma, gave me his phone card. When my call was done I wanted to return the card and pay him for the time I had used, but he was gone. It was simply a gift from a friendly stranger.

My call yielded no information about what had happened to our guide. We were stranded. A taxi took us to our hotel in Urgup. Then the hotel arranged for a new guide.

It was 2:30 in the afternoon by the time we got out to see what this part of the country had to offer. The experience was, as today's youth enjoy saying, awesome.

Nature created a landscape that looks like what a Disney architect might dream up. The ground has amazing rock formations rising up out of it. These outcroppings have basalt caps sitting on top of the point of upside-down cones, called fairy chimneys. Some were so large that dwellings, thousands of years old, have been carved out of them. In one area, Goreme, they were used as a religious retreat hidden from the Romans about 1,800 years ago to allow people to practice their religion undisturbed by the authorities.

There were multiple primitive churches constructed in the caves of these hills with murals that are 1,500 years old painted on the stone walls. It was impressive beyond words. We then traveled to a similar town called Uchisar to see more of these structures.

By the evening we were pretty tired, having traveled all day. On the way back Florence and Barbara persuaded our guide to make a stop in the town of Urgup so they could survey the local shops. They have a difficult time passing up any shops. A strange phenomenon occurs in their bodies. No matter how fatigued they might be, something is released into their circulatory system, possibly adrenaline, whenever a shop is nearby.

Our second day in Cappadocia brought us a new guide, Muzaffer Buyukbas. We could tell immediately how special he would be. We started our day in Zelve at a Turkish national park. Zelve was remarkable because of the very large number of breathtaking dwellings carved into the hills. Muzaffer told us that these dwellings, seen throughout Cappadocia, continued to be occupied until about 1950 when the government forced the occupants out as a safety measure. Little by little, erosion, water, wind, and weather had combined to cause portions to collapse and create a hazard for occupants.

After a while we went to one of the underground cities. It is suspected there are about one hundred of them. On the way we passed a celebration going on in the courtyard of an official building in a small village. It was Turkish Republic Day, similar to our Independence Day. Their national hero Ataturk established the new republic in 1923.

We decided to stop and watch the young costumed girls doing a Turkish folk dance when an elderly gentleman came over to talk with us.

He asked, "American?"

We acknowledged we were and he shook each of our hands vigorously. "Thank you! Thank you! Thank you!" was his only comment.

In charades we asked if we could take his picture and he was thrilled. He gave us a card with his name and address, asking us to send him a copy. We assured him that we would. Muzaffer said the information on the card indicated he was the local soccer coach.

We arrived at Derinkuyu, one of the underground cities, by late morning. Buddy and Barbara looked in at the caves and claustrophobically said they would pass. Florence and I joined Muzaffer. It was an underground city that extended for seven stories below the ground, offering its inhabitants, practicing Christianity, an opportunity to continue their religious activities in secrecy. Gaining access to the lower levels was not easy for one as tall as I. Even kneeling and bending I continually bumped my head.

Once out of the underground city, we headed for Ihlara Vadisi, the Grand Canyon of Cappadocia. When we arrived and stood at the edge of a precipice looking down into a vast canyon, Muzaffer gave us two choices. We could drive alongside the canyon for four kilometers or walk down the riverside, giving the impression it was an easy stroll down the river. The vote went three to one against the adventure. I, alone, decided to take the river walk. After all, adventure was supposed to be an important part of this year.

As it turned out Muzaffer had done me in, but the challenge was wonderful. I made my way across large boulders to the depths of the canyon.

Once at the bottom, I climbed over the rocks, through narrow spaces, and came upon small streams leading into the main waterway. At one point I could find no way to continue. Water too wide passed in front of me, with boulders too large to climb over on both sides. I retraced my steps to see if I could find a narrower portion to ford and found a spot with a muddy, steeply inclined area on both sides of the stream. In my evaluation it seemed one of two things was likely to occur. I would either slip into the water as I stepped down toward the stream, or, jumping to the opposite side, I would slide back and fall in the water anyway. Building up my confidence, I took my best Olympic leap. Miraculously, at least in my mind, I jumped over safely and remarkably remained dry. The distance I had jumped probably could have been accomplished by any nine-year-old, but to my old eyes it looked monumental. My walk through this desolate area continued.

I passed some local residents working in a field and then came upon two young children who were by my estimate about three and five years old.

"Photo! Photo!" they shouted at me in English.

I gladly acceded to their wish and took a quick candid shot. It became apparent that they were requesting a reimbursement for their professional film appearance. Obviously, from their sophistication in making such a request, this was not their debut. I looked into my wallet and handed one 20,000 lire. That's only twenty cents. The other then asked for money. I indicated in my sign language to divide the money. The next thing I knew, the second child burst into terrible tears. I coughed up another 20,000 lire.

At the end of the walk, an hour and a quarter later, there were my three partners in this small village with Muzaffer. They insisted I see the things they had scouted. Among these sights were the dung piles used for heating purposes. We passed hordes of chickens wandering freely around the village. They were lunching in the piles of dung. There was also a hotel with a sign that I loved. It read, "Six rooms and twenty-five beds."

It was time to have lunch, and Muzaffer took us to a restaurant along the stream that passed through the town. The food was wonderful. We had lentil soup, a salad, and then two of us had fish and two had chicken on a skewer. After we were done Florence said she believed the town waste was run into the river. Having heard that the fish being served were caught there, she decided to opt for chicken as her main course for lunch. Not to be outdone, I inquired if she noticed where the live chickens were lunching. As usual, laughter was the background sound during this entire trip. The other sound that could be heard, no matter where we were, was the wailing call to prayer, heard five times a day.

On our long return drive, we stopped in Urgup, where Buddy and

Florence had been negotiating for a rug. Awaiting their decision, Barbara and I walked around town.

In a small shop selling trinkets, Barbara found a doll she liked and asked the price. In that little store I had the greatest insight to the bargaining for every little purchase.

"Two hundred and fifty thousand lire," was his response.

That would be two dollars and fifty cents.

"Will you take two hundred thousand?"

He looked at me and quietly said, "Why?"

I was dumbfounded. I was flabbergasted. I hadn't the slightest idea as to "why" I had offered fifty cents less. I looked at him with the dumb look only a person offering fifty cents less could possibly have, and gave him what he had requested. Even while paying him I was embarrassed. It was the best answer I'd ever heard during negotiations.

* * *

The following day was full of unexpected adventures. It started in the morning when the airplane tickets to Istanbul couldn't be found. At the airport I explained our plight to the agent and was advised, less pleasantly than previous experiences in Turkey, that the airline made no provision for lost tickets. We'd have to buy four new ones.

"If you ever find the old ones, we will reimburse your money."

Unhappily I took out my credit card.

"I'm sorry, in Kayseri we accept no credit cards. You will have to pay in cash."

The sum was far more than I had in my wallet in Turkish lire. In the crowded waiting area, I had to do a semi-striptease to get money out of my money belt. This was going to be a bad day. I could feel it already. I gave her the money and we passed into a waiting room. Just before flight time, a clue came from Barbara about the disappearing tickets.

"Where are our passports? They're probably in the bottom of a suitcase."

Right in the lobby I emptied the suitcases. There on the bottom were our passports and the tickets. I returned to the agent, and got my refund sooner than she had expected.

Earlier, during our first stop in Istanbul, I spoke with a friend who was visiting his family in Turkey. A man in his seventies, he had invited us to dine with him in Istanbul on our return from Cappadocia. We were to have joined him during our first week, but he had forgotten and canceled the engagement. So it was postponed until after our return.

Before leaving I spoke to him once again, telling him of our trip up the Bosporus and our plans in Cappadocia. We agreed that on our return I would call and the family chauffeur would take us to the Asian side for dinner in a private home. It sounded very appealing.

When we arrived I returned to the hotel to contact my friend, while my three companions sought a gift for our hosts. When I called, a non-English speaking person seemed to say he wasn't there. I left a message, uncertain whether it was understood.

Meanwhile Barbara, Florence, and Buddy decided to bring flowers. They went into a neighborhood florist. Unimpressed with what they saw, they decided the only choice was a dozen roses. As the owner brought them out, they selected the least wilted. Each time a rose was selected, my traveling partners pointed to a petal that was limp or dying.

The owner would pull it right off the flower and say, "No Problame!"

He pulled off another, "No problame!"

Petal off, "No problame!'

"No like! No problame," petal off.

"No problame!" Off came another petal.

By the time they were done, the roses on the table looked like they would not survive a half-hour. My partners knew there was no way possible for them to take these sick-looking flowers to our hosts. Barbara and Buddy, the two who didn't have the courage to go into the caves with Florence and me, showed their mettle once again. Too embarrassed to tell him to forget it, they walked out and left Florence alone. Having more courage than the two of them together, Florence took the matter into her own hands.

Florence said, "Forget the whole thing," and exited the flower shop. All the way back to the hotel they burst into laughter saying, "No problem! No problem!"

Meanwhile, I was having no luck reaching my Turkish friend. Barbara, Florence. and Buddy, at their wits' end concerning what to bring, and not being aware I was having no success, stopped in a candy shop and bought a large box of chocolates to be our gift.

A call finally came from him and I sadly realized my friend was having a problem with his memory when he told me he had no knowledge of our Cappadocia trip. He said he was sorry we weren't with him earlier in the day during his ride up the Bosporus that morning, not remembering we'd taken the trip the day before going to Cappadocia. He had no recollection of any dinner engagement and said the family had left for Cyprus. That ended our plans for the evening and left us with a rather large box of chocolates.

Though dinner was now a problem, lunch had been very funny. Buddy and Florence, our dear friends, would not deny being rather frugal. A humorous story they tell on themselves relates to a trip they took with one of the least frugal couples in our community. Buddy made the reservations. Apparently the places selected by Buddy were so modest that the other couple could not tolerate them. As a result, Buddy said of that trip, he and Florence stayed in about seven hotels in different cities. Their traveling companions, on the other hand, stayed in almost twice as many, the ones where they were booked and the ones they moved into after checking out of Buddy's selections.

With that background one can get a better perspective of that day's lunch. The little restaurant selling pizzas where we had eaten on a previous day was very inexpensive. Buddy and Florence suggested we eat there again. We all agreed. Since I was in the midst of phone calls about dinner, they started for the restaurant without me. When I arrived I ordered my pizza and paid for it. As we walked out the owner indicated the bill for Buddy, Florence, and Barbara had not been paid. Buddy assured him that the earlier food was already paid for by him. The manager did not appear to be convinced, but accepted Buddy's position on the issue. The three of them had ordered salads with their pizzas.

The remainder of the story I got second hand. When Buddy returned to his room he found the bill he had paid at the restaurant. On it were the pizzas and not the salads. The manager was right and Buddy, as honest as anyone could be, felt guilty. So, he walked all the way back to the restaurant to pay the small amount of money that was due.

When Buddy explained the reason for the underpayment, he expected a very pleasant reaction for the fact that Diogenes' honest man had been found. Instead, as Buddy stated, the manager took the money, uninterested in Buddy's honesty, making clear he had known all along Buddy had underpaid him. No good deed goes unpunished.

But the excitement of the day was yet to come. We decided to take a last-minute walk through Istanbul and find some intimate place to have dinner.

Flashback

In my travels I've been somewhat surprised about a problem I would not expect to face. I'm a rather large person, standing at about six foot one, weighing 180 pounds. I wouldn't think I'd be the best target for a thief. And, in fact, I'm not.

The first time I was robbed traveling abroad was the most successful for what the police call the perpetrator. I was traveling in Mexico City with two young children. On a very crowded bus, being jostled around, my thoughts only concerned keeping my children safely with me. A pickpocket relieved me of my wallet and my money, traveler's checks, and credit cards. I was unaware it was happening. It caused considerable difficulty with the remainder of the trip until we were able to get some replacement traveler's checks.

My daughter, less than ten, did lessen some of the unpleasantness the next night.

After dinner in a restaurant she said, "Ask them if they take American Express."

"Stephanie, It won't help. I don't have the card any longer."

Once again, "Ask them if they take American Express."

"Stephanie, I just told you I don't have it," I responded somewhat exasperated.

"Just ask them if they take American Express. If they say yes, ask them if they took yours."

It broke us all up and put a much lighter feeling on the evening. It would turn out to be the last time anyone would be successful in a personal theft of my property during traveling up until the present time. That may not necessarily be the case in the future.

The second attempt came about five years ago in Paris. I was on the Métro with my wife and another one of our children on our way to the French tennis championships. My wallet and the tickets were in a hip pocket. We changed trains and I stepped from the platform into the Métro car. I felt a hand in my pocket, looked down, and noticed that it wasn't mine. The intent was to withdraw the contents as the door closed. The desired result was for me to be on the train with the thief remaining on the platform. I quickly grabbed his wrist and pulled him into the car with me. An associate, realizing his partner was in trouble, held open the door and jumped in as well. When the train started I pushed him up against the wall, shouting obscenities at him I am not accustomed to uttering.

Meanwhile my wife and son were in a panic, expecting him or his partner to have a gun or a knife. The two thieves, much smaller than I, were in a panic as well. They were obviously unarmed, as I'm still alive. They may have been more nervous than my family. With my boisterous shouting, they probably believed I would become violent with them.

In my broken French I was asking other passengers to get a *gendarme*. I must tell you that the entire episode looked like a scene from Laurel and Hardy. Finally, with no police or other help, I had to make a decision on what action to take. After several stops I physically threw them off the train onto a platform when the train stopped.

My third adventure happened two years ago. Again it was in Paris, my favorite city in the entire world regardless of these tales. And again it occurred in the Métro, one of the thieves' favorite haunts. I cannot emphasize too strenuously, no matter how safe one might feel in a big city, European or otherwise, always be on the alert for pickpockets.

On this occasion Barbara and I were with our dear friends Judy and Seymour Palans. It was late evening and we were returning from dinner to our hotel on the rue de Rivoli opposite the Tuillerie Gardens. We were walking up the Métro stairway in single file on the final level leading to the street. Barbara was in front, then Seymour, followed by Judy. A slight young man was behind her and in front of me. I saw him rummaging through her purse, which was on a shoulder strap and down her back. I grabbed him and shoved him up the remaining steps in front of me, shouting once again. Shouting seems to work well. Judy and Seymour were thoroughly confused by what was happening.

At the top of the stairs, attempting to frighten him, I said, "I'm going to kill you."

One and a half times his size, you could tell he knew exactly what I was saying as panic appeared in his eyes.

Barbara, getting a little more accustomed to these events, calmly looked at him and said, "He really is going to kill you."

It was almost midnight, once again with no gendarmes to be seen. What was I to do with this hoodlum? The traffic was coming closer as the light turned green at the next corner. I shoved him onto the rue de Rivoli, where he hopped, skipped, and jumped between cars, making his way to the other side of the street and then dashing off.

Barbara said, "What would you have done if he got hit by a car and you were arrested?"

As shifty as he was, I doubted he wouldn't make his way across the street, even in traffic. Besides, there would be worse places to spend the rest of my life than in France.

As a sequel to that, our dear friend Judy, who can make the sourest person laugh, brought us to hysterics the next evening. She had earlier told us her makeup purse with all its contents was lost. After this incident she concluded a similar theft must have occurred with another pickpocket. She assumed someone had put his hand in her purse, thinking the small makeup kit contained money, and removed it. She also advised us she had heard that pickpockets listen for those speaking English and make them the targets.

The next evening, on the Métro, with a straight and serious face she said to the three of us, "Speak French! I'm carrying makeup."

The Present

Having no luck in finding a place where we would like to have dinner, we turned back to our hotel, where the female concierge had given us good advice in the past. As we walked down a busy and crowded street Florence, Barbara, and Buddy realized the florist they had rejected was on that block. They were anxious to pass his store as quickly as possible, embarrassed by having turned down his flowers. Buddy and Florence crossed at the corner quickly, and Barbara reached the corner with me about three feet behind her.

Suddenly a young man dashed out of nowhere and grabbed Barbara's purse. It was on a strap over her shoulder and across her body. While trying to pull it off, he ripped her coat buttons and knocked her sprawling. Whether it was his intention or not, her fall came like a National Football League–quality block across my body. It thwarted my attempt to grab him. I hit the ground hard. Unable to get the purse, he began running down the crowded street on which we had just walked. I pulled myself up and began chasing him.

He was about eighteen years old. With a forty-plus-year advantage over me there was no way I could possibly catch him. As I ran, I yelled "Thief, thief!" as loud as I could. There I was shouting again. Suddenly, at least a half a dozen young men began the chase far in front of me. As the thief reached the corner his pursuers trapped and grabbed him.

While I was running out of her sight, Barbara was with a policeman. The two of them were charging up the street looking for me, certain I was in mortal danger.

As opposed to Paris, the streets of Istanbul are a convention of police cars and policemen. Before I reached him, he was in the police's hands. They utilized no brutality toward him in the street, but did place him in handcuffs. By then a large crowd of people had assembled. They were terribly upset about the incident. Their anger was directed toward the thief. One man actually had to be held back from attacking him. I understood none of the ongoing conversations. But all the people on the street, knowing we were Americans, were extremely kind to us. Shopkeepers offered Barbara a place to sit down and brought her tea to calm her. Needless to say, she was extremely frightened.

The police talked to the boy and then asked Barbara to accompany them, in the paddy wagon, to the police station. She was a nervous wreck and told me she didn't want to go, didn't want to talk, and wanted to be allowed to go back to her hotel. They promised to take her there after a few minutes at the station. Still nervous, she declined.

Barbara pulled me aside and said, "There's no way I'm getting into a paddy wagon in Turkey. I saw *Midnight Express!*"

"Let her be," I told the interpreter. "I'll go with you and provide the information."

They agreed and said they would take me to the hotel when we were done. At the station an interpreter gave them my story. The young man denied it, stating he was trying to avoid a passing car. I said the story sounded strange, as he kept pulling on her purse, running away once it couldn't be removed. They didn't believe him and took him away.

I had to wait my turn as there were two others who had been robbed. One was a woman tourist who had just had her purse snatched. They wanted her to see the young man in our case, but, based on his clothing, he had not been the one to steal her purse.

After a while they brought a typed document to me and asked me to sign it. I looked and saw that it was all in Turkish.

"I'll need someone to translate this for me before I can sign it."

By this time the translator had left. For the first time the police showed some annoyance with me. They seemed to be saying that it was just routine. I still refused to sign anything that I couldn't read. They then decided they no longer cared whether I signed or not, and I could leave. I asked to be driven back to the hotel as they had promised. In their broken English they made it clear. "No signature, no car ride."

... Off to See the World · 41

As I left the station, my left hip, elbow, and wrist were feeling the bruises suffered in the fall. I hailed a cab and went to find my companions. The three of them were thrilled to see me, worried the police were keeping me. I presumed they weren't too upset, though, as they were having drinks in the hotel bar. Barbara finally had calmed down.

For dinner we went to Yacob, where we had eaten lunch the first day we arrived in Istanbul. It was crowded and noisy. This happened to be the night that the Istanbul soccer team was beating the team from Manchester in a major upset. The customers in the restaurant were watching it on TV, and their screaming and cheering created a wonderful atmosphere. The evening ended much better than the remainder of the day had been.

* * *

In the morning Buddy and Florence flew to Paris and we were off to see more of Turkey. By car ferry we reached Bursa, a center for Turkish baths and revitalizing waters.

Up bright and early, I went for a Turkish massage. I had already lived sixty-three years having never had a professional massage. I had nothing with which to compare, and no idea of what I was supposed to do. No one spoke English, so everything was in charades.

I was sent into a cubicle to remove my clothes and wrap a towel around my waist, and from there into a domed area that looked like a mosque. I progressed into a second mosque-like room with sixteen stone basins along the wall with running warm water. In the center of this large domed room was a round pool about twenty feet in diameter.

They gave me a bar of soap and said, "Shower." It was a word they learned to use for their English-speaking customers.

I realized I needed to wet myself down with the running water, and wash. I dropped the towel and began the procedure when a second client came into the room. Immediately he indicated I had to cover my genitals with the towel. Apparently that was customary, though the sexes were separated. Privacy or shyness may have been the reason. Whatever, the local cultural behavior demanded I be covered. I did as I was told. When in Rome.....

After rinsing the soap off I stepped into the pool. It was as hot a tub as I could remember. Meanwhile others came into the room. I had washed down as I thought proper, but was amazed by their washing thoroughness. Cleanliness was not a problem here.

After a short while I decided to go for my "rubbing and massage" in a third, smaller domed room. It lasted for only about twenty minutes, which I believe is shorter than one might expect back home. Since it was my first time, it was more than adequate.

He began with the rubbing, *"kese."* With a giant loofa, held like a mitt, he rubbed the skin right off my body. I was shocked by the sheets of skin that peeled away, certain this would be the weight-reduction choice of the future. He then poured hot water over me to wash away the skin before I was told to lie down on my stomach on a marble slab, and received three blows to the back. I believe I heard my ribs cracking—or was it my sternum?—against the marble. Finally a substance was poured on me which made my skin tingle. As he went through the massage the solution bubbled up, much like suds.

Immediately I knew this was not someone I wanted to meet in a dark alley. His hands were unbelievably strong. Whatever the manipulations were, I knew I would never be the same, with the kneading and rolling of the muscles. Finally, feeling like a limp towel, a large quantity of hot water was poured over me to wash away the substance he had used. As I left, he stopped me so that I would be dressed properly for my exit. He draped me with heavy Turkish towels to dry myself, and with a third one created a turban on my head that hung along the sides of my face on each side. Looking in the mirror in this mosque-like setting I knew I wasn't Muslim, but was less certain I wasn't Turkish.

I wouldn't have missed it for anything. I felt very refreshed. The baths, the rubbing, and the massage altogether were only $13. The experience was worth a lot more than that.

* * *

We packed up and were on our way. This day had been set aside for driving from Bursa to Bergama, a trip I expected would take six hours. But when I looked at the map I suggested we should change our route. The decision proved to be a wise one. It began down the coast of the Sea of Marmara with exquisite vistas. Just before 2:00 we arrived at Lapseki, the location where a car ferry leaves. To our great good fortune, the ferry, which leaves only once every two hours, was scheduled for 2:00. We drove on board.

The opposite end was Gelibulo. The English translation is Gallipoli. We arrived on the south side of the Gallipoli Peninsula. In thirty minutes we were on the north side, which is bounded by the Aegean Sea. Gallipoli was the site of the terrible disaster, chronicled in books and a movie, of the attack by British, Australian, French, and New Zealander troops during World War I against the Turks, at that time allies of Germany. The battle raged for nine months with hundreds of thousands of casualties and almost 100,000 deaths, ending in a stalemate. A young Winston Churchill, secretary of the admiralty, was held responsible for the debacle, which almost ended his career.

We wandered around some of the thirty-one cemeteries. The site of the battles is on a beautifully serene setting at the edge of the Aegean, with monuments to thousands of young men who died there. The gravesites were lovingly cared for. Like Normandy, it was extremely moving. I am overwhelmed continually about the insanity of war and how many young people, of all nationalities, have been slaughtered because older leaders send them to kill one another. It was important we didn't miss this place. The emotions felt during a visit to Gallipoli, like Normandy and Anzio, gnaw at one's very soul.

This was certainly not the season for crowds of tourists. We saw only one other car there. When we got out at one cemetery a young woman began waving to us. Of all the unbelievable coincidences, and all the tourists in Turkey, it was Honde, our guide from Istanbul. She was there with a lovely English couple, Jan Kennedy and Tony Ball, whom she was guiding through the area. We stopped and chatted. Though it was hardly what I would have expected, we had many things in common with the British couple, including successful offspring in the theatrical business. When we mentioned our plan to go to London by the Chunnel in the spring, they invited us to call before our arrival, even though we had only just met at the cemetery in Gallipoli.

From there we took another ferry, farther down the peninsula, which took us to Cannukale on our way to Bergama, where we arrived at 8:00 in the evening. Driving down narrow, undivided, two-lane Turkish roads at night is certainly not the best idea.

As we drove into town we saw the sign for our hotel. In the darkness it was difficult to find the entrance, located in the rear. They spoke no English but checked us in and showed us to our room. We saw no other guests there. When we indicated we'd like to eat, they took us to an empty dining room and proceeded to bring food that was quite good. Fatigued, we went to bed looking forward to a new guide in the morning.

* * *

"I have taken three buses and traveled since early this morning. I have had no breakfast. May I sit here for a while and get a cup of tea to get back my strength?" were the words spoken in a rather strident manner at about 10:15 in the morning, an hour later than prearranged, by the guide who was to be our escort for the next three days.

Committed to having a wonderful experience, I took the conversation in my stride, assuring him it would be fine. We then went to an archaeological area called Pergamum. From there it was necessary to drive to Kusadasi, which would be our base for two nights.

The conversations between the guide and us in Pergamum were not particularly stimulating. He had a way about him that made us somewhat uncomfortable. Back into the car for the drive to Kusadasi, he slept all the way, saying not one word.

Uncertain as to the route we should take, I luckily awakened him at a crossroads.

He said, "Oh, yes, you turn here."

Had I not roused him, there was no telling how far we would have traveled. We finally arrived at the coastal town of Kusadasi, where the hotels, including ours, looked like they were from Miami Beach. I was sorry we hadn't booked our own reservations.

A not-so-great buffet dinner was improved by an interesting conversation with two young people sitting next to us. They had come from Germany with a group that had received a special package at this season-ending time. She owned a women's boutique in Munich and he was in construction. They spoke at length about the conflicts between East and West Germany and the many issues that had been raised by the reunification.

Finally, the problems with our guide needed to be resolved.

"Do we have to stay with him?" Barbara asked plaintively.

"As long as we pay him, we can do whatever we want."

"What do you want to do?" Barbara asked.

"Ephesus is the most important of these archaeological stops. Let's meet him in the morning, take that trip, pay him, and end it."

My only concern was Barbara. She can be so sweet, I could just imagine what might happen. I'd tell him we were going to let him go. He'd be upset and want to know why. Then Barbara, feeling bad, would say, "Oh, no, we don't want to upset you." If that happened, we would then not only be stuck with him, but I would be the bad guy as well.

* * *

All the advance information was accurate. Ephesus was incredibly impressive, and so was our guide, but not in the same way. Any concerns I had about Barbara were very soon dispelled. It began with him being rude to other tourists, ordering a person to move away from a ruin he was describing. He then chastised a group of young people who were laughing and having a wonderful time. Wonderful, that is, until we came along.

Then came the doubts about his knowledge. He pointed to three columns.

"Here is an example of the three types of columns, Doric, Corinthian, and Ionian."

"But two of those three are exactly the same," I said.

"Oh, yes, but they are different."

Barbara and I looked at each other and rolled our eyes.

"Here is the sculpture with the Roman with his foot on the ball. That was to indicate that they controlled the world."

"When is that sculpture dated from?"

"The first century A.D."

"But no one believed the world was round then."

"In Ephesus they did."

We pressed on further, and were continually told that the first place in the world this or that thing happened was in Turkey. To say that we were getting more and more annoyed with our guide and this entire experience would be putting it mildly.

"This was the home of Socrates. Do you know Socrates?"

"Didn't Socrates live in Greece?"

"That was a different Socrates."

That was enough. Barbara was ready to get rid of him on the spot. But at the end of our time he did something that almost reversed our feelings about what we should do.

Our early afternoon with him was something very special. We had known in the past the ploy of guides taking their clients to stores to buy products for which the guide gets a cut. For most experienced travel-

46 · Two Drifters . . .

ers, it is annoying to pay a fee to a guide and then be pressured into buying some local product. This time it turned out differently for us.

We had already purchased seven rugs in Turkey, but not on a whim. Before we left we had fully intended to take home a Turkish rug for each of our six children and one for ourselves. The place our guide took us to was called Selcukidi, very close to Ephesus in the town of Selcuk. In an isolated area, it had a magical feeling to it. Sequestered from its primitive surroundings, this compound sat like a Shangri-la. It was circled by a grove of several types of flowering trees, including many bearing mandarin oranges.

A beautiful young woman appeared from one of the buildings. She quietly introduced herself and asked us to follow her. She began by showing us how the fibers were dyed from vegetable colors in large vats. We watched each stage of the process up to and including the weaving of a rug. It was quite interesting, but probably not very different from many other rug makers. But there was something special one could sense there, a serenity in the environment which was more than enchanting. As it turned out we saw some of the nicest rugs we had seen anywhere. As might be expected, a long, hard negotiation ended with us buying a rug for about 70 percent of the starting asking price.

Then, without explanation, we were led into a separate lovely area. Tables were set and we were served a delicious lunch. The young woman told us this rug business had been started by her father. As the eldest of three daughters she was now running it. When we left she asked if she could give Barbara a gift of a bag of mandarin oranges. It was a very wonderful afternoon, even if our guide did get a share of the action. Back in Kusadasi we ended the relationship, paying him for all the days that had been originally scheduled. He got some paid vacation and we ended up with some peace.

The entire experience was a reminder of the risk of using guides while traveling. We've had wonderful experiences with some and terrible times with others. That was exactly what we experienced in Turkey. The time spent with Honde and Muzaffer earlier in the trip was nothing but a joy.

No matter how valuable a guide may be in some situations, time spent with a bad guide can be inexorably horrible and long. One needs to think very carefully before deciding. At times you can get as much information with a fine guidebook on your own, without the hassle that can sometimes be experienced.

I cannot in all honesty say there was nothing humorous about the time we spent with our last guide in Turkey. Actually one incident drove us into uncontrolled laughter. Our very unpleasant guide was unmarried. He insisted that we meet a woman friend of his and we were introduced to quite a wonderfully sophisticated and beautiful woman.

When she was out of our presence he said with extreme pride, "I have chosen her to be my bride. What do you think?"

Barbara had already become so annoyed with him that she had no inhibitions about speaking her mind. She quickly blurted out without a pause, "*Bonne chance!*"

The nuance of her words, "Good luck!" was the American expression signifying "fat chance." He completely misunderstood and took it to be a well wish for success.

"Thank you, thank you so much," was his response.

When Barbara and I realized the discrepancy in speech and understanding we fell into laughter. Fortunately, he took it to be joy on our part for his choice of a wife. The lovely woman apparently had no knowledge of the choice he alone had made. I would not want to hold my breath waiting for that marriage to transpire.

* * *

Barbara and I spent the afternoon strolling through Kusadasi, as the sun was setting, before returning to our hotel. It was so romantic. We still think we're newlyweds.

Like some of the other hotels we had seen in Turkey, there was a casino in the hotel at Kusadasi. But we're not gamblers. A card had been placed in our room by the hotel stating it entitled each guest at the hotel to ten free slot-machine coins each day. We had not taken advantage of the offer on our first day.

"Well why not, Barbara? Let's go down there and throw their twenty coins, ten for each of us, into the machine and see what happens."

"Sure," my sweet companion agreed. And off we went.

"I'll give you ten free when you buy one hundred," the teller offered.

"Where does it say that on this card?" I asked, quite annoyed.

"Nowhere, it's a mistake."

Barbara took it in her stride and went back to read. I, on the other hand, have an aversion to being treated dishonestly, no matter how insignificant the issue might be. The coins were worth only seven cents each, which meant the entire offer was only worth $1.40. But what was right was right. I went to the front desk manager.

"Where does it say on this card that one must buy one hundred coins to get ten free?"

He stared at the card for quite some time without saying a word. Then he asked me to follow him. We headed back to the casino cashier, where a conversation was held in Turkish while they were examining the card. Finally twenty coins were given to me. It was obvious that this was something that no one received unless they made a fuss.

I went back to the room to get Barbara.

"Let's go play the slots."

"How did you get those coins?"

"Oh! It was easy."

Down at the machines I told Barbara I wanted her to play them. She had had a funny experience at Harrah's in Lake Tahoe once when we were skiing. Given a similar opportunity for one free turn at a blackjack table, she drew blackjack. Barbara picked up her money, much to the dismay of the dealer and the other players at the table, and left.

Meanwhile, back here in Turkey, Barbara began throwing coins into the machine, at times winning one or two coins back. Then suddenly three of the same pictures flashed on the machine. The coins began falling. There were fifty of them.

"That's the last time that will happen," Barbara quipped.

"Then let's leave," I chimed in.

In total agreement we took the coins to the cashier and left with $3.75 of their money. What a killing!

* * *

The next day, without a guide, we went to Pammukale, thrilled to be on our own. After a few wrong turns, in a spirit of adventure we arrived at about 1:00 and went to lunch at a delightful guide-recommended restaurant, Gursoy.

The town was deserted, as the tourist season had ended. Shopkeepers were trying to make some last-minute sales, and guess where we found ourselves? In a carpet shop. The Turkish rugs were beautiful. Realizing we might never return, we were enticed to get the rugs then. The prices were extremely low due to the season ending, and the owner was willing to bargain as well. Barbara and I couldn't withstand the urge and bought three.

I was thrilled. Barbara on the other hand has a problem. She loves to buy, but then immediately suffers buyer's remorse. I never experience that emotion. It doesn't seem like much fun. We ended up in Turkey with six rugs for our children and five others for which we had no place. The major problem was how to carry all that back.

Pammukale reminded me of Yellowstone National Park, specifically the hot springs. There were terraces with small ponds of shallow water. Apparently, in the summertime the water is quite warm from the thermal streams which create these ponds. We took off our shoes, as is required, and walked across the "travertine" terraces.

In the morning we left for Izmir, our final destination in Turkey, a drive of about three hours. A very cosmopolitan city, it was the port from which our ferry disembarked.

An Aside

No one can travel to Turkey and not be amazed by the traffic. The cities were a constant bustle. Cars drove as if there were no regulations. Going through a red light was as common as brushing one's teeth. When I stopped at a red light, in the adjoining lane five or ten cars would pass right through.

In Izmir, the third-largest city in Turkey, there were very few traffic lights, and jaywalking was the usual means of crossing the street. That was to be expected because the crosswalks had absolutely no meaning. It was no safer crossing at the corner than to jaywalk. Cars, even police vehicles, went full speed through intersections, never stopping for pedestrians. The only way to cross the street, at the corner or the middle of the block, was to make a dash in between vehicles. Life is treacherous on the streets of Turkey if you're a nervous driver or not fast on your feet. But the locals don't seem to mind. No problem!

We planned to ferry from Izmir to Venice, a two-and-a-half-day trip, to avoid the long drive from Izmir through Turkey, and Greece to Patras, where we had started.

There was a significant amount of time difference between the two methods of returning to France, which would become quite important as the day progressed.

We had already decided to end our stay in Turkey with an authentic Turkish meal rather than what we had been eating in our prearranged

American plan hotels. After some scouting we found Deniz. It had been absolutely packed the night before with local residents and now at lunch with businessmen. It's a great idea to eat where the locals do.

After lunch we checked out of the hotel and went to the harbor, arriving at about 1:30 for a 4:00 P.M. departure. We already had a reservation, but no money had been collected. On arrival there was quite a surprise for us.

"Sorry, no credit cards."

"But—"

"Sorry, no traveler's checks!"

"But—"

"Only cash!"

"But I don't have a thousand dollars in cash."

"Go to the bank."

So we headed back to a bank to get cash. The traffic was horrendous and there was no place to park. Finally, we found a bank.

After standing in line for a while, we were told, "Sorry, we don't do exchange. Go to the bank on the next corner."

I hustled down to the corner and waited even longer before it was my turn.

"Sorry, our computer is down so we cannot exchange any money."

The time was passing as I went to a third bank and was finally told we could exchange our traveler's checks for Turkish lire. That was fine, as the boat line would take any form of cash. Since the traveler's checks were in Barbara's name, I went dashing back to the double-parked car and sent her off to the bank. I waited in the mass of automobiles in the center of town. By now it was 2:30 and I was getting more than a little anxious. At the dock they had advised me that we needed to be back by 3:00.

After fifteen minutes passed without Barbara's return, my anxiety level had reached a peak. I contemplated missing the ferry and being forced to make the long drive back to Patras, Greece. I was uncertain whether we could make the long drive, get a ferry from Patras to Ancona, and return to Entrechaux in time to be in Marseille for our plane back to the U.S. Even if possible, we'd have to get a reservation on the Patras-Ancona ferry, for which I had no guarantee. I quickly paid a man on the street some money to watch our car while I dashed to the bank to see what was transpiring. Since we were double-parked, he wanted the key in case the driver of the car against the curb returned. I began wondering whether our car would even be there when we returned from the bank.

Inside, Barbara was frantic.

"It's taking so long and they've said they will only cash $400 worth. I'll need to go to another bank to try to get the rest."

Four hundred dollars wasn't going to cut it. I explained to the teller we were going to miss the ferry if we had to look for another bank. Couldn't we get some special dispensation?

"Please!!!"

After a few moments of cajoling they agreed. We got the necessary $1,000. Happily the man with our car keys was still there, and we went rushing back to the harbor. We arrived just in time to pass through five different desks, checking documents, passports, and everything you can imagine, before we were allowed to bring the car on board. Getting out of Turkey turned out to be even more difficult than getting in.

The boat was much older and slower than the Superfast, which had brought us there. The staterooms were similar, but the longer trip was extremely tedious.

Fortunately the weather was beautiful, relieving Barbara's fears of storms thrashing our boat around the sea. We passed through the Greek Islands and then the Peloponnese.

The trip was somewhat of a challenge. Sixty-seven hours with very little to do presented us with the opportunity to use our wits. There were several small public spaces, but many of the passengers smoked, causing the lounges to be quite unpleasant. Some on board told us they had taken this trip previously in difficult weather, forcing them to remain inside, but due to our good fortune we were able to spend our days on the deck.

The deck was crowded with passengers reading, conversing in multiple languages, playing cards, or just relaxing. Lots of tea was being consumed, but not by us. We tried it and found it not nearly as good as what we had tasted in Turkey or Greece.

Though food was included in the price of the voyage one could sit in a private separate dining area and be served à la carte, paying for special meals. We tried it for our first dinner but realized it was the same food being served to everyone else. The only description that can be given for the food was "not so good." But with so little to do on board, you came to look forward to each meal because it meant more time was passing.

We met a retired Swiss couple who must have had some stature, eating all their meals at the captain's table. But, by far, the most interesting person was a twenty-six-year-old marine in the British military. A member of their commando Service, he was on his way home by motorbike across Europe for a two-month leave. A leftenant, he described some of his training, such as the three months in the mountains of Norway on skis. In conversation we learned of his two earlier adventures in the United States. One year he pushed rolling chairs on the boardwalk in Atlantic City, New Jersey. Another summer he rode a bicycle rickshaw in San Francisco, pulling passengers up and down the streets of Chinatown, earning a thousand dollars a week. He was a very impressive young man.

Exercise was an interesting challenge. The deck chairs were so crowded together, it was impossible to do any walking. Barbara and I went to the small top deck, which was usually empty, and began fast walking in a relatively small circle. Barbara went around twenty-five times while I continued for eighty. To get an impression of the size of the circle, eighty trips took forty-five minutes, which probably would measure about three miles. Our only companions were children playing and passengers walking their dogs.

On the last day we were in for a treat. We skipped breakfast, finished our packing, and went out on deck, because there was "Land, ho!", and what wonderful land, Venice, that place of pure enchantment. We looked for places we knew as the ship glided through the main waterway.

Barbara shouted, "Oh, there it is, St. Mark's Square!"

Getting off the boat was another matter. We arrived before 10:00 A.M., Italian time, but it was 11:30 before we actually drove away from the numerous control points. At that we were lucky because everyone who came from a member state of the European community remained in a huge line of cars declaring their imports. Being U.S. citizens, we weren't required to do that until we returned home.

Turkey was an amazing country to visit. It didn't feel like France or Italy. It's still developing. For us, as residents near the southern border of the United States, the rural areas looked much like Mexico.

Now we were in Italy, with still a long way to drive to our base in Entrechaux, France. As I was soon going to have to pay Italian tolls, we stopped at an ATM to get Italian lire. At this point my finances were in a state of absolute confusion. My pockets were filled with French, Italian, Greek, and Turkish money. Trying to find which to use, each time a payment was to be made, was nothing short of riotous.

We drove from Venice to Entrechaux, a considerable distance, in eight hours. How that was accomplished is worth relating. At home I drive within the speed limit. "You can drive a little faster than that. Nobody's going to give you a hard time for an extra five miles," Barbara would say when were driving back in Texas.

Riding on the autoroute is another matter completely. The listed speed limit is usually 130 kilometers per hour. That's approximately 78 miles per hour. I drove back from Italy at an average speed of 84 to 90 miles per hour, faster than I've ever driven in the U.S. Staying in the right-hand lane at that speed, I was constantly being passed by other cars. I cannot determine at what speed they were traveling, but without question it was in excess of 100 miles per hour. I must confess that in a couple of long straightaway sections, with no cars to be seen, my speed rose to near the 100-mile-per-hour mark as well. I certainly would not recommend that anyone go beyond the speed limit on those roads, especially not at night or when the weather is not perfect, but it is difficult to stay within the limit as the other cars whiz by you. I also would not recommend that anyone take those roads if they intend to drive at 60 miles per hour or less. Cars will overtake you so fast that slow driving may even be a greater hazard.

Arriving at Entrechaux felt wonderful. Though I have found no place better than being home in the United States, France definitely comes in second. Possibly it's because I can communicate in French better than any other language after English. Possibly it's because I have been there so much more than any other country other than my own. Whatever it may be, life feels so civilized there. The people are gracious. The country is beautiful. Everything is very, very clean. And the food is phenomenal, which brings me to how we ended the day on our return to France.

When we arrived at the house I made a quick call to Le Brin d'Olivier, our favorite local restaurant.

"*Je suis désolé! Complet,*" I was told

They were all filled for the evening. That's not difficult for a good restaurant in France, because of one of the wonderful customs of this country. A meal is an occasion, not just a means of satisfying hunger. When you come for dinner you spend the entire evening. They do not turn tables. Back home a waiter or waitress may rush you because someone else is scheduled to eat at that table. But that cannot happen in France. So there was no way of saying, Can I get a late reservation? It doesn't exist.

It was already 8:30 in the evening, and not knowing what to try, I asked in broken French if he could recommend some other place. The maitre d' recommended Le Moulin à Huile. Imagine, in this small city, there were a number of fine restaurants only about five minutes from tiny Entrechaux, which itself could boast of one highly rated restaurant.

Having traveled for so many years throughout the United States, and finding myself a great deal of the time in small towns, I understand what eating in those places can mean. Fast-food chains or family-style restaurants are frequently the only safe places to eat. In France it is quite different. Even in very small villages excellent food can be found.

The meal at Le Moulin à Huile began about 9:30 in the evening and did not end until shortly before midnight.

* * *

The time had come to sort out those clothes we'd take home for our three-week stay in the U.S. and those we would leave behind. In the evening we were able to get a reservation at Le Brin d'Olivier, where the owner asked if we had been to the food fair. We promised to stop there before leaving for the airport in Marseille the following day.

I should have known this wonderful adventure would not end without a very special treat. It was Armistice Day in France, honoring the memory of the fallen soldiers of the many wars France has had to endure. In the town square of Vaison-la-Romaine a celebration was being held with soldiers and veterans paying tribute to those who had died. The program ended with the playing of the French version of taps and the singing of the national anthem. It was extremely moving.

Immediately opposite the town square was a huge tent with signs saying *"Journées Gourmandes."* We paid the ten-franc (two-dollar) entrance fee for each of us and were suddenly in the center of a joyous environment, quite unlike the somber one we had just attended. Inside there were about one hundred booths. Restaurants and merchants of fruit, cheese, fabrics, breads, candies, and artworks were there. As well as samples, food was sold in full-sized portions to be consumed at tables set up throughout the tent.

Some individuals, who didn't even have business establishments, had booths where they sold their special dishes each year at this event. The fair was now in its seventh season, and a great success. We were told that on one of the five days that the fair was open, four thousand people had passed through its doors. It was packed on the day we attended. The smells, sights, and sounds were delicious.

For lunch we selected a stand that had a large oven outside the tent. The owners were making a paper-thin pizza, with a light sauce of onions and ham. As they cooked the pizzas, the dough bubbled up. Barbara ordered a plate full of fresh oysters from another stand and I chose *soupe de poisson* (fish soup) from a third. Those three dishes came from entrepreneurs who sold their wares at distant locations. The *pissaladières* were from Alsace. The soup came from southwestern France. And the oysters were from the coast. For dessert we bought a small wedge of honey cake cut from a cake that was two feet in diameter. Every morsel was more delicious than the last.

As I previously indicated, the tent was packed. Even with numerous tables it was still difficult to find a place to sit and eat the foods we had purchased. Spotting a table with four chairs, two of which were empty, we approached a middle-aged couple and asked in French if we could join them. Somehow they recognized that French was not our first language. In English they assured us it was fine for us to take the other two seats.

It turned out that they were a British couple who have a vacation residence in the area and holiday there several times a year. The one time of the year they assured us they never miss was when the food fair was in progress. The husband was quite outgoing and wanted to give us lots of pointers about the local restaurants that were worth trying. His wife seemed rather subdued and not very much into the conversation.

None of us knew one other's name, and we were certainly still in the category of strangers when an awfully funny thing happened.

Even having had almost nothing to say, the British woman suddenly looked at me eating and said, "Excuse me. You have a hair coming out of your mouth."

It had the ring of the famous Gilda Radner routine on *Saturday Night Live*, discussing a piece of spinach caught in the tooth of the person to whom she was speaking.

In this case, as the comment came from a complete stranger, I must admit I was a little taken aback. I put my hand up to my lips and was able to remove it and stare at it for a moment. One then has to know that I am as bald as Yul Brynner to understand the remainder of the repartee.

Regaining my composure quickly, I responded, "Well, it's not mine."

I believe Barbara was the only one who gave me a big belly laugh for that retort.

The trip to the fair, hair in the mouth and all, was a wonderful way for the first segment of our European adventure to end.

It was time to make our way to Marseille for the flight to Paris as the first step on our return home. No matter how marvelous the last six weeks had been, we were anxiously looking forward to our trip home and the chance to see our family, do some work, and pay a lot of bills. The first segment of this odyssey had been nothing short of the beginning of a dream come true. The second promised to hold wonderful surprises as well. We looked forward both to being home and returning to Europe.

Part Two

THE DRIFTERS
in France, Spain, and Switzerland

Barbara and I made our way to the airport, with help from our friend Seymour. We planned to ski during the second and third legs of this journey, and would also travel to Spain and visit at least two very sophisticated cities. That meant, besides ski clothes and boots, we'd need dressier clothes as well. Beyond that it was necessary to have a winter wardrobe. Fortunately, we left our skis at home, and would rent them in Europe. The first part of the trip, completed in early fall, had required much less clothing. This time we had six suitcases, four carry-on bags (mostly computer things), and four coats.

On our return to Europe I learned once again it's better to be lucky than bright. We were scheduled to fly business class out of Chicago for Paris. But our flight to Chicago was being delayed two hours. We would definitely miss our connection to Paris. The agent in San Antonio, who knew us quite well from all of our traveling, was exceptionally nice. I'm certain that he's very pleasant to everyone because that's his basic personality. But there is another factor involved that can't be discounted. *There are tremendous advantages in being a steady customer and known by the staff.* Whether it's a restaurant, hotel, or resort, if you're known by the staff, the quality of service received is multiplied many times over. It applies as well to airport counters.

"I've got an idea. We'll route you through Dallas instead of Chicago. You can make the next flight to Dallas and that will put you there about two hours before the flight to Europe. And since we had to change connections, we'll just bump you up to first class."

That was the beginning of a wonderful day across the ocean. Flying first class to Europe is very expensive, more than we could possibly afford on our own. But is it ever wonderful! From the beginning it was pure luxury. They pampered us with movies, food, and drinks. In no time we were in Paris, but with little sleep. Barbara can't sleep on planes.

As she puts it, "Someone's got to listen to every sound."

I can sleep on airplanes with no difficulty. But I was watching movies for the first five hours, with only a short nap before breakfast. We would pay for it dearly with jet lag.

Though our luggage wasn't in Marseille when we arrived from Paris, after lunch at the airport it arrived with the next flight. In the car Barbara turned into a zombie for the hour-and-a-half drive from Marseille to Entrechaux, where we both collapsed.

When we awakened it was almost noon. An invitation was on the entrance table, left while we were away. With scrambled brains, we put it into our plans for the day.

We found another letter when we returned to Entrechaux. It was from the English couple whom we had met at the food fair the previous month. There was a new list of suggested places to eat. It certainly demonstrated the thoughtfulness of these total strangers.

The invitation had come from Pat and Brian Stapleton, who have lived in Provence for a number of years. Quakers, they have spent their lives serving people throughout the world. Brian is an economist by education and Pat, a sociologist and English teacher.

Earlier years were spent in Africa and China, where Brian was an administrator and teacher. Pat now teaches English in Hungary, France, and elsewhere, to doctors, executives, and, as Brian likes to say, "women of a certain age."

In conversation you can just sense their strong sense of morality and service to mankind. They are very special people.

Today, as expatriates in the south of France, they have full and rich lives. In an extraordinary compound they created in Beaumont-de-Ventoux, they live with artist children and grandchildren. Pat and

Brian live in one structure; their son, daughter-in-law, and grandchildren occupy another. A third structure is an art studio, while another houses a public library.

Brian is big with a ruddy complexion, serious in his demeanor but with a ready smile appearing on his face. Pat is more serene but breaks easily into robust laughter. There is a special warmth always emanating from her. I can remember the first time we met, introduced by Barbara and Frank Alweis, who told them we were visiting Provence.

Hearing I was a physician, Pat had a brilliant idea. She was teaching English to a group of physicians in Provence. She invited us to have dinner with her class and to talk with them about our joint interest in health care. Her stated purpose was very clear.

"I want them to hear some bad English. You know, the American variety."

When reminded of that she said, "It must have been Brian who said that; I would never say that," and then laughed heartily.

Brian raises honeybees in Provence, and later I'll tell of my adventure into his world. With some anxiety, I was committed to trying everything in this year of Europe.

What we had been invited to on this Sunday was to be a lot less frightening than bees. In fact, we expected it to be quite boring and dull.

Let's start from the beginning. Just over ten years ago, Pat and Brian set up an English-language library in Provence. They went through the French legal process of creating a cultural association and gave it the name of the Beaumont English Language Library. They called it the BELL. Today it has 10,000 books, on loan to members who pay an annual fee. Through those fees, and contributions, new books are accumulated. A wide range of fiction, travel, literary criticism, biography, and children's books are available. The library opens every Wednesday for seven and a half hours and at other times by appointment.

The library also has Sunday events about once a month in the winter. At these programs, talks and poetry readings are presented. On this day there were poetry readings. The invitation was so very thoughtful, we knew we should attend, even with jet lag.

Some poetry readings I had attended in the past had been difficult, with my mind working at full throttle. My very tired brain was unsure it would survive.

To make matters worse, due to our diminished alertness, we got lost going to the Stapletons' compound, and arrived ten minutes late. The guests were well into the mood when these two strangers, from America no less, were knocking at the door. I mention our nationality because the group was mostly British. They believed, in relation to language, those of us from across the Atlantic were an inferior species, and they're probably correct.

Nevertheless, we quietly made our way to the chairs that had been set out for us.

We were in for quite a surprise. For the next hour and a half there was no way that we could possibly be bored, fatigued, or uninterested. The library members, a group of extremely talented individuals, ages thirty to seventy, were reading, or reciting from memory, poems that related to festivals, the obvious topic with Christmas approaching. The readings sounded as if they were being performed by members of the Royal Shakespeare Theatre. They were funny, touching, poignant, and any other emotion you can imagine.

Following the readings we met some of them on a one-to-one basis. We were discussing theatre when one of them mentioned she had seen Les Misérables three times.

Another woman commented in response, "I was a groupie once for two years."

She absolutely did not look the type.

"You followed around Les Misérables?"

"Oh, no," she said. "For two years a group of women and I followed a British production of Cyrano de Bergerac around the world."

"Cyrano?"

"Oh, yes! It was so spectacular that we went to New York and saw all nine performances of it there. Crazy, eh? But it was just a phase I was in."

One of those whom we met was a well-known mathematician with a wonderful sense of humor. He asked me if I knew how many types of mathematicians there were.

"No, I don't believe I know the answer to that question."

"Well, there are three. One type knows how to add and one type does not."

When jet lag set in again, we bid everyone goodbye and went home to collapse.

* * *

With a light drizzle canceling out tennis, it was the perfect day to start our new exercise program. Before leaving home Barbara had purchased a Walkman and a walking exercise tape. This was not our first Walkman. But when the need arises we can never find the last one. I'm certain when Barbara and I have passed away, and the children are rummaging through our things, getting rid of junk, the following conversation will ensue.

"Why do you think they needed to have so many Walkmans?'

"Maybe they were going to go into the business of selling them."

"It couldn't be very successful with only one of each style."

"Well, I'm certain there must be a reason. They were always so well organized."

Oh! How very little most children may actually know about their parents' frailties. The organization of our lives is not that wonderful.

With our new Walkman, Barbara wore the earphones and strutted down the highway with cars whizzing by. I followed her every step for the next thirty minutes.

After a quick lunch at Auberge d'Anaïs we were off to Avignon to purchase the things we had forgotten to pack ... well organized?

We planned to go to the cinema but were still in jet lag. The film wasn't scheduled for another two hours, but Barbara had a great idea. We went to sleep for an hour and a half in the car until it was time to start. Passersby must have thought we were homeless.

Flashback

Sleeping in the car was reminiscent of an episode almost twenty years ago on our honeymoon in Hawaii. Barbara had gone there on her honeymoon in her first marriage. She likes to be consistent. She showed me where she stayed then to demonstrate how wonderful her life had been before she met me. Nevertheless, our honeymoon was great.

Our plan had us returning from Maui to Honolulu in the evening for dinner at a great restaurant, then off to a nightclub before heading to the airport for a 3:00 A.M. flight.

On that last day we played tennis in the morning, packed in the afternoon, and took the flight to Honolulu. After a whirlwind week, and hectic day, we were a little fatigued.

When we were seated at one of the best restaurants in Honolulu, and had ordered only a drink, I looked at Barbara and saw her head nodding.

"Honey, are you O.K.?"

"What, oh, oh, what did you ask?"

She was nearly in a stupor, and I wasn't feeling much better. We had no luggage, as it had all been checked from Maui back to Texas.

"Just sit here one minute and I'll be right back."

The restaurant was in a hotel in Honolulu. I walked into the lobby and up to the desk clerk and said, "My wife and I have no luggage, but want a room for a few hours."

The desk clerk looked at me slyly and said, "Sure ... your WIFE, and you, with no luggage, can have a room for a few hours as long as you pay in advance."

I paid him and he gave me the key with a big smirk on his face.

"Thanks," I said. "Please wake us at 1:30 A.M."

With another smile he said, "You got it, sporty."

I went back, paid for our drinks, and took Barbara to the room, where we were both sound asleep in less than one minute. Smart-ass desk clerk!

Present

We did our first major food shopping on this Tuesday in the Vaison market and then went to one of our favorite restaurants in Vaison, Le Batelour, for lunch. Back home Barbara began preparing food for a dinner party planned for later in the week.

In the morning, under a beautiful sky, we played tennis.

Flashback

Getting on a tennis court hasn't always been as easy as it is here in Entrechaux. In the past, staying at our friends' home in Gigondas, it was necessary to go to the post office to arrange to play on the town court. The gates were locked and local residents paid a fee. Tourists could pay a short-term fee. On our first visit Bruno was a member and gave us a key. On our second visit Bruno told us to see Monsieur Ternier at the post office.

A woman was at the desk. In my broken French I asked for Monsieur Ternier, explaining that I was a guest at Monsieur Verlet's home. I told the clerk that we had played there three years previously, and wanted to make arrangements to get a key.

"*C'est un problème. Monsieur Ternier est en vacances. Il va revenir mardi*": Mr. Ternier won't return until Tuesday.

"*Allez parler au maire!*": Try the mayor's office.

So I headed for the *mairie*, city hall, and saw the mayor's secretary. She obviously wasn't going to be of much help as I related the story about Monsieur Verlet, playing here before, and looking for a key. She wrote out a note. And told me in French, "Take this to Danielle in the bakery." It was beginning to sound like a comedy routine, but I believed I must be getting somewhere because the key to every Frenchman's heart is a baguette.

Nothing is as important as a *boulangerie*, bakery, unless it's a *pâtisserie*, where cakes and sweets are sold. In the United States, McDonald's is in every town. In France there are multiple *boulangeries* in every town, more than any other establishments.

So I went to see Danielle. Whatever anybody else thought, she couldn't help me. She picked up a cigar box with a few papers in it, and turned it upside down. Only papers fell out, no key. With a friendly smile she shook her head, "*Il n'y a pas de clé*": no key.

But Danielle wasn't done. She told me to go to the *syndicat d'initiative*, or tourist office. Once again I told the entire story.

She said, "*D'accord. Ce n'est pas possible aujourd'hui, mais demain, pas de problème. Revenez demain matin*": You hit the jackpot. The keys are nowhere to be found today, but you'll be a winner tomorrow morning. ... And so it was.

Present

In the evening we had a wonderful meal Barbara had prepared from our purchases the day before at the market. Even if I lost on the tennis court, I was a winner at the dinner table. But the tennis did remind me of a kinder time in the past when, if you played with someone inferior, on occasion you would let up and allow them to win. I believe I did that with girlfriends when I was a teenager. It appeared Barbara never learned about that.

* * *

I found I could pay our rental least expensively with the exchange rate from ATM machines. However, there was a maximum allowable withdrawal per day. In order to obtain sufficient francs I'd have to go through the process at least ten times, a day apart. I needed to do that every day to accumulate the entire amount before leaving Entrechaux.

With that in mind we started out in a driving rain for Nyons. We had heard they had a lovely market and we needed a few more items for our upcoming company dinner.

The weather was so bad the stands were closing. Quickly we obtained what we needed. But, even in this terrible rain, I had to find another ATM machine to accumulate the francs needed for the rent. We found one located alongside a bank that had gone out of business. In this new high-tech era some things survive even going out of business.

After obtaining the cash we sought out a restaurant for lunch.

Flashback

In France I've always been impressed by how many times we have had difficulty with restaurants being closed. They all have very different schedules.

On our last trip to Provence I recall that we arrived in Paris planning to stop for lunch on the drive south. We stopped outside Paris at a town called Auxerre, in order to eat at a highly recommended restaurant. It was 2:05 in the afternoon. As we walked into the restaurant, with many patrons, the hostess stopped us and said, *"Je suis desolée, mais on est fermé à quatorze heures":* You are five minutes late. No lunch.

Fearful we'd find nowhere to eat, we went to a nearby restaurant where a French boy and girl had just been seated, lovingly looking into each others' eyes and the menu. At last we would have lunch. The waitress looked at us as we asked in our broken French to be seated. She looked at us and said, *"Fermé":* closed.

"But you just seated them."

That was followed by a long sentence beyond my ken. However, I knew the translation: "They are French." We ended up at a pizzeria.

I have to qualify both those stories by saying that our general experiences with the French have been marvelous. We've found them to be very gracious to us as tourists.

Our food problem for the day was solved but there was trouble ahead. The drive was long and after the transatlantic flight we were very tired. Feeling unsafe driving, we pulled into a lovely roadside rest area, parked, turned off the engine, and went to sleep.

More than one hour had passed when we awoke refreshed, ready to travel.

"Chug, chug, chug." Nothing! The car would not start.

"Chug, chug, chug." The engine kept turning over but would not start.

"What are we going to do on the highway with a stalled car?" Barbara implored.

In France it is almost impossible to make a call in a public booth without a phone card. There are very few phone booths that take coins. Fortunately, I had purchased a card at a newsstand when we arrived at the Paris airport. So I headed for the phone booth.

"Monsieur, I am leasing a Renault from you and . . . ." I told him the details.

He began laughing and in English said, "Everybody has that problem."

I was flabbergasted and responded, quite annoyed, "If everybody has that problem, why are you leasing these cars?"

"No! No! You don't understand. It is not a problem. It is the new security system. If you turn off the engine and don't turn on the alarm, after a while it sets itself and the car can't be started. Get in your car, set the alarm, and then turn it off. The car will work fine."

Sure enough, he was right, and our car problem had ended without difficulty.

But cars have presented us with several problems during our visits to Europe. Fortunately, we've never had an accident. Once, in Provence, while wandering through an area of vineyards, as I backed up, my rear wheels slipped over the edge of the side of the road into a ditch. It took some clever maneuvering to finally extricate ourselves.

On one occasion our car radio was stolen, necessitating a visit to the police station in Beaume de Venise to file an incident report. It was our only car-theft problem.

But the supreme story about automobiles is about a van six of us rented in Italy one year. I will not reveal the name of the company. As we began driving, it became obvious that the clutch was broken. Then there were defective seat belts. Then the windshield wipers didn't work. Oh, don't be mistaken, this was not one van. Each time we arrived in another town we went to the company and they gave us a different one, each one worse than the previous one. That trip we used five different vans until the completion of the rental. I can recall a wonderful stop where the agency was next door to Avis.

After we returned that van Barbara said to the clerk at the desk, "We've had so much difficulty. Can't we have that lovely van that's sitting out in front of your store?"

The man looked at her and said, "Oh, no! That beautiful van belongs to Avis."

But the end of the story is the best part. When we returned home, and I received my credit card bill, there was a huge charge for the rental. I had already reserved the van under a specific fixed price which was a fraction of what was billed.

When I called, the clerk politely responded, "Oh, yes, Dr. Keyser, you made arrangements for one vehicle, but you had five."

"Five rentals? Are you just pulling my chain or something? Every time we got a van...." I went on to tell her the details.

She was shocked and said the information couldn't be verified from the data sent from Italy. Within a few weeks, adjustments were made and we received the correct bill.

Well, that's the car story so far except for one really enjoyable experience. When leasing a car from Renault, which we have done many times, you are required to get it serviced every so many miles. They tell you in advance approximately what the cost should be. One year I took my car in to a dealer and the charge was considerably higher. Barbara marveled at what I was able to do with my very limited French. We negotiated until the price ended up where the company had told me it would be. The conversation and the negotiation were great fun, especially since it ended up as a victory.

Present

It was still raining hard. As I drove toward Dieulefit, Barbara checked our trusty Michelin Red Guide to see if they listed a good restaurant for that town and found one.

Barbara had an appetizer of mussels *farcie,* and I had calamari in a lovely sauce. We both followed with duckling in brown gravy with *dauphinois* potatoes and a vegetable which looked like oversized celery. They completed the meal with cheese and dessert.

From there we went to Poterie Milon in Dieulefit, which we had found the previous month, to buy "seconds," *deuxième choix* in French, for our own home. Unfortunately, there were very few dinner plates. We wanted eight and only three were available.

We decided to try again another time when the owner saw our frustration. She went to the stacks of perfect plates, considerably more expensive, and pulled out a sufficient number to give us eight at the price of the seconds. What a nice *cadeau*, or gift.

At home we had a dinner of meatball soup and a delicious salad with watercress, onions, and clementines, French bread, and wine. Another wonderful day for the drifters!

By noon the following day the rain had let up and we decided to walk to a lovely restaurant in Entrechaux, St. Hubert. Several other tables were occupied. Our meal lasted two and a half hours. When we left all the other tables were still occupied.

An Aside

No one who comes to this country will ever understand the French unless they understand the importance that food plays in their lives. In the United States the majority of people eat because it is time to do so. We eat seated, standing, walking, or even running. Fast-food chains thrive because we cannot consume our food fast enough to please us. We rush through the meal to get to the next activity, usually work.

In France eating is one of the main occasions of the day, and it is done leisurely. In most French cities and towns we have visited, it's a mistake to try to buy anything between noon and two-thirty or three. That's because almost every establishment, even the post office, closes. Business will not interrupt their afternoon meal. A store that closed during lunch hour in the United States would not likely remain in business very long.

I have mentioned that there is no such thing as turning tables in a restaurant there. It's because the French expect that the table they sit at will be occupied for several hours.

Depending upon what one orders, lunch will occasionally be two, more frequently three, and not infrequently four courses. It will always be accompanied by wine. The last course will usually be a very rich dessert, which in the four-course meal is preceded by a platter of cheeses. It is difficult to explain why the French are not obese.

Present

St. Hubert offered a menu with three possible meals. The cost of those meals ranged from 130 francs ($23 for three courses), to 180 francs ($32 for four courses), up to 280 francs ($50 for four gourmet courses) at dinnertime. But most French restaurants have a menu that is used exclusively at lunchtime. The fixed-price lunch at St. Hubert is 70 francs per person, about $12.50 for three courses, a glass of wine, tax, and tip.

They served us a salad of house pâté, greens, radishes, and tomatoes. The second course was a pork loin with three vegetables laid out like a picture. The flavor of each item was exquisite. To complete this meal there was a homemade apple tart. This is a restaurant in a small town, Entrechaux, where the length of the business community is about three city blocks. The town would not be large enough to have a McDonald's back home. In France a high-quality restaurant such as this in a small village is not unusual.

After lunch we drove to what the French call a "hypermarché." These superstores, like a Wal-mart in the U.S., sell everything. But the portion that is the food area, which we would call a supermarket, dwarfs the largest ones we have. A woman who was working in the store as a supervisor actually moved around on roller skates.

* * *

Barbara was preparing for our dinner guests, the Stapletons, while I was making calls arranging for skiing trips. In the middle of her preparations Barbara threw together leftovers for a great lunch. She can turn the most insignificant food into a special meal.

By late afternoon I was in the kitchen too, having been assigned dessert. Barbara's menu included a chicken dish with prunes and capers and a marvelous sauce. She also made a casserole of zucchini combined with a million other things.

I was making spiced baked apples from a Pierre Franey recipe. Barbara recommended I stuff them with dried cranberries. Her suggestion turned out beautifully.

Finally I said, "Let's go for a walk. It's gorgeous outside."

Barbara chose the direction, and what a choice. We walked down the loveliest of roads, with hills in the distance and surrounded on all sides by dormant vineyards. The sun was shining. It wasn't cold, just nicely crisp. It couldn't have been more invigorating.

By 7:00 our guests came and we spent the next hour over drinks while they regaled us with stories about their adventures all over the world. After a while we had dinner and it was about 11:00 when the evening ended.

In the morning we went to a charming Christmas fair, a Nöel, in nearby Mirabel aux Baronnies. They sold oysters, sausages, omelets, cookies, and honey. Christmas there is not as commercial as at home. The holiday is important, but without the pressure.

From there we drove to Nyons for lunch. In Provence when one says the name of the town of Nyons, the "s" on the end is pronounced. In Paris an "s" on the end of a word would always be silent. There is a definite difference in the dialects.

On this Sunday afternoon the town was very quiet. Wandering among the shops, we noticed three young people standing on a corner chitchatting away.

"*Excusez-moi, y a-t-il une bonne pizzeria près d'ici?*" Not just "is there a pizzeria near here?" but "is there a GOOD pizzeria near here?"

Barbara and I found our way to the recommended pizzeria and, as expected, it was *oh la la!*, with fresh tomatoes, mushrooms, olives, and a fresh basil sauce.

Flashback

Once in Vaison, traveling with friends, I wanted a fresh tomato pizza.

As the last to order I said, "*Je voudrais une pizza avec des tomates fraises.*"

A look came over her face. It was difficult to determine if it was just quizzical or she wanted to say, "Are you some kind of idiot?"

Clearly not yet making contact with her, I decided to try again, understanding that she must be having a problem with her French.

"*Je voudrais une pizza avec des tomates fraises!*"

"*Quoi, des tomates fraises?*"

It suddenly dawned on me. *Fraise* means strawberry. She wondered what strawberry tomatoes could possibly be. It was no wonder this poor waitress was in a state of utter confusion. She did finally break up completely when I changed my order.

"*Je voudrais une pizza avec des tomates fraîches*": I'd like a pizza with fresh tomatoes. It was just another one of the many times I'd made a fool of myself with the language. Fortunately, those to whom I had spoken usually were very kind.

Present

Something else interesting happened in that pizzeria in Nyons. Two other couples were having lunch when we arrived. It was a typical French restaurant, small and quaint, with lovely country table settings. After we had been there for about ten minutes we realized there were others there as well. But we hadn't seen them. They weren't people.

Under each of their tables sat a dog, absolutely still. It is a phenomenon seen throughout France. People take their dogs with them to dinner. The dogs were so well behaved it was impossible to realize they were there, except when they entered and left.

I believe in the United States one can't bring animals into restaurants. At least, I've never noticed any other than seeing-eye dogs. French dogs, very well trained, seem so happy to be with their masters, and never cause any disturbance. It is quite remarkable.

* * *

We began our first-ever ski adventure in Europe at the ski station Les 2 Alpes. In France they call them ski stations instead of resorts. Barbara and I have skied for twenty years all over the United States, but skiing in the Alps is awesome.

It took three hours to get there, about one hour beyond Grenoble. On this glorious sunny day we stopped at the tourist office to get an idea of the mountain layout. Then we had to select a ski shop to get our rental equipment.

All the shops providing equipment looked exactly the same, so we chose Magic Sports, and it turned out to be magic. The couple running it were darling. Besides getting us fitted, they gave us help finding our way around, including a place to have lunch.

For the best skiing we were advised to head for the glacier area. After climbing many steps we reached the takeoff site of a *cabine*. A cylindrical-shaped structure, it moved swiftly along a cable high above the slopes, carrying about twenty skiers.

On dismounting from the *cabine* we went out one door and back into the same building through a door a few feet down, entering a second *cabine* of a much larger size. I would estimate this one held about forty passengers. But we still had not reached our destination. A third *cabine* we took was of a similar configuration to the first.

It appeared we would then need to utilize a T-bar. Barbara is a fine skier, but she hates T-bars. So we avoid T-bars to keep her happy. On this day Barbara didn't need much to keep her happy, as the mountain was elegant.

Fortunately, there was an alternative option to the T-bar, an underground funicular. It looked like the trams in airports. We took the funicular and were at the top in a few minutes. Now the question was, "Where do we go from here?"

Everyone getting off the funicular appeared very young. They were heading for what I believed was a "black" run area, the most difficult. We were not up to that for the first run of the season, so we went in the opposite direction, and soon we were all alone.

The Alps were different from anything we had ever seen before. There were no trees. Instead the ski runs went through the middle of craggy mountaintops. In Colorado, mountain peaks are at a distance. Here they were adjacent to us, and it was breathtaking.

As exciting as the environment was, there was a problem. We had been told that in Europe the runs were not well marked, and we'd have difficulty finding signs with the name of the slope or its degree of difficulty. Here it was not difficult. It was impossible.

We were in the middle of a moonwalk with no directional signs. There was not a tree or a person to be seen. The peaks next to us were sharply pointed with ragged edges. Though it was extremely beautiful, for the moment it was scary not knowing which way to go.

After a while we found our way to the top of the third lift. The skiing between that point and the top of the second lift was grand. We could hardly stop talking about how unbelievable the experience had been.

The day was long, as their lifts stayed open until 4:30 P.M., later than ours back home, especially at this time of year when the days are so short. Both fatigued and exhilarated, we drove back to Entrechaux, had a simple dinner, and fell into a deep sleep.

I was awakened by a knock on the front door.

"Monsieur, vous avez un problème avec votre voiture."

It was a friendly neighbor I had seen several times before. "Oh, God," I thought. "Don't tell me someone has broken into the car?"

I went out to face the problem. There, sitting on the roof of our car, were goggle cases and a neck gator. It was then I realized how tired we were when we arrived home last night. Unloading, we had left them on the top. I was thrilled that this was the extent of our problem and thanked him profusely. The residents of Entrechaux knew a lot more about "those Americains" living in La Grange (the name of the house) than we ever imagined.

By 10:00 A.M. we headed to Vaison and the Tuesday market. We were leaving for two and a half weeks in Spain and needed no food, but loved to wander there. We met Pat and Brian, which was fortunate. I had promised to provide a title for a presentation I was to make for a Sunday program at the Beaumont Lending Library in late January. The title was "Light Perspectives on Thirty-five Years as an Obstetrician." I wanted to keep them laughing.

It was midnight by the time we went to sleep. We were very excited about our next adventure. Barbara had been to Spain once, many years ago, and I not at all.

"Good night, precious. I can't wait to see Spain," I whispered to her.

Spain would turn out to be even more special than I had imagined in my wildest dreams, and so very different than anything else we experienced in this magical year.

* * *

It began raining quite heavily as we drove along the coast of France. The weather made us question our plan to take the autoroute to Perpignan, then leave the main road to drive through the Pyrénées. Three days and two nights had been allotted to reach Madrid.

The downpour was so heavy it seemed foolish to use small roads or get out of the car to see anything. Using plan two, we stayed on the autoroute and drove straight to Lérida (Lleida in Spanish). My first day in Spain gave me culture shock.

The shock resulted from the fact that Lerida was definitely not a tourist town. It is a lovely city, where almost no one speaks any English. In the guidebook I had purchased, there was not even a listing of Lérida. Apparently, tourists don't go there very often.

We had dinner at a restaurant called Forn del Nastasi. Not one person working there spoke a word of English. We had no Spanish menu book (Spanish-English translation) to help us order from the menu. We decided then and there to purchase one as soon as we reach Madrid. No other city before that was likely to have one for sale.

Over dinner Barbara and I agreed, "There'll be very little we can do in Lérida tomorrow. Let's try for another long drive and get to Madrid a day early."

It was holiday time, but fortunately they had room in Madrid for an early arrival.

When dinner was over we were able to tell them we wanted to add a tip to the credit card amount. Barbara speaks some Spanish. But he told us in Spanish he was not allowed to put it on the charge. We explained we had no pesetas with which to tip him.

"Would it be all right if we give you dollars?"

Then he gave us the most unbelievable answer.

In Spanish, interpreted by Barbara, and with a gracious smile on his face, he said, "Noooo problame, forget the tip. You'll give it to me next year at the holiday season."

"Next year! No, not next year. We definitely won't be here next year."

It's difficult for me to remember anyone back home ever saying, "Forget about the tip." We happily gave him dollars, returned to our hotel and quickly went to bed, full of excitement and anticipation about the next day's arrival in Madrid.

Up early, I went out looking for money, a telephone card (an absolute necessity), and gasoline. The money and the telephone card were quite easy. But the gasoline, ah ha, now, that was interesting. I could not find a service station anywhere.

I said to myself, *Don't be an idiot, Herb. There are cars riding all around you. They're not driving on water, or fumes, or even electricity. Find a gas station!!!*

When I returned the receptionist said, "Of course not. There aren't any. By law they must be located outside the city limits. That's the only place you can get gasoline."

The drive through Aragon was very striking. The rolling hills had reddish-orange soil, uncultivated and laden with small rocks. There were windmills galore. In one area there was a rock formation the Spanish had cut through in order to build the highway. It was a multi-colored swath, resulting from different layers of silt being laid down on the land over millions of years. It looked like a giant sculpture on each side of the road.

The strangest thing suddenly appeared on a hilltop several miles in front of us. At first it was just a black speck. Then it began to take form. It was a giant animal. As we got closer, we saw a black bull, twenty feet high, cut out of sheet metal and supported on a rack. What was this sculpture doing in the middle of nowhere? No other manmade things were seen on the highway, except for directional signs, and absolutely no billboards.

After driving another ten miles or so, "Wait a minute. There's another bull."

As we drove toward Madrid I would estimate we saw a dozen of these. At 3:00 we pulled off at Catalayud and stopped for lunch. One has to go with the local customs when it comes to the timing of meals. By a wonderful stroke of luck we found a very nice restaurant in a hotel. The town is small, but the waiter spoke English quite well.

Aside from the food being excellent, he provided a great piece of information.

"Why are the bulls on the hill? Does it have something to do with bullfights?"

He laughed and said, "No, not at all. Osborne!"

"Osborne? Osborne? What's Osborne?"

He left and returned with a bottle of liquor labeled Osborne, a Spanish company.

"There are forty-five of the bulls here. They used to have their name, Osborne, on them but the government forced them to take it off. Now it is just the plain black bull."

An Aside

The waiter at this restaurant, in a tiny town, strutted around the dining room like a peacock. He was so proud of the work he was doing. On this afternoon he was dressed in a tuxedo. This was not the first time we had seen such a thing in Europe.

It reminded me of doormen at fine hotels. They've been at their jobs for years and have great pride in their work. It mattered not how few people came into the restaurant. This was his domain and he exhibited that in all of his actions. It's a lesson worth learning.

The Present

So they did have outdoor advertising on the highway. But very subdued. After lunch we continued toward our destination. In Madrid we found just what we expected, heavy traffic and crowds in the streets. We were in complete confusion trying to find our hotel. At stoplights, with our heads out the window we asked, *"Dónde está Hotel Villa Real?"*

Everyone was helpful, but in Spanish, so we only understood a portion of the directions. Each time we became confused, we received more directions farther down the road. Finally, we pulled over to a policeman and asked where our hotel might be.

He didn't say "dummy," but he might have thought it as he pointed to the building we were stopped in front of ... "Hotel Villa Real." Well, one can't be brilliant all the time!

The hotel was grand. Travel in Spain was so inexpensive, even with the highest rating the price was great at 17,000 pesetas daily including breakfast, about $130 a night. Try to get that in the top hotels in New York, Los Angeles, or Chicago.

Due to the holiday, dinner reservations were difficult to obtain. The concierge sent us to Rincon for a superb dinner. At midnight we returned to find a message. It confirmed the special reason we wanted to be in Madrid. The message was from Uriel Segal.

Uriel Segal is a world-class symphony conductor. From Israel, he was the director of the Osaka Symphony in Japan. As their first conductor he established that orchestra, taking them in 1995 on a worldwide tour, including Los Angeles and New York City.

Uri, as he is known to us, also is the conductor and music director of the Chautauqua Symphony of the Chautauqua Institution, a self-contained cultural center in western New York State, where Barbara and I spend our summers.

We first met Uri a number of years ago when he was the guest conductor of the San Antonio Symphony. We heard of his arrival through an intermediary, Harvey Biskin, the orchestra's tympanist, and invited him to our home for a Hanukah celebration, as he was far from home. He, his very wonderful wife Ilana, and their children became dear friends.

Uri was in Madrid to conduct their symphony. We planned to have dinner with him each evening, go to the rehearsals in the morning, and attend several performances. He suggested that while in Madrid we see the flamenco dancers. We made a reservation for midnight, after the concert and dinner, which would not begin until 10:30. I was certain it would be 2:00 in the morning before we returned to the hotel. I hadn't stayed up that late since the high school prom. WHAT A COUNTRY!!!!

After breakfast we went with Uri to Madrid's new concert hall, Auditorio Nacional de Música. Nothing is more fun than being on the inside of something when you're actually an outsider. Uri took us through the performers' entrance, and we sat on the sixth row of the auditorium, watching the orchestra and chorus rehearse.

Uri spoke English and Italian to the orchestra, as he wasn't as comfortable in Spanish. He spoke to the choirmaster in German, that gentleman's native tongue.

I got lost in the cacophony of languages, as repeatedly Uri would say, in some language, "No," throwing up his hands to stop them. There was a great deal of laughter, as through their language barrier they tried to sort out the errors. Uri, apparently an easy conductor with whom to work, uninvolved in temper tantrums, just moved steadily along.

All went well, until 1:00 P.M. that is, when the orchestra's contract called for the rehearsal to end. Like back home, the union holds the line. The rehearsal problems related to the choir, although the problem wasn't the music. They were performing Mendelssohn's "Elijah," repeatedly sitting and rising. The moves were disturbing the mood of the piece.

The orchestra wanted to leave, as their practice time had been delayed by the directions for the choir and it was not their problem. Negotiations went on and it was agreed the orchestra could leave. Uri and the choir director would resolve the problems.

By 2:00 P.M. Uri, Barbara, and I were on our way, strolling through the central area of Madrid, looking for a *tapas* bar. They were all over, selling a selection of delicious hors d'oeuvres. In comparison to other prices in Spain, they were somewhat expensive.

The rain still had not let up. And on our return from the rehearsal Barbara left her umbrella in the taxi. Well, actually, she left *my* umbrella in the taxi. The problem was she had left my raincoat in Entrechaux when we loaded the car. But, being as sweet as she is, I could hardly be upset. So, after lunch, I went shopping on the streets of Madrid. Luckily I found an umbrella and even a Spanish-English menu book to help us in restaurants.

The concert turned out to be a lot longer than we had expected, and we didn't start dinner until almost 11:00 in the evening at La Trainera, a great seafood restaurant. By the time we were done, it was 1:00 A.M., so we canceled our plan to see the dancers.

In the morning Uri went with us to the Prado Museum. Since this was my first visit to Spain, I had never seen it. I had been told that the lighting was bad and I'd be disappointed. The reports were completely false. If it had been bad at one time, now it was superb, with a mind-boggling collection. Uri had told us it was his favorite museum.

While there, we met the soprano from Uri's concert with her husband, wheeling a baby carriage. She and Uri began discussing a serious problem about the baritone. He was ill and they were concerned about the concert. Uri considered shortening the program, relieving the baritone of some arias. Ultimately, it was a lot worse than Uri had expected.

After the Prado, Uri went back to the hotel to work on the problem and get some rest, while Barbara and I decided to walk around Madrid. We lunched on *paella* with the *Madrilenos* out shopping. We even tried the Metro to see what it was like here in Madrid.

Their Metro, inexpensive at fifty cents, was very clean but limited in scope. By comparison, the Paris Métro reaches every location quite easily. Then an interesting happened. Looking to the left for the approaching train, it appeared on the right.

A man, noticing I was examining a Metro map, asked in English, "Can I help?"

The system was quite simple so I responded, "No. It's very easy, but *muchas gracias*." I turned away, looking at the map, and then quickly turned back.

"There is a question I have. Why do the trains run on the left side of the tracks?"

He laughed and said, "I wondered about that when I came here until I was told the Madrid Metro system was designed by English engineers, and that explains it."

It's quite possible the story is apocryphal, but it certainly was funny and explained why it ran opposite from any other I had ever seen. It had been a long time since I had been in London, so I didn't recall, but I assume it runs on the left there as well.

In the evening at the concert hall an announcement was made in Spanish, and we realized what they were saying when only three soloists appeared on the stage. Uri had been working feverishly, cutting different portions out of the piece. By the time we heard the concert for the third time, we were surprised to find it had been shortened by fifty minutes. It was so abbreviated that we wondered how the audience might have felt.

Barbara and I were seated with charming Israeli friends of Uri. Their names were Rachel and Yochanon. After the concert we all ate at a marvelous restaurant called Arce.

Parking in Madrid was almost impossible. Yochanon and I left our companions at the restaurant and went searching for a space. We found a multifloor parking facility and pulled into the end of a line of cars waiting to get in. A sign in front said *"completo."* Every time a car left, another was allowed in. After thirty minutes of patiently waiting, we entered the building. Yochanon's conversation was so interesting, the delay seemed quite tolerable. Meanwhile, our companions were doing something in the restaurant.

When we entered the parking building we circled and weren't surprised to find no spaces on the first floor. On the second level we found the same condition. But when we arrived at the third level we were quite shocked. The attendant at the entrance obviously had no concept of what was happening inside. On the third floor there were enough open spaces to accommodate fifty cars. We parked and finally got to the restaurant, where our companions were laughing and drinking wine. They never missed us for a moment.

The chef came to every table before dinner to discuss what dishes each one of us would like, making multiple suggestions. I believe some of the dishes were actually concocted to the customers' taste. It was a very unusual dining experience.

We had arrived at 10:30 P.M. When we left at 2:00, some diners were still there.

Barbara said, "The only reason there aren't more people still in the restaurant is that the remainder have already left to go to the discos."

Uri, needing to get down from the high achieved during every concert, asked if he could smoke his Cuban cigar. We all concurred, but said that for half a concert, the most we'd allow was half a cigar. Uri sweetly took a lot of needling for the abbreviated performance.

After breakfast Barbara and I went on a museum tour. We started at the Reina Sofia National Museum to see Picasso's "Guernica." Then, by Metro, we went to the huge 2,800-room Royal Palace. As Barbara likes to say, "Who cleans all the bathrooms?"

Our last stop was the Museo Thyssen-Bornemisza, all its contents from one collector. It is almost impossible to think of an artist from Rembrandt, through all the French impressionists, to the most famous modern painters, who was not represented.

In the evening we had a final dinner with Uri at Casa Botin, before he left Spain.

Driving around Madrid on our last day, I realized the city was more beautiful than I had ever imagined. The wide, treed boulevards had large traffic circles with towering monuments. The driving was much easier than in Greece or Turkey, as they didn't seem to drive as fast. But I believe I heard more honking of horns than anywhere else.

On our last evening we planned to go to a church concert and then to the finest restaurant in Madrid, Zalacain. We went to the listed location, and drove around in circles for an hour, asking locals about the location of the church without success. So by 8:30, we gave up and arrived at the restaurant just before 9:00. The restaurant was dark.

"Do we have the wrong reservation?" I asked out loud of some nonexistent person, concerned that the entire evening was going to be a cipher.

We wandered around the building, and two minutes before 9:00 the doors opened and the lights went on. They really meant business. No dinner before 9:00 P.M.

Zalacain was more than special. We started with small puffed pastries filled with chicken, ham, and bacon, followed by soup. Neither of these two dishes was part of the menu. They are just what restaurants in Europe consider little gifts. Then there were four more luscious courses. The wine, which was quite inexpensive, was delicious. The restaurant itself was more expensive than we were accustomed to in Spain, but the same meal would have been considerably more costly had it been served in New York.

We were excitedly looking forward to the morning when we would drive to Granada and spend Christmas Eve at the world-famous Alhambra. When we awoke it was raining as it had been every day since we arrived in Spain. There was a potential problem in store for us, as reports indicated that the continuous rain had caused major road damage.

Our plan was to take a slight detour and go through Toledo, an hour from Madrid. As we approached its outskirts, I asked Barbara to tell us what we were about to see.

"Please pull out the guidebook, honey, and look up Toledo."

Our English-language guidebook to Spain was our bible in finding our way around. An English-language guidebook was not an easy thing to find there.

"Where is it, Herbie?"

My mind began racing. I didn't remember seeing it when we loaded the car. I pulled into a service area and unpacked the entire car. Panic was setting in. If it was hard to find an English-language guidebook in Madrid, in small cities it would be impossible.

We drove into Toledo and found a telephone booth.

"We were at your hotel until this morning. Could you check our room and see if there is a guidebook to Spain?"

Barbara reminded me that the maid put whatever was out into a drawer to keep the room neat. I suggested that possibility to the receptionist, and was told to call back in five minutes. My anxiety level was a little high. What would we do without it? I called again.

"Oh, yes! The book was in the drawer and we will hold it for you."

After a discussion with Barbara, in which she laughed and said, "It's just part of the experience," we were on our way back to Madrid. Two hours had been killed.

We picked up the book, had lunch, and were on our way again. But we were in for another disappointment. I had assumed Christmas Eve would be special at the Alhambra. It turned out not to be the case. Nothing happens there at Christmas Eve. No church services are held. No caroling can be heard. And the restaurants open and close early so their employees can go home. We barely made it in time for a dinner which was only fair.

Thus a rainy day, with a lot of driving due to an error, and nothing very inviting at the completion, was coming to an end. But the hotel, one of the state-operated facilities (*paradores*) in Spain, was quite beautiful. That was the highlight of this less than super day. But I knew the next day would be better, because Barbara always helps me keep everything in perspective. The forecast still was predicting "possible rain showers."

It was Christmas Day and, the rain finally stopped. We taxied to the highest point of the city, in the old town. It was on the opposite side of a valley from the Alhambra, which we could see in a broader perspective, as well as a grand view of the city.

We were so high it was easy to understand why we were advised to go there by cab. Going on foot to the top would have been more of a challenge than we needed.

We did walk down the narrow cobblestone streets to the center of town for lunch. With everything closed, we meandered through grounds of the Alhambra, leaving the interiors for the next day, and at night dined at Bogavante, Granada's best restaurant.

* * *

The interior of the Alhambra was well worth the wait. The 1,500-year-old palace is so beautiful and intricate that it is difficult to comprehend how such a building could be produced without today's technology. Barbara was mesmerized. For a very long time she stood on the spot where Isabel spoke with Christopher Columbus.

"It's unbelievable to me. I'm standing where they spoke to each other."

By 1:00 in the afternoon we were driving past the famous beach towns Marbella and Torremolinos. Torremolinos looked like every beach town we had ever seen, so we decided to bypass Marbella. Our primary goal was to see the White Villages in the province of Cádiz, which one of Barbara's dearest friends, Beth, had told us not to miss.

Though the weather was now perfect, this was where road problems had been reported. It didn't help that we were falling behind in our schedule, as the distances were longer than I had expected. We passed Gibraltar and were close enough to see it jutting out of the water before we left the main road for the beginning of an amazing adventure.

Traveling into a beautiful mountainous area, the condition of the road became extremely bad. Very narrow, it went winding up one mountainside and down another. At several points a portion of the road had actually been washed away by the flood and there were protective guard rails set up to keep one from going over the edge. But still the road continued on and up. Barbara became extremely anxious. And while I reassured her, I privately hoped we would soon reach our destination and get back on a safe roadway.

After seeing the first village we had no choice but to continue on to the next, as it was the only direction we could take to reach our final destination. Unfortunately, our map was far from great and I was having difficulty determining our exact location on the small, unmarked roads. By my estimation, ultimately the road would lead to the autoroute.

Another problem was now developing. It was 6:00 P.M. and we knew daylight would end by 6:30. Luckily I had found a way to bypass the second White Village. But as darkness approached, the worst possible thing I could imagine happened. We came to a total roadblock. We had driven hours through these mountains, and now we were stuck. All the way up not one car had come from the opposite direction. It appeared we might be left out in a deserted area with roads that were so treacherous it was not inconceivable one could go crashing down the side of a mountain.

You can imagine my surprise, with night falling, to see sitting at the roadblock a car driven by a young German and a female companion. He spoke perfect English.

With an inadequate map for small roads, I had no idea how to find our way in the dark of night. However, the young man had a detailed map of the region and told me to follow him. He would get us out. Barbara's panic subsided, and I was relieved because I was truly lost. In the dark, the road conditions in these mountains would be frightening.

With the Christmas season going on, Barbara's mind began to float back to a story she had read they day before about the fiftieth anniversary of the film *It's a Wonderful Life*.

I was following him down the dark road when Barbara asked, "What's his name?"

I could hardly believe the question.

"What's his name! Are you kidding? What's his name." I was concentrating so hard on the driving, I couldn't imagine why she asked that of me.

"How in the world am I supposed to know his name? He's just very nice. And he's going to get us out of here so we're not stranded in these mountains overnight."

Then Barbara, who's quite a lot more spiritual than I, suddenly said, "Clarence."

"Clarence! If his name is Clarence, he's probably the only young man in Germany with that name. It can't possibly be a common German name."

"I'm telling you he is *our* Clarence. There we were, not a car seen for an hour, and in terrible trouble. Then, out of nowhere, a person just as sweet as can be comes to rescue us from our plight. His name IS Clarence, and now at Christmastime he is doing his good deed to gain his wings. I know it. I know it for sure."

He said he was headed for Jerez. That was perfect as just before Jerez we'd reach the autoroute to Sevilla, where we could turn off. As we reached the autoroute, he waved and sped away. I was hoping he'd stop so I could thank him, but he was far out of sight.

"He's not going to Jerez. His job's done and we have been touched by an angel."

I can't verify whether he's in Spain or Germany now, or in heaven as Barbara has assured me, but the experience was one not to be forgotten. Wherever he is, I'd like to thank him profusely, whether his name is Clarence or a more common German name.

By the time we arrived in Sevilla it was 9:00 P.M. We came down a wide and beautifully treed highway. I could tell this was going to be an exquisite city like Madrid.

Having trouble with the street signs, at a plaza I lowered my window and asked a pedestrian in my awful Spanish to please tell me the location of Hotel Alphonso XIII. Believe it or not the idiot American had done it again. With a hearty laugh he pointed straight above my head to the sign. We were sitting directly in front of our hotel.

The Alphonso XIII is called one of the most beautiful hotels in the world, and the description is not exaggerated. Yet the cost was very reasonable by U.S. standards.

Seville, with its streets lined by orange trees, is exquisite. I kept wondering why the oranges weren't pulled off the trees by street people and beggars. Questioning the concierge at the hotel, he laughed and explained, "These oranges are not edible. When spring comes the trees blossom and the oranges are then used to make perfumes."

The streets were crowded during this holiday season. Although this is a city which 1,500 years ago was ruled by the Moors, and is just a short distance from Africa, we didn't see any blacks among those out walking. Coming from San Antonio, a tricultural city, Hispanic, Anglo, and Afro-American, such a homogeneous society was somewhat lacking.

Though we had a lovely lunch at Albahaca, Barbara and I agreed, among the countries we had visited, our clear choice for the best food was France.

We had the typical very late Spanish evening. At 9:00 P.M. we went to the class restaurant of Sevilla, Egana-Oriza, and it indeed lived up to the claims. It was 11:00 when we arrived at El Arenal for the best flamenco music and dancing in Seville, the heart of flamenco music in Spain. The hour-and-a-half show ended at 1:00 in the morning.

Back at our hotel people were getting ready to go out. Questioning the receptionist he said, "Oh, of course, they're starting to go to discos." By 2:00 we were asleep.

We were back on the street in the morning. It was raining again, and the crowds were gone. Maybe it was the weather, or were the Spaniards sleeping off a very late night? The rain didn't stop us. We did some shopping on the walking mall and visited the Alcazar, a palace built in the thirteenth century, where the detail was absolutely gorgeous.

When the sun broke out, I said to Barbara, "Let's take a carriage ride."

We had no idea how lovely the ride, which goes primarily through Parque de María Luisa, would be. The elderly carriage driver gave us a running account of everything we saw. María Luisa was a Spanish princess. What we were seeing, and it was nothing short of phenomenal, was the site of the 1929 World's Fair in Seville.

I've seen a number of the World's Fairs since my first in 1939, in New York. Some of the 1939 structures still stand, but most of the fairs I have seen leave only a structure or two remaining after the fair. The philosophy was quite different in 1929. A number of the pavilions still exist. Our driver told us the Spanish pavilion took fifteen years to build. It's not difficult to believe. In separate alcoves there are fifty colored mosaics, representing each of the Spanish provinces. It is shaped in a semi-circle which surrounds a pool with bridges traversing it. There are multiple staircases with decorative tile balusters and railings. Each look at this immense structure revealed one remarkable detail after another.

The park was filled with lush plantings. The orange trees I previously described were all over. We were told that the fragrance in Seville in April, when the blossoms open for one month, is intoxicating. Like Madrid, Seville is a city not to be missed.

But it was time to leave this grand city and head east to Barcelona for New Year's Eve. In a driving rainstorm we got to Carmona by lunchtime and Cordoba by evening.

Flashback

One thing that rainy weather, day after day, promotes is making love. To get some perspective on what I am about to write, let me begin by saying my wife and some of my daughters can tell you the exact garments of clothing they wore at an event attended years previously. On the other hand I have difficulty remembering what I wore yesterday.

I cannot tell you how many times my wife and I have made love. And I certainly cannot remember any specific details about those times, though divine, except for a very few occasions. I can remember the very first time we made love and I will never forget making love with great difficulty on this trip during the ferry ride to Greece in a bed about twenty-four inches wide. But the time that we made love during our first trip to France, more than ten years ago, is the single most memorable time in our love affair.

We had traveled to Paris, and in a last-minute decision decided to drive to the Loire Valley for a few days, without reservations anywhere. As the first day passed, and it was getting near sunset, I suggested we stop in the next town and find a place to stay. It was springtime and the season was busy with tourists. The only place with space had a name like L'Hôtel de la Gare, "the hotel of the train station," and was located across the street.

It was not exactly a starred residence. Its restaurant had a window with Coca-Cola and beer decals. A charming Frenchwoman had many roles there. She managed the restaurant, waited the tables, was the hotel desk clerk, and helped us with our baggage.

We were fortunate to get the last room. It was small and on the very top floor, reached by a winding staircase. It was so clean that, as Barbara would say, "You could eat off the floors." The slanted dormer walls made it difficult for me to stand in any location.

With the bed immediately adjacent to the door, we went to sleep in the Loire Valley. When we awoke in the romance of France and the Loire, our sleeping garments were soon removed and we began our forever memorable episode of tender lovemaking.

At the height of our passion in our birthday suits, the door suddenly opened. Barbara turned her head, saw the chambermaid standing next to her, and let out a scream that was heard almost to Paris. The chambermaid, totally unflustered, and as if to say, "I've seen better and I'm unimpressed," let out a guttural, "Huh," as she closed the door.

Barbara was in an absolute panic, as if she were fifteen years old and caught in the act by her mother. She jumped out of bed, rushing for her clothes.

"Oh, I've got to get out of here quickly."

"What's the problem? Do you think they're going to report us to the authorities for indecent behavior of a husband and wife in their bedroom?"

Barbara heard none of that and was dressing as fast as possible. Certain that our lovemaking was over for the day, I followed her lead. We were ready to leave when I went to open the door and found it locked. Analyzing what was going on, the scenario became clear. In this very old building the doors were opened or locked by key from inside or out. Last night we had opened the door and inadvertently left the key on the outside. In the morning the maid had come to do the room. Seeing the key in the door, she turned it and entered. Realizing that Barbara was now committing that dastardly act, and wanting to protect her from future intruders, when the maid closed the door she locked it.

To me making love had hardly been a problem, even with a guest viewer. The real problem was language and our lack of it. There was a phone in the room, so I called the same woman who ran everything. I was more able to understand her than to make myself understood. It is possible that the chambermaid had already made her aware of her great find that morning, because during the entire conversation she never stopped laughing.

I assume there was only one key for the room and she came to the conclusion we had it, but were too dumb to place it in the lock and turn it. While I was trying, without success, to explain our plight, she said in French, "Open the window, take your key, and throw it out on the street. I'll go out there and pick it up and come up and open the door."

"Idiot" was an understood but not spoken word.

After some period of time, with the continuous laughter, I was able to clarify the key was on the outside of the door. Within moments she came and helped us make our escape, still laughing. I suggested to Barbara that we have breakfast there before leaving.

The woman manager and the chambermaid kept walking through the dining area. Barbara was certain she heard snickering every time they passed. She ate very quickly and insisted we had to get out as soon as possible. Within a very short time we were gone.

I can't recall where we stayed the next night, but I called in advance to one of the finest establishments in the Loire Valley. I had to make up for Barbara's embarrassment at it being discovered that she was not still virginal, all her children notwithstanding.

There are many things I don't remember, but I'll never forget that lovemaking.

Present

It was still raining, as it had almost every day since we arrived in Spain. The weather had been bad throughout Europe, with many deaths attributed to it. But, with no guarantees, we always took the weather as it came and moved ahead. I can't imagine we would have done anything differently on this trip had the sun shone every day.

Flashback

I can recall vividly a weather experience we shared with our friends Judy and Seymour in the Dordogne area of France. There are so many wonderful places there.

We had decided to see the Padirac chasm one day and stopped in Rocamadour to have a picnic lunch in that city built into the side of a mountain. Barbara and Seymour, both wine lovers, bought a bottle of red wine to share. While Judy and I ate baguettes with ham, cheese, and tomatoes, Seymour and Barbara bought a large tin of foie gras. The two of them then consumed about 5000 calories each of foie gras and wine, with enough fat to choke off the arteries of an army. They gluttonously relished every moment.

After the chasm we were fatigued. On the way back to our lovely hotel, we came upon an outdoor *fête du fromage* (cheese festival) in temporary tents and bought a few items.

Back at the hotel, we sat in front of a large picture window and saw the weather suddenly change. The sky turned black with severe winds and rain. The following morning we were told a tornado had struck, and I wondered about the tents at the cheese festival. As we drove, for miles around, trees were down with the roots torn out of the ground, and the roads blocked. It restricted some of the things we could do, but it didn't stop us much.

Thank God, that's the worst weather disaster we've ever faced in our travels.

The Present

On our way to Barcelona we stopped in a small town, Valdepenas, to have lunch. We arrived in town shortly before 1:00 in the afternoon. The traffic congestion was impossible, and we drove in circles trying to find a place to park. A car in front of us had the bumper sticker "I love Valdepenas" in Spanish. But we didn't share in that philosophy.

Finally we turned down a street with cars parked on both sides and a single lane in the middle. At the end of the street, there was no outlet. By this time there was a line of cars behind us. I had to get out of the car to tell the others. One by one, each car had to back out. It took fifteen minutes just to escape from that street, and an hour and a half until we found a restaurant and a parking space. Valdepenas was not our best stop.

Flashback

Driving in Europe is always a challenge. In many towns the streets are barely wide enough for one car. With traffic congestion very severe, especially on market day, I'll never forget an incident in Aix-en-Provence, one of our favorite cities in Provence.

Saturday is market day in Aix and it was our first visit. It's necessary to get there early, as they end at noon, but we didn't arrive until 10:30 in the morning. Not knowing the city, I said to Barbara, "Let's park as close as we can to the center of the city."

That was a terrible mistake! A car can't be parked in the center of Aix on market day. It's necessary to park outside the center and walk in, actually a short distance. We were trapped in small streets with people walking in between cars. We got stuck behind trucks unloading, unable to move forward or back. Then we made a terrible mistake. We turned into a pedestrian-only street. There were no more cars, only masses of pedestrians walking in front of, behind, and on both sides of the car. They looked into our window to see who these crazy people were. We moved inches at a time, hoping somehow to find an exit. There in front of us was a large cylindrical stantion, one foot wide and two feet high.

The situation was now impossible. There was no way forward. Still surrounded by pedestrians, I inched slowly backward, trying to get out of this mess before we were attacked by angry shoppers. I expected that any moment we would be dragged out of our car.

Then a man came shouting at my window, telling me to move forward. I tried to explain I was blocked by the stantion. He waved us forward, shouting, "*Compression!*"

I hadn't the foggiest notion what he meant. Barbara was in a panic. I was too, not willing to let on. I assumed another mistake meant capital punishment. I drove up to the obstruction. Then, *voilà*, just about a foot away, the barrel lowered itself into the ground.

Of course, it's a trick I've done many times in the past, but I didn't want to have to use it with all those people watching. We got out of the pedestrian area and soon found a parking lot. There was one small problem. By that time the market was over, so we had to return on another Saturday. The next time we were wiser about the traffic on market day.

Present

If Christmas Eve in the Alhambra had been a major disappointment, New Year's Eve in Barcelona was not about to duplicate that.

Driving into another large city, as usual the help offered by locals was way beyond the call of duty. I leaned out my window, asking another driver the way to our hotel. He began giving instructions and then stopped, saying they would be too difficult to describe.

"Follow me."

He drove in a very circuitous route which could not possibly have been where he was going on his own. We were led right up to the hotel and then he was on his way.

The Palace Hotel was simply grand. We checked in and I went scouting for local information and newspapers. Meanwhile the concierge got us tickets for *West Side Story*, in Spanish. This special New Year's Eve presentation was almost completely sold out.

The show began after 10:30. Oh! These Spaniards. Shortly before midnight, after Maria sings, "I Feel Pretty," the curtain came down. At each seat there was a bag of colored paper rolls, hats, paper necklaces, New Year's Eve horns, and a bag of grapes.

The orchestra went up on the stage, joining the performers. Horns began blowing. Ushers with supermarket carts filled with bottles of champagne came down the aisles, giving everyone a bottle. As the countdown for midnight came, a bell chimed twelve times. In the Spanish custom, with each ringing a grape was to be eaten. There were twelve in each bag. The noisy, joyful audience was dancing in the aisles. And we joined them at our seats in a box above the orchestra. The festivities continued for half an hour. After the confetti and rolls of colored paper were cleared from the stage, the cast reprised "I Feel Pretty," and went on with the show, ending at 2:00 A.M. We finished that special evening walking back to our hotel. By 3:00 A.M. we were just getting into bed. It was probably the most wonderful New Year's Eve we had ever experienced.

We got up with difficulty at 10:30 A.M., after the breakfast buffet had ended. The maître d' agreed to give us juice and coffee, and brought us a bill for $35, the charge for two full buffet breakfasts. Some things are just a little too much, so I went to speak with the manager. He concurred it was absolutely absurd and threw away the bill.

The sun came out and we spent the day on the streets of Barcelona, in an area called Rambla. There were beautiful flowers, bird and animal vendors, and outdoor artists.

We wanted to see the buildings of Barcelona's most famous architect, Gaudi, unlike anything we'd ever seen. But on New Year's Day we could only see the exteriors. Barcelona cannot be appreciated unless the Gaudi architecture is part of the experience.

Gaudi died in a street accident in 1926. A church he designed, which was in the midst of construction at that time, is still being built seventy-three years later.

We returned to the hotel, via the Metro. Then at 10:30 we dined where the concierge recommended, La Dama. On arrival the restaurant was empty, but by midnight it was packed. The Spanish march to a different drummer when it comes to the clock.

Barcelona was phenomenal. We loved Madrid, and then we thought Seville was even better. Barcelona became our favorite, primarily due to Gaudi and other architects.

It took a while to appreciate special things. At almost every corner the buildings were not at ninety-degree angles. Every corner was cut off in a forty-five-degree diagonal. With the setback at each corner, the intersections became circles. The look was grand. The buildings are old, with intricate facades. But nothing compared with the Gaudis.

We went to a museum of Gaudi's architecture. It might more properly be called his art, for they are like sculptures. The museum was excellent, providing great detail as to the logic and architectural theory of the buildings, of which there are many in Barcelona.

As advised by the guidebooks, we attended a concert at the Music Palace. Built in 1908 by a friend of Gaudi, it has the feel of his work. The best description was Barbara's.

"I feel like I'm in the center of a wedding cake."

The walls and ceilings had ornate decorations. Among the ceramic flowers and human forms were animals and muses coming out of the walls. The muses had the lower halves of their bodies designed in mosaics, while the upper halves were in relief. Between breathtaking forms there were large splashes of Tiffany glass with floral decorations.

After the concert we dined at Barcelona's finest *nouvelle cuisine* restaurant, Jean Luc Figueras. Barbara is a great eater, but doesn't like desserts. At this dinner we ordered one dessert and Barbara couldn't keep her eyes or her hands off it. I felt deprived, as she usually leaves it all to me. There was a slice of the most delicious carrot cake in the center with a scoop of lemon sorbet and strips of mandoline-sliced carrots over the top. A large scoop of a plum sauce could be combined with the cake or the sorbet or both. On the other side, in a lake of luscious *crème anglaise*, was a piece of delicious chocolate cake.

* * *

It was time to leave, but I knew I would not soon forget Spain. In the morning, I told Barbara I was going out and would return to join her for a late breakfast. I wanted to find two items for Barbara before we left Spain. I knew this would be the last chance.

After our experiences she said, "I'd love to have a book of Gaudi's architecture to remind me of the things we've seen, and I wonder if there's one about the Music Palace."

I was committed to finding them even though it was raining cats and dogs and the wind was fierce. The concierge sent me to a store three blocks away to solve my problem, Librairie Catalano. I found two books there. One was a book on Gaudi which had been translated into many languages. But they could find no copy in English. The pictures were wonderful, but it would be so much better if we could read the descriptions.

Their only book on the Palau de la Música was in Spanish as well. So they suggested a store two blocks away. Through the rain I made my way to Librairie Castell.

"Do you have the Gaudi book in English?"

"No, we're sorry. But you can try another bookstore one block away."

Undaunted, I got the same response at the Librairie Bosque, with one difference.

"Two blocks from here, I think you will find it at Happy Books."

To my delight they had the Gaudi book in English. I bought it and went back to purchase, in Spanish, the only book on the Music Palace. The weather was still vile.

92 · *Two Drifters* . . .

By the time I returned to the hotel an hour had passed. Barbara was in the lobby and came quickly over to me, giving me the biggest hug.

"Oh, I'm so glad to see you. I was sure you were dead. I was going to call the police or the embassy, certain you'd been run over in this weather by a car, like Gaudi. I thought, like Gaudi, no one would recognize you and leave you to die unidentified."

"No, sweetheart, I'm not dead. I'm always coming back like Skimbleshanks."

To understand that you have to know one of Barbara's nicknames for me is Skimbleshanks, of T. S. Eliot and *Cats* fame. Skimbleshanks was a cat who always was making certain that everything was right. Barbara says that describes me. She knows that whenever I disappear for a little while, I'm out making some preparations.

Flashback

Many years ago I arranged a ski trip for some couples in Vail, Colorado. The first morning I was out before anyone, buying ski passes and picking up newspapers. On my return I made certain everyone had their equipment. All dressed, we went to the gondola to go up the mountain together. As we stood in line, my friends, looking at me, began to laugh. I stood there wondering what was causing the hysterics. I asked what was so funny.

"Look at your feet," they chimed in.

As I looked down I saw that the idiot arranger of activities was standing in the ski line in his après-ski boots. I had never taken them off and put on my ski boots while I was assisting everyone else. Sometimes Skimbleshanks is, more than anything, a little forgetful.

Present

Barbara loved the books. We had breakfast and, with the rain slowing, we were on our way. The return trip was fine until just before our planned exit from the autoroute in France. We had a two-hour delay. All traffic was forced to leave the autoroute. It was evening and the rains returned as we drove through flooded side roads and finally home.

The following day I discovered what the problem had been. The rain and snow were so terrible they had to close the road because cars were spinning out of control.

The weather didn't change, making it perfect for staying home, unpacking, and listening to beautiful music. We went shopping for food and Barbara made a lunch and dinner with soups and wonderful salads, supported by great bread, cheese, and wine. The house had a wonderful warm and cozy feeling on a nasty, rainy day.

* * *

American newspapers had stories about Europe's horrible winter with weather-related deaths. When friends called concerned about our welfare, I quoted from Twain.

"Reports of our demise are greatly exaggerated."

Opening the curtain I saw the sun ... and snow falling in full force. The trees were covered. It was beautiful and shocking. This was the south of France, not snow country.

I called the Stapletons, and they assured me this was very bizarre weather. They promised the sun would melt the snow momentarily. In fact, that is what happened.

After lunch, we drove to Avignon. That city has always been a minor car problem for me. The town is old and has a medieval wall surrounding the central portion. From our direction one can enter through the wall quite easily and park in a parking structure under the Palace of the Popes, the primary sightseeing location in Avignon. However, at times it would be more convenient to park nearer the center of the town. That presented two problems, finding one's way to the center of the city and getting a parking space.

Flashback

Several years ago, while staying in Gigondas, we decided to eat in Avignon. After minimal difficulty we found ourselves in the center of town, near the restaurant. After a twenty-minute search, a car pulled out of a great space. We parked and went to dinner.

We had a long, leisurely, lovely meal. With our stomachs full and our hearts warm, we walked to our car. Now the problem began. Apparently we had parked in a private lot in front of apartments with assigned

Barbara and I standing in the courtyard of the rented Entrechaux house that served as our base during the year abroad.

Jack Frishman, who taught Barbara how to ski; and his always effervescent wife, Belinda, on a rainy day at the Louvre museum in Paris.

Sylvia and Hugh Wolff share a beautiful day with us at Luxembourg Gardens in Paris.

Twice we shared a picnic at the beautiful Roman aqueduct at Pont du Gard.

A pyramid in the Louvre courtyard.

The best part of this sign is "6 rooms, 25 beds."

A Turkish exotic dancer embarrasses Buddy Kost as she hugs him and collects money in her bra at a restaurant.

Rural Turkey: the retired soccer coach who couldn't stop telling us how thankful he was for America.

Three local women, rural Turkey.

A sign I couldn't pass up on a street in Istanbul.

A charming narrow trolley car on the streets of Istanbul.

On a boat ride down the Bosporus, in Istanbul, Turkey, Barbara is seen in front of an outdoor cook on the dock, preparing, in her words, "the best fish I've ever eaten."

Ice cream on the Bosporus, Turkey.

A spectacular view of the main thoroughfare in Ephesus.

Brian Stapleton preparing to spray smoke on the beehives.

Cowardly me in my white suit being protected from bee stings.

Brian and Barbara, on our way to the hives.

The wonders of Cappadocia, Turkey.

A Turkish senior citizen rides his donkey.

Two wonderful boys, one with a bare bottom. Rural Turkey.

At an Entrechaux dinner. Left to right, Florence and Buddy Kost, Pat Stapleton.

Barbara sitting at the dinner table in Entrechaux with Barbara Alweis and Brian Stapleton, now both residents of France.

A two-hour trip on France's high-speed train, TGV, brought Judy and Seymour Palans to a reunion lunch in Lyon, after we had driven several hours from Entrechaux.

The Beldens, who joined us in Belgium and toured the canals and streets of Brugge.

Bruno Verlet, with Barbara; and Helene Verlet, with me. These longtime friends frequently hosted us in France. Bruno is seen in Paris's Bagatelle Gardens and Hélène at a French castle near Fontainebleau.

A rainy day in Portofino, on the southern coast of France.

The inspiration for Monet's water-lilies paintings, at his residence in Giverny, France.

Architect Antonio Gaudi's still unfinished church in Barcelona, Spain.

Amazing Gaudi architecture in Barcelona.

Uri Segal of Israel, a world-famous symphony conductor and dear friend, on the podium at a rehearsal in Madrid. Together, between performances, we roamed tapas bars by day and shared dinners until 2:00 A.M.

Barbara, at Christmas in Granada, Spain.

Sheldon on the boat to Murano, the glasswork island, in Venice.

Ah, Venice!

Pat and Sheldon Goldberg at a coastal town in Italy.

Barbara and me, with Barney, at the base of the Matterhorn in Zermatt, Switzerland. Barney is the one in the middle.

Barbara looks down on gravestones at emotion-filled Gallipoli, on the Turkish coast.

Here I am wading, pants rolled up, through the warm waters of Pammukale just after dumping one terrible guide.

spaces. Now our car was blocked by several cars with nothing in front of us but metal stantions and the sidewalk. Barbara was distraught.

"We'll never get out. We'll have to find a place to sleep here in Avignon tonight."

I surveyed the situation, and then pulled the metal stantions out of the ground.

"What in the world are you doing?"

The sidewalk was rather narrow, so I asked Barbara to stand there as I got back into the car. At the end of the sidewalk was a nonremovable pole. The space between it and the building wall was also rather narrow. I drove the car onto the sidewalk. After some maneuvering I turned the car around, and drove toward the narrow space between the wall and the pole. Barbara's job was to determine if I could inch through it. There was very little clearance. With the side-view mirrors retracted back, I drove through and onto the street. The metal stantions replaced, we went home. Getting out of that mess was a lot of fun, but harrowing. It was awfully nice to be Barbara's hero, at least for a few hours.

Present

We had been invited to dinner at the Stapletons', together with a French doctor and his wife, and decided to go to a nearby winery to buy wine for our hosts. A sign indicated it was down the block. When we got to where we thought it was located, a sign said it was still two kilometers away, a mile and a quarter. Our plans immediately changed.

We decided to make it our exercise walk for the day. Changing into our walking shoes, we bundled ourselves up for the cold air and were on our way, surrounded by vineyards and vistas of hills and snow-capped mountains including Mont Ventoux.

Twenty minutes later we arrived at Cave de Saint-Gely, also known as Domaine de Champ-Long. Looking over the wines, we selected the top of the line. The price for the full bottle was under seven dollars. Other, lesser wines were priced from three to five dollars.

While there Barbara noticed something we had never seen before. Locals were in the shop buying wine. They were, however, not buying bottles. They brought their own plastic containers, which were filled from large vats. The price of the wine was by the liter, one and a third times the size of a normal wine bottle. It cost them $1.10. Amazing!

Flashback

The first time we stayed in a house in France presented the opportunity to use the *supermarché*. My French was almost nonexistent, but I was prepared to dive right in.

We noted a great system with shopping carts. All carts were returned to their proper area. The technique was simple. When a cart is taken from the storage area a ten-franc piece is inserted into a mechanism. When the cart is returned, the ten-franc piece is retrieved automatically. One wonders why it isn't utilized back home.

I had learned that bottled water was normally ordered in restaurants. They were charging about twenty francs ($3.75) for a large bottle, more than a quart. That seemed steep, but it was the going rate. I entered the *marché* and found the water, for us to use at home.

"*Pardonnez-moi, monsieur, combien d'une bouteille?*": How much is one bottle?

"*Un franc, dix centimes.*" One franc, ten centimes!

God, it's so difficult for me to make myself understood in French.

"*Non! Non! Le prix, le prix pour une bouteille?*": No! No! The price for one whole bottle?

Damn it! Same smile and same pleasant response, "*Un franc, dix centimes.*"

One more time. Maybe I should try another language. "*Tout bouteille! Tout bouteille!*": The whole bottle, not just a sip.

"*Un franc, dix centimes.*"

Slowly the fog disappeared over the American imbecile's head. The markup in the restaurants was about twentyfold.

When I returned home, without even a "hello" or "how are you" I blurted out to Barbara, "That's the last time I ever order bottled water in a restaurant."

When I explained my frustration, she shrugged her shoulders and said, "Everybody's got to earn a living."

Present

Our evening began at the Stapletons' home at 7:30 P.M. The other guests, Brigitte and Christian, were expected later, as Christian was still in his office seeing patients. They arrived about 8:15, which gave Barbara and me a few moments to tell of our trip to Spain. Pat and Brian have been to just about every place in the world. There was hardly any place we could describe which they had not seen in their wonderful experiences.

Christian and Brigitte were a darling, quite handsome couple. He was born in Versailles and grew up in Paris. She was raised in northern France near Lille. In the 1980s they came to Malaucène, where he now practiced general medicine. They had three children, a fifteen-year-old girl, a thirteen-year-old boy, and a ten-year-old girl.

They both had studied English, but, like us, had difficulty with the foreign language. We all tried to communicate in the other's language, making the evening great for the four of us and a challenge for Pat and Brian. They explained to us what we didn't know in French, and to Christian and Brigitte what confused them in English.

The main dinner dish was Oriental, with pork, spinach, dried Chinese mushrooms, ginger, and pepper, followed by a two-part dessert. One was a *gâteau de Noël*, an English version of an American fruitcake. Then there was a delicious persimmon pudding.

On our return from the Stapletons' I ran into difficulty with the telephone. Each night I checked our answering machine in Texas to see if any messages had been left. That night I was having difficulty getting through to the telephone service. Finally, the system straightened out and I made my calls. By 1:00 A.M. we were tucked in.

At 2:00 A.M. the phone rang.

"I understand you are having difficulty with your telephone."

"Who is this?" I asked.

It was a private company called by the telephone service to manage problems they can't resolve. I asked if she knew it was 2:00 A.M.

"Two A.M.? Where are you?"

"This is France you're calling."

"France! France! Are you kidding?"

"No, I'm not kidding and it's 2:00 in the morning."

"Oh, God! I'm so sorry. Goodnight," she said as she hung up.

In the morning we shopped in Vaison and purchased postcards, but the next day they were nowhere to be found. As we racked our brains trying to figure out where they might be, I remembered we had stopped in a shop to buy a belt that was on sale.

On my routine trip into Vaison, I stopped at the belt shop. Alongside the register were our postcards. I wasn't surprised to find them still there in this small town in France.

Flashback

This wasn't the first time something was lost or broken during European travels.

One morning in Gigondas we had a more serious problem. Breakfast was done and we were preparing for an outing. Barbara was dressing and I was in the kitchen doing the dishes. At that time my computer and printer did not have built-in electrical converters to change the voltage from 110 to 220. As a result we had separate converters.

Barbara came down to the kitchen to say, "You're not going to be happy about this. I dropped the electric converter (the one I needed for my printer) and it broke."

I responded, "There's no use getting upset. We'll buy another one in Avignon."

Many shops and several cities later we found it was impossible to buy an item in France which converted electricity from the French current to ours. Fortunately, with tape and thread we got the broken parts to stay together and last the remainder of the trip.

Lost items have been a problem on occasion. One day we were going to lunch with friends in Carpentras, twenty minutes away from the house. When we arrived I decided to give the waiter my credit card in advance and tell him to charge the meal to me, but my wallet was gone. Now I was not only in the position of not being able to treat, I couldn't even pay my half of the bill. Besides that, if the wallet was lost I was in for a lot of difficulty with a lost driver's license, credit cards, and money.

I excused myself and said I'd be gone for a little while. The wallet wasn't in the car, so I dashed home. I had been working at my computer before leaving and headed to that room. There on the floor was the wallet. I returned to the restaurant, gave the credit card to the waiter, and went on with the meal. Everyone asked me what was the problem.

"Oh, nothing, I just forgot something I had to do. Let's just have a great lunch."

The funniest loss occurred one night while Barbara and I were having dinner in a restaurant. She put her hand up to an ear and said, "Oh, my God, my earring's gone."

We searched around the area of the table, but nothing was to be found. We looked around the restaurant without success. We went out to the car but there was no earring.

"That was a gold earring I've had for years and loved," Barbara said very sadly.

"Then we'll replace it, honey. Don't be upset."

We returned home after dinner and parked the car in its usual location a little distance from the house, and walked on a dirt pathway between the car and the house.

The next day when walking to the car Barbara said, "Wait a minute."

She bent down toward the dirt road and said, "Look! Here it is! My earring."

But that's not the end of the story. The earring had fallen off because the back had come off. So we went to a local jeweler asking for a new back for her gold earring?

The woman looked at it and said in French, "That will be no problem. But did you know this is not a gold earring? It's just gold-plated."

Well, not every story can end up perfectly.

That's almost the most spectacular retrieval we've made of a lost item, but not quite. Once Barbara, while shopping, found that one lens was missing out of her glasses. She recalled that the last time she had touched them was when she changed to sunglasses when leaving a shop. We went back to the store, and believe it or not, Barbara saw her lens lying in the street up against the sidewalk in front of the store. Can you top that?

Present

Barbara heard a sale was going on in stores throughout the country. From our past experiences Barbara had found there was no store where she found more things that she liked than Printemps. They also gave a 10 percent discount to foreign travelers, and another 13 percent, the value-added tax, was refunded if more than 1,200 francs were spent.

We had been told there was a Printemps in Marseille, but couldn't find the store. A shopkeeper said they had moved to a shopping mall. We continued our search and were thrilled that we did. The prices were 40 to 50 percent off plus the additional 10 percent tourist deduction and 13 percent value-added tax taken off the balance. It was irresistible. Barbara found a jacket, slacks, and a purse. I found a chair and read the *Herald Tribune* while she shopped.

* * *

It was time to take our second ski trip in Europe. At nightfall we arrived at Bourg-Saint-Maurice, near Val d'Isère. It was the culmination of another wonderfully fortuitous event. As you may recall, on a street in Athens, a couple stopped when they saw us examining a street map. They helped us find a restaurant, and then these total strangers told us they ski in France every year and would love to meet us. Subsequently we made contact and arranged to meet them in Bourg St. Maurice.

On arrival we called Frank, who met us at the hotel where we had our reservation. After unloading, Frank and Anna, his wife, said we should come for a *raclette* dinner where we met Frank's older brother Jacques and his uncle, Louis. A stove in the center of the table held new potatoes. Around the sides were square pans, in which one placed a slab of cheese. When the cheese melted, it was poured over the potatoes. They also served prosciutto ham, *mortadella* and Italian salami, *cornichons*, and pickled onions.

For dessert there was a homemade *mille-feuille* (a thousand leaves) over a mouthwatering sauce, accompanied by clementines, pears, and apples.

Jacques and Louis, who spoke almost no English, were the most darling and gentle men one could imagine. The two bachelors live on a farm in the Pyrénées, near Biarritz, raising organic produce. They told us of their travels in France, Spain, and Canada.

After four hours of dinner and talk we returned to our room to prepare for skiing the next day with Franck. Anna couldn't join us, as she was in the process of renovating their house. It had been occupied for the past fifty years by Franck's parents. Rebuilt after World War II, the original farmhouse had been destroyed by the Germans during the war. Now Franck and Anna were modernizing it as a permanent vacation property for them and their son. The second floor was occupied by Jacques and Louis. Arrangements with contractors had to be completed then, as it was their last day before returning to Athens.

Unfortunately, our ski adventure was not to begin that day due to a dense fog. For us it was "noooo problame." We wandered around the charming village, bought little gifts for the grandchildren, and then had a great lunch. Even without skiing it was a lovely day.

In the evening we dined out with the family. Barbara sat next to Louis and Jacques and later told me that talking to them was wonderful. I was at the other end of the table between Anna and her mother. Three languages were being spoken. Frank, Anna, and their son conversed in Greek, French, and English. Anna's mother spoke only Greek. Jacques and Louis spoke exclusively French. Barbara and I used English with a bit of French. At one point the waiter told Anna's mother a story he thought was funny, in French, his only language. Anna's mother laughed heartily with him.

I turned to Anna and said, "I thought you told me she could only speak Greek."

"Of course! She doesn't understand a word he is saying. She looks at him and smiles like she understands. But she doesn't."

Anna was very interesting. Besides working as an economist, she's a flamenco dancer and singer. No less busy at home, she makes her own clothes, bed linens, and window treatments in her apartment. What she did best was tease Frank, and he, in return, did the same to her. We were fortunate to have spent these days with this loving family.

* * *

The next day the weather was perfect, giving us the opportunity to ski Val d'Isère for a day before leaving for Zermatt. We obtained rental skis and lift tickets and rode the Funival, a funicular (train) which went up the side of the mountain. When we got on the train I asked a young woman standing next to me if she knew the mountain.

"Oh, yes, I work here."

She was English and very sweet.

"Why don't you follow us?" she suggested. "I'm taking my father to the top of the mountain."

After that train we took a chair lift to another train, the fastest lift in the world. Several hundred people got on with us. We went zooming through a tunnel directly through the center of the mountain. Finally a cable car took us to the very top. We were in an area called Tigne, above the mountain peaks, looking down upon them. The feeling was astounding and what I imagine mountain climbers must feel when they reach a peak.

I cannot possibly describe to you the surge of excitement I felt. There were no trees. We seemed to be immediately adjacent to mountain peaks. It was the most spectacular skiing experience I had ever had.

This was going to be a long day, even longer than we had expected. We planned to drive from Val d'Isère to Zermatt in Switzerland, supposedly a three-and-a-half-hour trip. It's not possible to drive into Zermatt. You must drive to Täsch and park your car. From there you take a train for fifteen minutes to the Zermatt train station, where the hotel picks up guests at the station as long as they arrive no later than the 9:00 P.M. train.

As it turned out the drive took five hours. We arrived just before 9:00 with the train ready to leave in five minutes. I rapidly unloaded the car and dashed to park it almost a block away. I ran through the cold night air and when I returned, barely able to breathe, the train had left. Fortunately, the trains ran every thirty-five minutes. I called the hotel from the station and they were extremely nice, promising they would come to meet the later train.

"We've got one other problem. We're starving."

"Don't worry. We'll make certain that the hotel grill stays open to feed you."

They did all they promised and we had a lovely meal that ended about midnight. The hotel, Mont Cervin, was absolutely beautiful and very expensive. We couldn't fit it into our budget during high season, but during low season we could manage.

As you might imagine we slept late after that very long day and stuffed ourselves at the lovely buffet breakfast of wonderful fruits, cereals, eggs, meats, and pastries.

Zermatt, a quaint Swiss village, was nothing like Val d'Isère. The mountain is smaller with shorter runs and less sophisticated lifts than in France. But for the first time we had the unique European experience of taking a real railway train ride up the mountain. A local skier, about age seventy, sat next to us. Going up we got closer and closer to the Matterhorn.

"Quickly, come to this side of the train. That's the best view of the Matterhorn."

"Now come over here and look at this."

He told us all about the mountain and kept instructing us to jump from one side of the train to the other to see the specific sights. It was a joy being with him on the train.

He then told us about language in Switzerland. I had thought there were only two spoken there. We found out there are four. Besides German and French, Italian is the language of a small portion of the population. But the third most frequently used, more so than Italian, is an ancient tongue similar to Italian. I never got its name quite right.

When we reached the top we met another man who led us down his favorite runs.

Unfortunately, skiing conditions weren't great, with lots of hard-pack snow. After a late lunch we went in for a hot shower and rest before an Italian dinner.

The following day brought another wonderful experience. I woke Barbara early because we wanted to go over the top of Zermatt and ski down into Italy.

Taking a completely different route, we started with a small cable car, changed to a larger one, and finally shared a giant cabin holding over a hundred people, which took us to the top.

We then experienced something we had never encountered in our twenty years of skiing, a single continuous run lasting forty-five minutes, ending at the Italian town Cervinia. The run was wide and long. It is hard to describe the elation one gets from such a run.

When we arrived in Cervinia we found a wonderful Italian restaurant for lunch, but outsmarted ourselves a bit. Not wanting to carry our skis while seeking a restaurant, nor leave them unsecured, we stored them in a ski shop in the town. After lunch we returned for our skis, and found the shop had closed for lunch and wouldn't reopen for another hour. After twenty minutes I located the proprietor and retrieved our skis.

To return from the Italian side we took three cable cars and skied to Trockener Steg. The instructions for returning were working out perfectly, until … From Trockener Steg we were told to ski to Furgg to end our day. We would descend by cable car because the concierge had made it very clear that skiing to the bottom from there was too difficult.

When we arrived at Furgg the lifts were not well marked. Looking for the Furi lift to ride down, we mistakenly arrived at Schwartzsee. We asked and an amiable German responded.

"We want to get to the Furi lift."

He assumed we wanted to ski to the bottom of Furi, rather than its top, and began leading us. With a smile he said in broken English, "Nooo probleme. Follow me."

I knew it should be nearby, but stupidly we followed. Something was wrong. He led the way, waving us on with encouragement. Occasionally he'd stop, point to pristine surroundings, and say the other English expression he had learned, "Oooh my goodness."

Suddenly we came to the end of the great skiing into a narrow pathway that was steep and slick. Barbara began having a great deal of difficulty.

"*Wunderbar!* Noo problame," he exclaimed with a smile and a positive attitude.

Barbara slid into the side of the road, and when I reached her she was in tears.

"Nooo problame," he came and said to her as he helped lift her.

She fell some more as he shouted encouragement, adding, "Ooh my goodness."

Barbara was crying and shouting at me, "I'll never forgive you for this!"

"Nooo problame, *wunderbar*," he continued.

I wasn't helping, as I couldn't stop laughing. This warm, friendly German skier was totally ignoring what was happening and cheering her on as if all was fine. He was in his glory. Barbara was semihysterical. And it looked like a Laurel and Hardy movie. The difficult skiing finally ended and we came to a spot requiring a long, difficult uphill walk.

"Nooo problame, *wunderbar*, ooh my goodness," our unofficial guide still kept saying with a smile that never let up.

Ultimately we came to the end of the roadway and back to a cable car to take us down. By this time, even Barbara was occasionally laughing at what was happening.

Flashback

Barbara began skiing with Jack Frishman, one of the nicest men in the world. She took lessons from Jack for years and would only ski with him. When we started skiing together, Jack was always with us. While Jack was teaching her, I was watching and learning. There was nothing Jack would tell Barbara that she wouldn't believe. He was her idol on skis. One day in Aspen, when we were together, Jack told us we would go down the mountain at the end of the day on a ski run we had never seen. He promised we would love it. A roadway during the summer months, it was a narrow ski path in winter.

When we got there, there was NO snow. We had no way to get

down the mountain. With skis off we began walking until a truck came with just enough room for Barbara. Jack and I walked the entire way. Barbara and I have never forgotten that day.

We still see Jack and his wonderful wife Belinda whenever we can, but never stop teasing him about that ski run. From that incident we thought we had learned never to trust anyone who says "Follow me." Apparently we didn't learn well. Nevertheless we got back in one piece, Noo probleme! *Wunderbar!* and Ooh my goodness!

I must admit that Jack and this charming German skier weren't the only ones to do Barbara in while skiing. I'm included in that group. One day, after a late dinner in Vail, it snowed quite heavily and we were a great distance from our condominium. The buses had stopped running. I said I knew a short-cut and we began walking in a dimly lit area and got lost, ending up in snow well above our knees, resulting in a very difficult return to our condo. We laugh about it now, but there was little laughter that night. Barbara hasn't forgotten my shortcut.

The Present

We went out for a fondue dinner. Who could come to Switzerland and not have some fondue? But in the same sense, who wouldn't have Swiss chocolate here? I assumed we would find them left on our pillows. But guess what, no chocolates were left at all.

The following day we had lunch on a mountain terrace with a breathtaking view.

As we sat down at our table Barbara said, "Someone left their sunblock."

I read what I could on the label of the tube on the table, and not to be outdone by Barbara, I added, "It's not even a good-quality sunblock. It's called mild."

We both ordered what any self-respecting Swiss skier would order, bratwurst. And, when the plates arrived, asked the waitress, "Could we have some mustard?"

She handed us the tube which, in our minds, contained sunblock. We noticed, the "sunblock" could be found on all the tables. No wonder it was labeled "Mild."

Our last day was like all those that preceded it, absolutely cloudless skies with temperatures in the Thirties, a boon to the sellers of sunblock, not the mustard type of course.

At our last lunch I got a shock. My credit card was gone.

"Oh my goodness," I said in the words of our German guide of several days before. Unfortunately, I couldn't say, "Nooo problame," because there was a real one.

I pondered where I might have left it. When we got off the mountain we took an electric taxi to our hotel. The taxi took us to the furthest point he was allowed to travel and we walked the two blocks to the hotel in our ski boots, carrying our skis and poles.

I dropped off the equipment and went to the restaurant where we had eaten the previous night, only to realize it was located exactly where the taxi had just dropped us. Though annoyed with my stupidity, I found my credit card had been left there. As I returned to tell Barbara the good news I heard someone calling me. I turned and saw a young man waving.

"I was your waiter last night and found your credit card. It's at the restaurant now."

I thanked him profusely for his good deed and told him I had retrieved it moments before. It seemed like everyone wanted to be certain my day ended with "nooo problame."

On our last night we ate at the best restaurant in town, Le Mazot.

Leaving from the Mont Cervin Hotel was especially charming. They had a horse-drawn carriage to transport their guests back to the train station.

In general, I would say the advantages in France over Zermatt were threefold. The French ski stations we tried had more opportunities for varied skiing. After a few days in Zermatt the skiing became a little repetitious. We also felt that the food in France was much better. Finally, in Zermatt, prices for everything were extremely high.

An Aside

In Zermatt it's worthwhile to have some valuable information. At the train station, there's no one to help with luggage, which when skiing can be cumbersome. There are rolling carts, but they can't be used unless you have a Swiss five-franc piece to release the cart. When the cart is returned the money is refunded. But you MUST have the coin.

One car of the train has an open section, for the rolling carts. Take the cart with you on the train. On arrival take the cart to the taxi stand, and return it for your refund. Not knowing about this, people drag luggage back and forth down the length of the platform.

Another rule is to buy a combined ski ticket for Switzerland and Italy at the start. Some of the best skiing is on the Italian side. Without the combined ticket, each day you ski on the Italian side you must purchase a supplementary Italian ticket at a cost of $50 extra per person.

Finally, there are three areas in which to ski. If your hotel is in the center of town you can walk to the train station. That is what we did the first day. If, however, you are using either of the other two mountain accesses, getting there can present a problem.

The bus stop from our hotel was a long walk with skis. Going by taxi was quite expensive in relation to the distance. One company charged three francs per person, about $2.25 each way per person. Another charged $3.75 per person each way.

Wherever you eat you will find the meals very expensive. A meal for two can run into a hundred dollars or more quite easily without splurging on your choices or wine.

Hopefully this information may make a visit to Zermatt more easily managed.

Present

We left Zermatt at 12:45 P.M. and didn't arrive in Entrechaux until after nine. Quite tired, we got up late, unpacked, and in the late afternoon went to Vaison to pick up last-minute gifts. While there we stopped in a shop that was new to us. No name was out front at all, and a sign said it was open only three afternoons a week. How strange!

Apparently a women's-wear factory near Vaison subcontracts for major designers. The leftovers of their runs, some with designer names, were sold at this "store" at a major discount. We left with sweaters and a beautiful scarf, all for about a hundred dollars.

Our hectic plans for the next day began with lunch at St. Hubert, a movie at the Avignon cinema, and an evening concert in Vaison followed by dinner at La Bartavelle. Barbara says my energy level is going to kill her. But she can keep up and more. But there was a problem. We hadn't any idea where the concert was being held. I inquired in shops, but no one knew the location other than the general direction. When we arrived at the area a cherubic-looking man about seventy years old, walking his dog, approached us.

"Pardonnez-moi, où est le concert?"

"Aha!"

He knew just what we wanted and pointed us in the right direction.

* * *

On our last full day of the second part of our European adventure we went to the monthly Sunday meeting of the BELL, Beaumont English Language Library. The guest speaker was to be, of all people, me. The topic was "The Lighter Side of Obstetrics." Pat told me that one person called to say that she was not attending.

"There's nothing funny about having a baby," she complained to Pat.

Though hardly an unbiased observer, I felt there was sufficient laughter to call the afternoon a success. Everyone said they enjoyed it. But that seemed almost obligatory. I was certain from the introduction Brian gave me that they had gotten their money's worth.

"Dr. Keyser, in the battle for better health care for years, believes everyone has the right to be heard. He believes in free speech. That's why he is speaking free today."

Brian may have gotten the biggest laugh of the day.

* * *

We drove 9500 miles in the first half of our journey and were on our way home once again. Arriving in Orly airport earlier than we had expected, Barbara suggested we go to Paris. We took the Air France bus into the city and went to the Left Bank.

After dinner in a small restaurant we walked toward the Seine. A sightseeing boat came brightly lit down the river. Opposite the Louvre, we crossed a bridge over the Seine. Romantic is hardly an adequate description. A taxi drove us through the Louvre grounds, alongside the pyramids, and back to Montparnasse to get the airport bus, and then the Hilton shuttle.

Two taxi drivers were standing at the pickup point for the Air France bus. They made no effort to get us to use their taxis instead of the bus when we asked if we were in the proper location. Their only concern was that we get on the correct one.

When we got on the bus we were the only passengers.

"Where are you going to?" he asked us in French.

"To the airport Hilton," we responded.

There was no further conversation. When we arrived at the airport instead of the Air France dropoff point, he took us directly to the Hilton and wished us *"bon voyage."* Parisians are rude and unfriendly? Please tell that fairy tale to someone else. Barbara and I have found the people to be wonderful wherever we go. Whether it's France or any other country, treating others decently is all that is necessary to get the same response.

Part Three

THE DRIFTERS
in France and Italy

Traveling to distant locations, with multiple plane changes, is fraught with the threat of total chaos. The travel on the first two legs of our trip had been relatively uneventful, until we reached this crazy day. Our slide into Blunderville began when our flight to Europe was canceled due to a strike threat. Our super travel agent gained us two seats on another airline, when space was at a premium. When we arrived at the airport we found our plane was an hour late. But that was the least of our problems. Checking luggage all the way to Marseille had been a blessing on the previous trips on our preferred airline. On the new airline it would be taken only to Paris. There we would have to retrieve our luggage and personally carry it to the airline flying us from Paris to Marseille.

As previously, we were to pick up a leased Renault in Marseille. The desk there, moderately busy, opens only when a customer is scheduled to pick up a car. The delay in our Paris flight made our chances for making the Paris-Marseille connection slimmer by the minute. Moreover, it was Saturday, with no way to reach the Renault desk by phone.

We landed in Paris forty minutes before our scheduled departure to Marseille. But we were not through with confounding problems. Our plane couldn't get into its slot at the Orly airport, leaving us on the tarmac for another twenty minutes. I was still hoping we could pick up our luggage, dash over to Air-Inter, and make our connection.

Out came the luggage, piece by piece, or more like piece by piece minus one. Now we had to report the missing bag, and by then our flight was gone. But that was only the beginning. We had to transport the luggage down long corridors to another terminal. In the process we were required to give up our rolling carts and carry the four bags, plus four carry-ons, all by hand. But it could have been worse. We could have had five pieces if one hadn't gotten lost. After the huffing and puffing we finally made it to a connecting flight.

In Marseille the Renault attendant had long since left. A note said he would return, "In an hour." Finally, we got the car and drove to Entrechaux safe and sound.

But the question of safety brings up another point. When Seymour drove us to the San Antonio airport, a homeless person at a traffic light was requesting money.

Seymour casually said, "I wonder if for a buck she'll guarantee a safe flight." Now, Barbara is a nervous flyer and a suggestion that anything might go wrong is out of order.

"Quick! Stop! Let me give her a dollar. I can't take the chance, now that you've said that, in case not giving will make the difference," Barbara hollered out.

The dollar was given, but would two dollars have guaranteed our luggage?

In the morning the airline called and notified us, "Your luggage has been found and it will arrive in the Marseille airport by 1:00 this afternoon."

"Great. And when will it arrive in Entrechaux?"

"On Tuesday."

"On Tuesday, are you kidding?"

"No, I'm sorry. That's our first delivery time. But you can come and pick it up."

We had planned to start driving to Italy that day, and the drive to Marseille would be a three-hour round trip at least, but it was better than leaving for Italy without it.

"I'll be there."

So we planned to pack for Italy, then drive to Marseille to pick up the suitcase, have lunch, and start for Italy early the following day. But trouble was lurking. We found a few things missing, not unexpected in back-and-forth trips. We needed an umbrella, an alarm clock, and electrical adapters. We would stop in Avignon on our way to Marseille.

While driving we looked for a place to have lunch. Shortly before Carpentras we saw a sign for a restaurant. I had just passed it slightly when I stopped and backed into the parking lot and ... CRASH!!!! I heard an awful noise and looked back. The entire back window was shattered into a million pieces, leaving our station wagon completely open to nature. Apparently a sign, which couldn't be seen through the rear-view mirror, had its lower corner hit the top of the window frame and shattered the window.

Great! There was no way we could drive to Italy in that state, and it was Sunday. Now we'd have to wait until Renault opened on Monday. I didn't know how long it would take for repairs. I began wondering if we were meant to get to Italy at all.

Thoroughly exasperated, I drove to Carpentras, where we lunched at Café van Gogh. It looked raunchy, but so did the great restaurant where we had eaten in St. Rémy, in the fall. The food was wonderful. Barbara ate *salade paysanne* with goat cheese crêpes and smoked ham on the greens, followed by marinated mussels. I ordered a *salade niçoise* and *soupe de poisson*. All of that plus wine cost $30 for the two of us.

Our *supermarché* stop to buy the missing incidentals also failed, as the store was closed on Sundays. We continued on to Marseille, picked up our baggage, and returned home. Feeling truly down for the first time on this trip, and jet lagged, we went to sleep.

* * *

I began the day anxiously at the Renault dealer in Vaison. Apologetically, they told me they didn't have the replacement window and would call larger dealers in Orange, Carpentras, and Avignon. The answer was always the same. I was feeling pretty low.

Then they contacted the main Renault office. The response was no better. No one in the area had the part. We had already lost one day in Rome due to the baggage. Having never been there, the thought of losing another day was discouraging.

Since we were traveling east, the dealer made the following suggestion. The parts could be sent to the easternmost location in France, Beausoleil. We'd drive there immediately and drop off the car. The dealer would lend me a car to drive to Santa Margherita, an hour-and-a-half drive, where we had planned to spend the night. Then, the following day, I would drive back to Beausoleil, pick up my car with the window replaced, return to Santa Margherita to get Barbara, and go on to Rome. It would be a long day, but at least we would keep to our schedule. We decided to go for it.

When we got to Beausoleil, things began to sour again.

"Pas possible de finir à midi": It can't be done by noon. *"Peut-être à quinze heures"*: Maybe by 3:00.

"Oh, no," I thought. "I'll never get to Rome tomorrow."

After considerable negotiations we agreed I would call at 9:30 to see if the job could be completed by noon. They gave us, as a replacement, a tiny old Renault with so little power I couldn't keep up with the traffic. We chugged along like a Model T Ford, arriving in Santa Margherita two and a half hours later. Even if the repair was done by noon, I doubted I could get back by then, as I had to wait until 9:30 for verification that the job could be completed. I didn't believe this old jalopy could make it that quickly.

A cultural phenomenon complicated the problem. In France businesses close for lunch at noon, not opening until two or three or later. I knew that meant I could very well be stranded in Beausoleil for hours if I didn't make it back by 12:00.

Hoping things would work out, we checked into the lovely Grand Hôtel Miramare and went out to dinner at Trattoria Cesarina at the recommendation of our concierge. What we found was quite a surprise. When I asked for the menu before being seated, the animated and annoyed owner said, "There is no menu. Do you want to eat or read?"

It was in broken English and Italian. Somewhat intimidated, we sat down.

"I will bring you white wine and water. Do you want water with gas or not?"

"Can I have red wine?"

"Red wine with fish!!!!"

He was getting angrier, and I, more intimidated. I agreed to everything, but the die was cast. He didn't particularly care for me. But!!! He was crazy about Barbara and spoke to her in endearing terms, referring to me by saying *"lui,"* Italian for "him." The derisive comments were made with a shrug, as if to say, "Him, that piece of nothing?"

When he left the table to get our food, Barbara decided my new name should be "Louie." The entire evening was a hoot. He brought us four delicious courses of fish in different styles, including one with ravioli, and ended the meal with wonderful Italian pastries. The food, his commentary, and the whole atmosphere was terrific. By the end of the meal he was even befriending me and joining in our laughter.

* * *

At 9:30 A.M. I was advised the repair would be completed by noon. Leaving at 9:45 I had two hours and fifteen minutes to reach Beausoleil. On the highway, traffic suddenly slowed down due to a five-car collision. Once past that point I pushed the old car to its maximum. As I approached Beausoleil the hour was reaching noon. With a last dash, I arrived at five after twelve. The doors were locked and I was beside myself. I'd have to wait at least two hours for them to reopen. A few choice words may actually have been heard slipping through my lips until I heard my name called by the garage owner as he emerged from a car. He was leaving for lunch when he saw me drive up and turned his car around to reopen and give me my repaired station wagon.

I was thrilled and kept saying, "*Grazi, grazi, multo grazi, multo multo grazi.*" Thank you, thank you, thank you very much, thank you very very much.

As I left they waved and said, "*Au revoir.*" I could hardly contain my laughter. I was thanking them in Italian, forgetting I had left Italy, returning to France to get the car.

From a public phone I called Barbara to say I was on my way back for a late lunch together. Barbara had spent the morning and early afternoon walking through this lovely town on the water. We ate in a small pizzeria and were on our way toward Rome.

Before the fiasco of the car we had planned to see five towns called Cinque Terra on the Italian coast. We decided to make an adjustment and see just two of them. They can only be reached by driving through La Spezia. When we got there the traffic was terrible, delaying us an extra half-hour. The towns looked so similar to the coastlines in California and Maine, we decided to move on. Already way behind schedule, though we would have liked to stop and smell the roses, this didn't seem like the time or place. When we got back to the Autostrada, an hour had passed and we had not seen very much.

Looking at the map Barbara said, "Herbie, I've seen it but you haven't. You have got to see the Leaning Tower of Pisa, because we're going right past that town."

I left the Autostrada again at Pisa. We weren't off for five minutes when we faced a line of cars as far as the eye could reach. No one was moving, not one inch. We made a maneuver through the traffic and after half an hour we were back on the Autostrada. As we left we saw that the highway was closed by an eighteen-wheeler jackknifed across the road. I never did see the tower, but Barbara assured me, "It definitely is leaning."

What a day! I had driven to and from Beausoleil, and tried to see Cinque Terra and the Leaning Tower and had seen neither. It was late and we still had a long way to get to Rome. Arriving there after dark, we were totally lost. It's very difficult finding one's way at night in a large European city when it is completely new to you.

Driving down one of the major thoroughfares, Barbara and I saw one of the most unusual sights we have ever seen. In the distance there was a giant billboard, larger than normally seen on a highway. There were two big horses, one actually mounting the other. It was a sight to behold, probably twenty or thirty feet high. We passed it so quickly we couldn't tell what they were advertising. Barbara suggested it might be an ad for condoms.

With the car window opened, we asked everyone for directions and finally found our hotel at 10:30. We were given the last room in the hotel, Scalinata di Espana. The hotel is wonderfully located but the room was postage-stamp size. They promised to change our room in the morning. The desk clerk then sent us to a late-night restaurant for dinner. In Rome we were looking forward to fewer problems and wonderful experiences.

Flashback

Several years ago Seymour, Judy, Barbara, and I went to Paris. We had never seen the hotel we had reserved. Unpacked and unhappy, Barbara said the place was intolerable.

Judy chimed in, "I'm so glad you said it because I really wanted to."

I didn't believe we could get out of the reservation. Barbara and Judy said they wanted to find a hotel we liked in the past. I left the problem for them to resolve and went to get concert tickets, asking them to meet me at the hotel they preferred, The St. James and

Albany. When I arrived there, the desk clerk knew who I was. They had given him a description of a tall, bald man. He told me "the two women" had gone for the luggage.

I returned to the original hotel, where I found Barbara, Judy, and Seymour in the lobby with the suitcases packed. The desk clerk took one night's payment and said he hoped Judy's asthma attack would improve in the new hotel with air-conditioning. It was the first I'd heard of Judy's asthma, which remarkably disappeared once we left the hotel.

The Present

Barbara and I started the day at the Colosseum and the ancient Forums, followed by lunch at Osteria da Nerone. From there we headed for the Trevi fountain. Unlike the stories I've heard, I saw no one throwing coins into it, which brought me to one of two conclusions. Either the economy was bad or the tourists had no interest in returning. The story is, if you throw a coin into the Trevi fountain, you will revisit Rome.

Our next stop was the Piazza Navona, where, we were told, the best gelati was sold. We bought some and sat down in the shop to eat it. The tables were empty and we soon found out why. A waiter tapped us on the shoulder, telling us to leave. We couldn't sit down at their tables unless we paid the "inside" price for the ice cream. It was the first time I'd ever been thrown out of a shop after purchasing their product. By contrast, in France, people commonly buy breakfast pastries at a patisserie and bring them into a cafe, where they order coffee to have with them. No fuss is made about food being brought in by the customer. The episode in the gelateria was quite a turnoff, but when in Rome ...

The evening presented new problems. We planned an early dinner followed by a symphony orchestra concert. We had come by taxi because the concierge advised us against using our car in Rome. When the concert ended at 11:00 P.M., there were no taxis to be found. Interestingly, in contrast to New York, very few taxis were cruising the streets.

We were far from our hotel and decided to walk a mile to the closest Metro station, where we arrived at 11:35 P.M. A guard told us they closed at 11:30 P.M. There were no more trains. We had walked in the exact opposite direction of our hotel, which was now three miles away. As we exited the Metro a taxi miraculously appeared. What luck!

In the morning we began our sightseeing with a tour of the Vatican. The enormity of the center of the Catholic Church was so impressive. St. Peter's Basilica is one of the most remarkable churches we've ever seen. We remained in the area for a lovely lunch at Tre Pupazzi, and then went window-shopping on the world-famous Via Condotti.

At Prada, Louis Vuitton, and Gucci there were long lines of shoppers waiting to be allowed entry to purchase their very expensive products. I wondered why almost everyone was Japanese. The answer was quite simple. The prices of these items apparently were greatly inflated in Japan, so this was an opportunity to get them at a significant discount.

In the evening we heard the Mantua Chamber Orchestra play a Mozart concert. Having learned the taxi system the night before, after the concert I called for a cab. In three minutes it came and took us to the hotel without the stress of the previous evening.

* * *

Pat and Sheldon joined us in Rome to travel together for a week. They arrived in the morning by train from Paris and described their overnight trip. With the dining car full, the conductor suggested they join someone sitting alone. Their dining companion, who couldn't have been nicer, was Tom Stoppard, one of our favorite playwrights.

As usual they were great fun, teasing each other at every turn. Sheldon had spent two and a half years in Italy during World War II, moving with the American army through Sicily, southern Italy, and then Rome. He speaks Italian well and had the best time talking to everyone. Sheldon has a wonderful knack of laughing with the people he meets in conversation, especially about accidentally switching into Spanish. Barbara has the same problem with Spanish and French. I'm lucky. I get my English mixed with nothing.

Pat kept ribbing Sheldon about what he should be buying in order to be dressed properly. I can relate to that because Barbara is of the firm conclusion, were she not with me, I wouldn't be allowed on city streets due to a lack of sophistication in assembling a wardrobe. Obviously, manner of dress is less important to Sheldon and me than to our mates. But Sheldon and I still consider ourselves to be the pictures of sartorial splendor.

While in Rome Sheldon asked Pat if it wouldn't be a fine idea to find his girlfriend of fifty years ago. She didn't think so, as they've been married for forty-five years.

For dinner we went to Al Ceppo, a restaurant for locals rather than tourists. Most of the parties were large groups of friends and families, eight, ten, and twelve. The food was excellent, but it was necessary to know Italian. There was no English translation of the menu and almost no English spoken. Sheldon was a big help, but his knowledge of food terminology was not as good as his conversational Italian. I had no idea whatsoever what I had ordered until it arrived. It turned out to be calamari in a wonderful sauce.

* * *

Getting out of Rome by car was not half as bad as I had expected. The desk clerk at the hotel provided us with excellent instructions. We were on our way to Anzio and Nettuno, site of the American World War II Memorial cemetery.

I always experience overwhelming frustration and despair when I visit cemeteries such as Normandy, the Vietnam Memorial, and Gallipoli. The sites are beautiful, but their message causes great anger to well up in me, about the loss of so many young lives. These places should absolutely not be missed, to be certain that we never forget. In Nettuno there are 8,000 grave markers lined up as far as the eye can reach and a very moving memorial.

Anzio is the site of the British Memorial.

Patricia, using a new book, found a wonderful suggestion for lunch in Nettuno. The restaurant is Rodo. It is small, with a simple ambience, but the food was marvelous.

The owner, sensing our concern about leaving a car full of luggage, seated us in front of a window where our car was parked. The proprietor and his family were so excited about the reference to them in the guidebook they treated us royally. They had never seen the book and loved speaking Italian to Sheldon about it. The relationship between Sheldon and the restaurant owner was considerably different than my encounter with the restaurant owner in Santa Margherita. There was no mention of *"lui"* here.

Everyone who meets Sheldon falls in love with him and his ebullient personality. Of course Pat, who's been married to him for forty-five years and loves him dearly, doesn't think he's as cute as the rest of us do. No one's a hero in his own hometown.

The next challenge of the day was to make it to Caserta, where

Sheldon had spent a significant portion of his time in Italy organizing shows for the soldiers. Sheldon wanted to see the army headquarters, which at that time was in the old Palace of Victor Emanuel. During his stay in Europe in World War II Sheldon was as a musician. Though only a corporal, he was the leader of an army band, the members of which were in some of the best big bands in civilian life before they were drafted.

Barbara, who has known Sheldon for forty-five years, tells a wonderful story about him. As a Canadian, his family sent him from Canada to live with relatives in the United States, fearful that he'd be drafted during the early years that the British Empire was at war. That was before the U.S. entered the war in 1941. But Canada never had a draft, and he was drafted into the United States Army, where he served during the entire war.

Going toward Naples we saw prostitutes on the highway, not a city street. They appeared every few miles. It was my first time ever to see that on a highway.

I was concerned we wouldn't reach Caserta in daylight. It wasn't as if we were just going from one point to another. We were smelling the roses. We had spent over two hours in Nettuno having the best time over lunch, not thinking about time at all. Then we got into some bad traffic. What else would you expect when you are trying to make time?

At one point Pat completely broke me up. Recognizing the time problem, and not wanting Sheldon to be disappointed, she said, "Do you recognize this part of Caserta?"

Before Sheldon could respond I said, "We haven't reached Caserta yet!"

"Herbie, you are so dumb. Why didn't you keep your mouth shut? It's been fifty years since he's seen it. Maybe he would have thought we got there in case we don't make it on time." Though the joke was at his expense, even Sheldon thought it was funny.

Finally at 5:30 P.M., half an hour before sunset, we reached Caserta. We found the old palace. But fifty years had passed. It was now an Italian military installation and admittance was not allowed. Sheldon talked to an older guard at the gate who recalled it had once been American headquarters. Just seeing the old familiar surroundings made a big difference for Sheldon. I was pleased knowing how much it meant to him.

* * *

We arrived in Ravello in the dark after climbing up a long, winding road. Pat, sitting in the front seat, was nervous about the road, or was it the speed I was driving? I had no concerns, having driven in much more difficult locations in the past. The streets were so narrow the car could barely pass. Finally, we reached the hotel parking lot. A woman met us and said the bellman wouldn't be available for twenty minutes. In this off season only one person was on duty. Pat suggested that we take whatever pieces we could carry ourselves. The following conversation was absolutely hysterical.

The hotel was in two separate sections. In the off season, only one section was open. The parking lot was adjacent to the closed section, requiring a walk to the lobby.

Sheldon asked the woman, "Where is the hotel?"

"It is about a three-minute walk."

Thinking of carrying the luggage Sheldon said, "Three minutes?"

"Maybe four."

"Four?"

"Maybe five."

"Is it easy?"

"Yes. ... Until the steps."

"Steps?"

"Maybe ten. And then the hill."

"Hill?"

As each thing was added we began laughing harder and harder. The wonderful thing is that the woman talking to us was laughing, as well. But the laughter was hardly over. The march up to the hotel wound around and around. Each time we reached a corner we saw some other surprise in the approach which broke us up again. The trip actually involved a rather steep uphill climb all the way and the total number of steps was thrity-nine. Carrying all that luggage it took us about fifteen minutes to reach our destination.

In the morning we went to the ruins of Pompeii. Impressive is an understatement to describe what happened here almost two thousand years ago. The city was quite large and it would take at least four or five hours to get through it all. It was easy to get lost.

Sheldon had seen it fifty years ago and had some faint recollections. He told us he remembered there was a brothel in ancient Pompeii identified by the original pornographic pictures on its walls. He wanted to show it to Pat. We followed the recommendations in the guidebook but no brothel appeared. After several hours, Sheldon and Pat got tired, and went back to the entrance to wait for us until we were done.

The very next location where Barbara and I stopped was the brothel. The pornographic pictures were there just as Sheldon had said. But Pat never saw them.

* * *

The following day we went toward the Amalfi coast. Barbara and Pat had looked at pottery in Ravello but decided the prices were inflated in that resort town. Viettri, noted for its ceramics, was where we were headed. I was still nervous about leaving a car loaded with luggage while we shopped. The warnings are constant about thefts. Fortunately, I found a lot opposite the pottery shops, which were lined up one after another. Every few minutes Sheldon or I checked to be certain the car was still intact.

Barbara and Pat were amazing. They must have gone into each shop at least five times. Comparing prices, patterns, and colors, they finally made decisions. Then it was time for Sheldon and me to negotiate prices. After a brief conversation we would reach an agreed-upon price. During our negotiations Barbara came to the counter with some other small pieces she wanted. The owner indicated she could take them as a gift. The final price was at a 10 percent discount. When the owner threw in the extra pieces for nothing, it probably indicated how much we were overpaying. Nevertheless, the shopping and the negotiating were all part of making the experience fun and memorable.

An American shopper said she was going to lunch. In jest I asked if I was invited.

"Sure! We're going to Wendy's."

It's difficult to understand how one travels thousands of miles to Italy and eats at an American fast-food chain. Back at the car I told the story to my companions.

"I think we must have purchased the wrong things," Pat said.

"What makes you say that, Pat?" I asked.

"If she's buying what we're buying, we must be buying the wrong things."

Later on this trip I would find myself shocked by the huge crowds of Americans at McDonald's on the Champs-Élysées in Paris. Economics cannot be the reason, as it is easy to find very inexpensive

French food, even cheaper than American fast-food chains. One would hope that tourists would experience the different culture they are in. But there's no accounting for taste.

When the laughter settled, I gave my three companions an assignment.

"I think we should eat about 1:30. We'll be somewhere between Naples and Rome by that time. Select a town or a restaurant and I'll get off the Autostrada."

Vittore was their choice. They knew of no restaurant, but the hilltops looked interesting. It was Monday and the restaurant signs indicated they were all closed. I saw a policeman and pulled over, asking Sheldon to get a recommendation from him.

He pondered for a moment and said a name that began with an "S."

It was three kilometers down the road and had a parking space directly in front, where we could watch the car, probably unnecessary in this small town.

The owner spoke perfect English. He said his mother had been born in Bayonne, New Jersey, and he had grown up there.

Twenty-seven years ago he opened his restaurant in Italy. On the wall there was a clipping from *Newsday*, which stated that the greatest pizza the reviewer had ever put in his mouth was made by this man. Now in this town, the size of a postage stamp, he prepares delicious Italian food. For dessert, we had ricotta cheesecake, which he had second thoughts about selling. He said it was too warm, having just come out of the oven.

"It will really be much better tomorrow," he insisted.

I had trouble believing the cheesecake could be better. Ricotta cheesecake is one of my very favorite desserts. I told him I'd return tomorrow, and really wished I could.

The name of the restaurant was Sordella 1919. We never did find out whether the 1919 was an address or a date.

On the Autostrada the crew had a new assignment. Guidebooks and maps were dispersed. They had to choose a place to stay overnight that could be reached before dark.

Pat chose the Villa Rigacci in Vaggio, not even on the Michelin map. We arrived at 5:30 P.M., just before dark. It was a luxury hotel at a very reasonable off-season rate.

Pat's find for a place to stay continued to be wonderful in the morning with a fine breakfast. Before leaving she got the name of an antique shop, Delle Arte, where she might find ceramic numbers for her home. Not only did the owner want to sell us things, he insisted on showing us his house, attached to the shop, and gave us the royal tour.

Sheldon, Barbara, and I were finally able to extricate ourselves from his clutches, but he had Pat entranced with the things he was selling. She decided on a large antique platter. Sheldon, glad to buy her anything, kept telling her there was no room for such a large piece in the car, to say nothing of, "How are we going to get the darn thing home?"

Pat insisted, "I'll carry it on my lap."

Somehow in the car Barbara and Pat made room for it between them. But on the way home, on the plane, the platter broke and all Pat's efforts were for naught.

When we reached Venice, Sheldon negotiated the water-taxi fee, in Italian, and we arrived at the Flora Hotel. After lunch we strolled in the Piazza San Marco. For us, Venice is the most romantic city in the world, with the possible exception of Paris.

Flashback

Venice evokes wonderful memories. Once we arranged a special package deal in Italy with four friends. Booking three rooms for fifteen nights, all with the Orient Express Company, they gave us a great price and we were able to stay where we wouldn't even consider today because of the prohibitive rates of $500 to $700 a night per room. On that trip we stayed at Splendido in Portofino, the Villa San Michele in Fiesole outside of Florence, and the pièce de resistance, the Cipriani in Venice. The Cipriani was unbelievably glamorous. With Venice flooding due to heavy rains, we walked through the Piazza San Marco on wide boards placed on racks above the flooded piazza. When the water receded, the six of us danced our way through the piazza while holding umbrellas to protect us from the rain. We were duplicating Gene Kelly's role. Venice was magical.

While there I kept a diary. Seymour and Judy's son had taken us to the airport and named the six of us after some cartoon characters I didn't know. He called us the Farkels, who apparently bumble their way through life, and this is the diary I wrote of that trip.

The Farkels Go to Italy

Judy, Seymour, Millie, Oscar, Barbara, and Herbie Farkel make an uneventful trip to Chicago where they face a three-hour layover until their flight to Europe. A two-week gin game begins at the Admiral's Club. Oscar Farkel breaks out to an early lead. Seymour has played with Oscar before. Seymour plays this day with a smirk on his face. It is that look that Mona Lisa always has. He knows sooner or later the numbers will change. Some think when Seymour plays gin rummy with Oscar a charge of petty theft should be filed.

By the time the flight is ready to leave they make a mad dash. Herbie Farkel leaves his Italian phrase book behind. For the remainder of the trip he will fumble through broken French and Yiddish. Certainly there will be no worthwhile Italian spoken.

The Farkels can only swing for four business-class seats, so Millie and Oscar are relegated to steerage. They say that they are pleased with their accommodations, as Chateaubriand is served. Others in that section call it chicken fricassee.

The real fun begins on the arrival at the airport. The plane is packed with several hundred passengers. But only two people lose their luggage, Judy and Herbie Farkel.

"Don't worry, the pieces are in Düsseldorf," the airport supervisor notifies them.

Herbie thinks that is nice. Even though he has never been to Dusseldorf, his luggage has. Judy and Herbie will have to make their way without clothes until tomorrow when they will be delivered to Portofino. Finally the Farkels get out of the airport, but that is only the beginning of their trials and tribulations.

"Brand X" rent-a-car provides them with a van that shimmies and shakes, has windshield wipers that break in a rainstorm, and hazard lights that get stuck. The van appears to be one built immediately after World War II, or maybe during.

The immediate problem is how the Farkels can all go to lunch in Milan while the car is loaded with luggage. They have been warned about the dangers of leaving a vehicle filled with luggage unwatched. A plan is made to leave it securely in the underground parking garage. On returning from lunch everything is found safe and secure. The Farkels' secret plan of diverting the thieves by locking all the doors while keeping the car windows open is successful. (Well, maybe leaving

124 · Two Drifters . . .

the windows open wasn't exactly planned.) The Farkels consider getting a patent on their security system.

When they finally arrive in Portofino, they go to the Hotel Splendido. The next morning after breakfast on the balconies of their rooms, the Farkels make their way into Portofino. The first activity of the day is a boat ride to San Fruttuoso. Unfortunately, the boat cannot get into the port due to rough waters. Out of anger Seymour and Herbie Farkel grab the captain and pull him to the floor of the cabin. Admiral, as he is known only to his closest friends, Oscar Farkel takes command of the vessel and goes to sea. The women rest in the back discussing what shopping they can accomplish in Hong Kong. But Oscar finally relents to the screams of the captain and returns the vessel to Portofino.

The Farkels are spotted by the locals as American tourists. Word reaches a local art gallery. They immediately change the prices on the paintings. When Seymour and Judy Farkel make their appearance, a zero has been added at the end of each price. They immediately outsmart the dealer by making an offer of 60 percent of the asking price. Since the owners have already marked the price up tenfold, after pleading poverty, they agree to rip off the American tourists. As soon as the Farkels leave the shop, word is passed to a restaurant on the waterfront, "The Farkels are coming!" Of course, they are prepared.

At the restaurant a rather unexciting meal is consumed to the extent of 276,000 lire (approximately $180). Oscar Farkel comments that they are paying for the view. Three feet in front of where the Farkels are sitting on the sidewalk, people are walking past. The view in front of the restaurant is being offered to them without charge. But the Farkels understand that from the restaurant the view feels like it must have more value.

Finally, a young waiter who has been trained at the Portofino school, known as CTF, persuades Herbie and Seymour that the 66,000 lire (approximately $45), called "service and cover," all goes to the owner and some fellow in the kitchen who washes the dishes. They provide the starving young student from CTF with an additional 10,000 lire.

Editor's note: The private institution known as CTF is more widely known as Con the Farkels. Score: Italy 1, USA 0.

Dinner at the Splendido is marvelous. Millie and Oscar Farkel challenge Barbara and Herbie to a tennis match at 8:00 A.M. It turns out to be a trick match with Oscar and Millie not showing up. They are testing Barbara and Herbie to see if they can play doubles alone. Herbie and Barbara continue the Farkel tradition of confusion. They play the match and cannot figure out how to have the ball returned to them after they hit it over the net.

A trip to Cinque Terra is canceled due to rain, and the Farkels load up and head on their way. They are determined to find out whether Florence is ready for them.

"Florence," one Farkel says. "I thought we were going to visit David."

Another responds, "Oh! I think that's his mother."

The trip, of course, is not uneventful. In the rain, the windshield wipers stop working. Oscar Farkel climbs up on the hood trying to fix them. Of course the car is not moving. Seymour Farkel asks if Oscar is willing to remain on the hood while the car is in motion and keep the window clear. Oscar considers it, but rejects the plan.

He says to Seymour, "What do you think I am, some sort of Farkel?" A garage is finally found and the wipers are repaired. Oscar decides to change the wiper blades as well. Millie, not understanding the generosity of the Farkel spirit, angrily asks Oscar why he doesn't change the tires to please Brand "X" car rental. Oscar promises to behave himself the remainder of the trip, but Millie is still pissed. Finally after a harrowing ride through the streets of Florence and Fiesole, the Farkels arrive at Villa San Michele.

The Farkels head for Florence trying to buy their way through the Ponte Vecchio. Though not many purchases are made, the Farkels do enter the Guiness book of records for the number of times they walk across the bridge looking at the exact same items.

A great lunch is had at Il Latini. Wonderful dishes are shared by all. Finally the Farkels return to Brand X rent-a-car for the daily exchange of vehicles, fourth day, three vans. Brand X is running out of vehicles in Europe. The Farkels are making themselves known. Even the ugly Americans are calling the Farkels ugly. But the Farkels know better. They have class. The Farkels decide to go their separate ways. Oscar and Millie Farkel are out making offers on twelve-foot sculptures and large pieces of furniture which they plan to hand-carry on the plane back to the United States. Oscar has told the local Florentians that he is a commander in the Texas militia (maybe he's not an admiral) and is here to present honorary awards to shopkeepers who provide a satisfactory discount. The Farkels end up purchasing most of the purses in Florence. They get every color of every size.

Barbara and Herbie make a move toward the museums, to see

Michelangelo's David. By a clever maneuver they go there in the van, and drive around for an hour searching for parking. Fortunately, they only have to waste five minutes looking at the sculpture. The crowd mills around, oohing and aahing. Herbie hears a faint moan from Barbara. He turns and hears Barbara, in between sighs, say, "He's not circumcised."

The next day the Farkels hit the road together. Oscar Farkel is today's tour guide. He is taking the Farkels to places they've never been. He describes those places. He has never been there either. They start off their ride singing. They join in typical Farkel flair.

Herbie Farkel says, "Let's do it in the style of the famous Italian, Art Capello."

Shortly after the trip begins, Seymour Farkel who has used every toilet in Italy, hears a calling. At a wine-tasting site he hopes facilities are available. With no intention of buying wine, Seymour approaches the owner, a middle-aged spinster, offers her a few thousand lire, and smiles while whispering "Toilet." She assumes he is making improper advances and begins to call the carabineri. Seymour finally agrees to accept a bottle of wine for his money. Fortunately, she allows him to relieve himself. Fiercely, while singing old great songs off-key, the Farkels advance further into the interior of Tuscany.

The weather becomes increasingly inclement while Oscar continually encourages Seymour to drive down country roads with hairpin turns to see something special. Primarily, what the Farkels see is rain and more rain. But they keep driving because they know that somewhere down the road is that special something that draws Farkels, food!

They finally arrive at Locanda dell'Amorosa, in Sinalunga, for a lovely lunch. Alas, the storm reaches a fever pitch and the highways are flooded. Seymour has the good sense to pull off until the disaster mitigates. As they near Florence, they reach a fork in the road. Against the consensus Oscar Farkel says go to the left. Some forty minutes later, with more rain beating down, after a turnaround, they arrive back at the same location. Finally the Farkels, fresh from singing the fortieth chorus of "When you walk through a storm, keep your chin up high, and don't …" arrive back at the hotel. They have completed their ten hours of punishment, to which they are entitled, because they are Farkels.

Judy, Seymour, Oscar, and Millie Farkel go to bed without dinner. Barbara and Herbie, maintaining the true Farkel spirit, order room service. Skip a meal; are you crazy?

For lunch the Farkels return to Il Latini. In front of the restaurant Seymour Farkel spots another couple from San Antonio. For that he has been named the winner of the special award which has been designated for the individual who first spots a San Antonian. Herbie had previously attempted to be the winner of the grand prize by stating that he saw Seymour Farkel. Oscar Farkel, the *commandatore*, disallows that. Consideration is even given to smacking Herbie on the head for such improper machinations.

Seymour, Judy, Barbara, and Herbie then wander around the Lorenzo street market buying typical Farkel *shtik drek* (junk). At 4:30 P.M. they rush to meet the hotel van to return them to Fiesole. They don't get that van or the 5:30 van either. You guessed it! The Farkels are standing on the wrong corner. Great going, Farkels! You've done it again.

The evening brings them to the farewell banquet at the Villa San Michele. The food is divine and, of course, Seymour Farkel receives his grand prize from the commandatore, 1,000 lire. Don't complain, sixty cents is sixty cents.

Finally the Farkels invade Venice. The Farkels could have come to Venice on any day. So, of course, they select the day of the Venice marathon. The runners are moving beautifully. The cars are not moving at all. By 2:00 P.M. the Farkels arrive at the exquisite Cipriani. Then it's back to mainland Venice and the Farkels' favorite pastime, window-shopping, followed by window-shopping, and to finish out the afternoon, a little window-shopping. Today is a rather unusual day for the Farkels. They don't do a lot wrong. They all go their merry way. Seymour and Judy accidentally meet Barbara and Herbie at the Accademia, Venice's main art gallery. The collection is quite remarkable, like the Farkels.

Afterward they go to Do Forni for a lovely lunch. The afternoon is spent wandering through the alleyways of Venice without the Farkels making a spectacle of themselves. Dinner is consumed at Al Mercanti, one of the nicest meals on the trip. The day ends with a late-night ride home on the launch. Tomorrow the Farkels will hire a guide.

Since the cost is quite significant, their plan is to see if they can torment him sufficiently, so that he quits before their sightseeing is completed. Certainly no matter what happens the guide will be entitled to one of Commandatore Oscar's awards.

Herbie Farkel arises at the crack of dawn for a meeting with Oscar in the pool. The race down the length of this Olympic-size swimming pool begins at 7:30 A.M. When Herbie has completed several laps he is uncertain as to whether he is in front or behind. It takes Herbie a while to realize that Oscar Farkel has not shown up. Herbie is really sharp.

After breakfast, it is off with the guide for the day. Franco Nogara doesn't realize he is going to have the Farkels all day. He treats them like they are normal and they have a great day. His knowledge of Venice is quite amazing. He takes them to a wonderful little spot for pizza, Al Sole di Napoli at Campo San Margherita. The tour ends at about 4:00 P.M. and the Farkels are tired and ready to cave in. After a while they regain their energy. Oscar and Millie assume the group responsibility for shop "until you drop."

Seymour Farkel makes an amazing comeback in the gin game. Oscar Farkel says this is one of the greatest days in the history of gin playing, telling Seymour it will not go unnoticed by the *commandatore* when awards are presented. Seymour sneers.

After dinner the Farkels decide to have coffee in St. Marks Square, where musicians are playing. Millie selects a wonderful group that has developed a new technique in which all the musicians seem to be playing different melodies or maybe just in different keys. The atmosphere is romantic. Two lovers are sitting in the corner. He has a handlebar mustache and a ten-inch cigar. They look like two KGB agents. She snuggles up to him and inserts her tongue into his ear and mouth. He reciprocates by blowing smoke in her face while alternately shoving his cigar and mustache between her lips.

Seymour Farkel notifies us there is good and bad news about what is happening. The bad news is the music will stop at midnight. The good news is the music will stop at midnight. The Farkels wander off to where another group is playing. In the middle of St. Mark's Square, the three couples pair off and dance under the stars. Others walk past them and smile at the romance exhibited by these *alta kockers* (senior citizens). One person passes by, glances their way, and says fondly, "Did you ever see such an ugly umbrella?"

The Farkels are fazeless. Nothing can deter them from their appointed task, to have fun. The night ends with them laughing and giggling their way through the hotel hallway until finally, as it becomes uncontrollable, Barbara Farkel makes a mad dash for her room. Again the laughter has overtaken her bladder and she is in the process of leaving a token of her laughter behind for the hotel.

The next morning it is raining, and windy. The moon is in its highest tide position, the water rises 1.23 meters, about four feet. Oscar and

Millie Farkel decide not to brave the weather and stay around the hotel after breakfast before heading into town. The other four Farkels, possessed of slightly less sanity, unbound courage and, of course, Farkel fearlessness, begin to prepare for a wild adventure in Venice. The Cipriani, understanding even crazy American Farkels must be served, provides high boots for each kook to put on before leaving for Venice. The launch itself is high above the normal position at the dock. When they arrive at Venice, five minutes later, the waves are washing the water onto St. Mark's Square. Elevated walkways have been assembled for crowds of Farkel-like tourists who are inching their way along this three-foot-wide walkway in both directions. Some, who are more courageous, have their shoes and socks off, pants and skirts above their knees, wading through the water. It is an amazing sight to behold. Barbara, Herbie, Judy, and Seymour make their way through the throngs to Ca d'Or, a gallery where they see masterworks five and six hundred years old. Afterward they meander through high-water areas to find their way to a recommended restaurant, Al Graspo de Ua. There they meet Luigi, their waiter, who develops a wild-eyed lust for Barbara and Judy. He says he will bring them special foods. No one is quite certain what he desires in return, more than a good tip. The meal is wonderful and the Farkels eat and return to their favorite adventure, window-shopping. Finally, before taking the launch to the Cipriani, Herbie and Barbara purchase a print of Venice to be a reminder back home. Judy and Seymour Farkel have already done the same in Portofino, but theirs is real art. You know, the kind with paint.

Oscar Farkel confiscates a little more of Seymour and Herbie's money at the gin table and then everyone prepares for the farewell banquet and awards dinner that night at the Cipriani itself. The excitement and electricity are already filling the air, like a cross between the Miss America Pageant and the Academy Awards. Who knows what will be served, maybe buonny rabbeet? The Farkels are capable of anything ... and nothing.

The *commandatore* Oscar Farkel presents Herbie with a special blue ribbon for organizing the trip. After dinner the Farkels, realizing how spectacular the Venetian portion of the trip has been, decide at Seymour's suggestion to take one final ride on the launch across to Venice and back. Under the late-night sky, with lights brightly shimmering, they think about five of the most spectacular days one could possibly spend.

Present

I'm amazed how many times shoppers can look in the same store windows they have looked into one hour previously. Each time something different is seen. Like reading a great novel or seeing a spectacular film, a different nuance is appreciated each time. After window-shopping Pat, Barbara, and Sheldon found things to purchase in Venice.

Pat wanted to stop by a restaurant in Venice which had a fabulous review.

"I am definitely going to choose this restaurant for our dinner this evening. Let's stop there and make a reservation."

She didn't realize the restaurant was quite far from the center of Venice, so it was a long walk. We finally came to a large piazza that was empty. Pat began to laugh about the fact she was standing in front of a very dingy place with a name similar to the one she was seeking. Sheldon and I looked it up again in the guidebook.

"That's not a similar name. That's the exact name. This is it."

Its front door appeared to be falling apart. We walked into a rundown room with unappealing food in a case on one side and two men sitting at a table drinking. We looked at each other, asked about the food being displayed, thanked them, and left.

"I change my vote. I'm eating somewhere else tonight," was Pat's first statement.

Instead we ate near the Piazza San Marco, a huge plaza surrounded by spectacular buildings, with a central area occupied by thousands of pigeons being fed by a mob of people. The pigeons are so accustomed to people that, if one chooses, masses of pigeons will sit on his arms, shoulders, and head while being fed. Watching them on others is great fun.

The children are always trying to catch the pigeons. I can assure you not one of them has ever been successful.

On that particular evening there was something added, a remarkably eerie sight. Fog in the air caused a strange glow through the lights of the piazza. The large walls of the spectacular church and the Doges' Palace had the most beautiful luminescence. It had an aura of unreality. Wonderful!

In the morning we headed for Murano, a small island off the coast of Venice, famous for glass-blowing, and stores selling glass in every form imaginable. To get there we took our first ride on the Vaporetta, Venice's water-bound bus system.

We were on the island less than ten minutes when we wandered into a shop where we made most of our purchases. As it turned out the owner was a close friend of the family that bought our previous home in San Antonio. What a small world! We bought things for ourselves and our children and had a great time wandering through the stores.

In another shop Barbara found more gifts. After they were wrapped she noticed a pencil made of glass. When she asked the price he kindly indicated it was hers as a gift. I guess we overpaid again.

An Aside

Sheldon carries with him a pillbox with days listed on separate compartments into which he places the different medications he is taking. When he saw how many pills we were taking, Barbara twelve and nine for me, he suggested we get such a case.

"Are they for elevated cholesterol?" Sheldon asked.

"No, I don't take anything like that."

"High blood pressure?"

"No!"

"Arthritis?"

"No!"

"Diabetes?"

"No!"

"Would you be upset if I asked you what illness you have?"

"No!"

"Well what is it?"

"The Nineties."

"I never heard of that. What kind of disease is it?"

"It's not exactly a disease ... It's more like a time. You see, all I'm taking is multivitamins, vitamin C, folic acid, selenium, ginkgo, and on and on."

"Ginkgo? What's ginkgo?"

"Recent studies have shown that it provides help for your memory."

"Really," Sheldon said, a little incredulously. "Have you ever purchased any of your 'medicines' in Europe?"

"No."

"Well, they're much cheaper here."

With that, the next thing I knew Sheldon was leading me into a pharmacy in Venice across from our hotel.

In Italian, Sheldon asked if they sold gingko. The pharmacist responded affirmatively in Italian. Sheldon then asked what it does for you. In Italian, with a big grin on his face and all the accompanying highly suggestive gestures, he told Sheldon that it would significantly increase his sexual prowess. Both he and Sheldon were laughing with great gusto during the pharmacist's description of what Sheldon might expect.

After Sheldon translated for me, being somewhat confused by his claim, I asked him, through Sheldon, if it wasn't true that ginkgo was supposed to aid one's memory.

When Sheldon translated my question there was a long pause. Then with gusto the pharmacist gave an answer that left them both in stitches. When able to speak once again, Sheldon translated for me.

"Oh yes, of course, it makes you remember how wonderful sex was."

We all had a hearty laugh, but neither Sheldon nor I bought any of his wares.

Our two weeks in Italy were ending. On this long day we were planning to drive all the way from Venice to Entrechaux. The weather was glorious and we stopped for lunch in Portofino. Pat and Sheldon had never been there and were absolutely taken by its beauty. It was impossible to eat and run there, so we spent an hour after lunch walking through that beautiful town. By now our schedule was getting into trouble.

Once in France we went to a telephone box and called Brin d'Olivier in Vaison for a 9:00 P.M. dinner reservation. As we had promised Pat and Sheldon, the meal was superb. Open for two years, the young owners told us they were hoping to appear in Michelin this year. What a joy to see a young, hard-working couple making a success. The evening ended as so many others on the trip with a feeling of great satisfaction.

I don't believe I'd ever seen a more tired group of people than my companions. The day began early in the morning, ending after midnight. I knew they'd sleep well. The next morning, with the house still at 8:00 A.M., I made coffee and waited another hour for the others to awaken.

Together we made one last journey before taking Pat and Sheldon to the train. Pat wanted to see the Saturday-morning Arles market, about one hour from Entrechaux.

Flashback

About six years ago Barbara and I went on a Saturday morning to the Arles market for the first time. It occupies a wide street for a number of blocks. One portion concentrates on clothing, and a second large area has food, flowers, and antiques.

The antique section of the market is on a small walkway off from the main street. The walkway has steps leading up above the level of the rest of the market. As in every small city and town in France the steps are quite old, with some broken areas that demand careful watching. After all, Arles' ancient Roman arena is thousands of years old.

When we came to the antique section, Barbara placed one foot on a broken step and turned her ankle, falling to the ground. She gasped in pain as the ankle swelled rather quickly. In my best obstetrical form I checked to see whether she had broken anything. I certainly don't consider myself an orthopedist, although my mother had once told me to go back to school and become one instead of an obstetrician. A friend had told her that orthopedics was where all the money was in medicine. I should have taken her advice.

My best guess was that nothing was broken. But the main point of this story is the antique merchants came to her rescue. They couldn't have been nicer. They brought ice for the swelling, not wanting her to leave until certain she was fine. If it happened in the U.S. she would have received the same treatment because of their concern about a lawsuit. In Arles it was only genuine concern. Nobody here thinks in terms of lawsuits.

Present

We went through the market with no difficulty, seeing everything before they shut down, and falling nowhere. Pat and Barbara found some items to bring back home.

Not knowing where to have lunch, we stopped in a little sidewalk café. I had learned, even in France, it is possible to get bad food. Whenever we follow our rule of eating only at Michelin-rated restaurants, we never get into trouble. I'm not referring to the starred restaurants, which can be very expensive. These are only a tiny fraction of the restaurants they recommend. The rest are uniformly good. But we broke our rule and had to pay for it. Sheldon suggested we forget the Michelin guide, and the food was atrocious.

From there we took them to Avignon to catch their train.

* * *

It was my birthday and I couldn't imagine a more lovely way to spend it. It would have been nice to have the Sunday *New York Times*, but that wasn't possible. We got up late and, after breakfast, played tennis. We spent the day eating and listening to beautiful music while I sat writing in a sun-filled room. For me that kind of day is difficult to beat.

Flashback

During our many trips to the area we have had the good fortune to be at some wonderful concerts. One was a choral performance in an old church in Vaison with about sixty singers, mainly senior citizens. Interspersed between the French songs they sang "We Shall Overcome" in English. As a finale they brought the house down with their version of "Home on the Range" in French.

I remember, as well, we had the opportunity several times to hear chamber music in Grignan, a town north of Vaison, at a very impressive château that belonged to Madame de Sévigné. A close friend of the French royal family and a prolific letter writer, her correspondence with her daughter has become quite famous.

The most exciting one, we attended by a stroke of luck. We were in Bordeaux, in southwestern France, at the time of an annual music festival in May. Barbara and I tried to get tickets, and found them sold out. But the box office told us there would be one final concert the following day at a church in a nearby town, Bazas, less than an hour away.

The concert was performed by two separate brass ensembles, placed in multiple locations throughout the church. The beautiful sounds of the trumpets and trombones reverberated throughout the church. It was a concert Barbara and I would never forget.

The Present

By early evening Barbara began preparing my birthday dinner. At my computer I heard her calling me for help.

"There's no gas on for the burners. You turned it off when we left for Italy."

"I don't think so. I turned off the heat, but I don't believe I turned off the gas."

"I'm certain, Herbie. It's under the sink. Please turn it on so I can start dinner."

I dutifully followed instructions, went under the sink, and turned the lever. Barbara hit the flint. The burner went on and she said, "You see, I told you so!"

I returned to my computer believing once again she had shown me the way.

Barbara suddenly came dashing out of the kitchen saying, "We have no water. Something must have happened to the line outside."

I went to the kitchen to help this disastrous situation. Barbara was already pouring our bottled drinking water into the pots in which she was preparing dinner. I turned the faucet and found her to be absolutely correct. There was no water. For a moment I began to ponder and then a light bulb lit in my brain.

I went under the sink, reversing the lever I had previously turned to start the gas. Turning the faucet, the water came out and the burners continued to flame. Obviously the gas line was never off, but as instructed, what I had done was simply turn off the water.

"I guess the gas was on," Barbara said sheepishly.

* * *

I called Pat in Paris. They had arrived with all their packages intact. She told me that as a result of our disastrous last lunch, Sheldon had decided to buy a new Michelin guide.

With the sun brightly shining it was a perfect day—well, almost perfect. One thing occurred which was somewhat traumatic. It was like being in a classroom and suddenly being called upon to respond when you're not fully prepared. A telephone call came.

"Tomorrow's the day, Herb. The weather has warmed up sufficiently and it's time for us to see them as the winter hibernation is ending."

136 · *Two Drifters . . .*

It was Brian Stapleton calling. I knew this day was coming. But now that it was here, my anxiety level rose considerably. He had scheduled our visit to the hives of hundreds of thousands of honeybees for the following day.

"Should I be wearing any special clothing?"

Casually Brian responded, as he has been doing this for years, "No! Just be able to tuck the bottoms of your pants into your socks. I'll take care of the rest of the clothing."

I couldn't imagine how anyone could be so relaxed about going into this den of terror without any concern. I decided to secretly bring the Benadryl I carry traveling. It's a drug for counteracting allergic reactions. I'm not certain it would suffice if I were to be bitten a hundred times. I had mixed feelings of excitement and imminent disaster.

The day started at the Vaison market. Along with the normal groceries we found gifts in the way of olivewood spoons, an additional adapter we needed for the electrical outlets, a folding knife for picnics, and a plumber's helper. You can find everything in there. But the most important aspect is the visual impact. The market is like a work of art.

The shopping done, we headed for lunch because a condemned man needs a very special last meal. Going into the beehives, this could be my last gustatory treat. We went to Brin d'Olivier. It began with a taste treat, olive bread followed by fabulous appetizers. In Barbara's case it was *tapenade* on *blinis* with a salad. For me it was a delicious pissaladière, with a salad. Then we had pork on a skewer with onions and tomatoes in a honey sauce. For dessert they served us *fromage blanc* with a red fruit *coulis* on top.

The time had arrived for us to go to Pat and Brian's home. Brian was all ready for our outing. We proceeded to a location near one group of hives. Barbara made it clear she was not going near them. She and Pat went for a walk as Brian and I went to the hives. To reach them we drove through the indescribably beautiful Beaumont Valley. Driving, it is a dead-end valley. But one can walk over the small mountains at the end. Later, when we all got together, Barbara described their walk. At one point Pat stopped and talked with an elderly couple seated by the roadside though they were complete strangers.

Meanwhile Brian and I took the car up the side of a hill on what appeared to be no roadway whatsoever. He had driven it probably hundreds of times in the past and knew exactly where he was going. Arriving at the destination, Brian told me to put the bottom of my pants into my socks, and gave me a white gown to pull over my head. The top was like a helmet that came over my face with a mesh area in the front. My arms went through the sleeves with gloves sewn into the end. The gown then came down to below my waist.

Once we were both dressed Brian took a pot, with an attached bellows, out of the car trunk. He filled it with dried straw and grass and lighted a small flame. Squeezing the bellows, smoke puffed out of the spout on the pot. He added more straw and lavender, continually squeezing the bellows. I learned this made it safer dealing with the bees. The smoke encourages them to settle on the frames and fill up with honey so that they are able to survive if the suspected fire causes them to fly off and find a new home.

We approached the first hive and my anxiety level rose with each step. It was a box approximately fifteen by twenty inches on the top and a little more than a foot deep. First Brian puffed smoke into the front opening of the hive where the bees enter and exit, and then handed the smoke pot to me. He raised the top and nothing much could be seen except another lid. He had a tool with him that looked like a large chisel, and with it pried up the second lid. My assignment was to immediately begin puffing the smoke directly into the hive as soon as the lid came up. I was ready to perform when suddenly the shock came.

"Oh, no," Brian exclaimed. "Robber bees!"

Hundreds of bees began flying out of the hive. Brian said the queen and workers were gone. They had been driven out of the hive by these others that did not belong there. This hive was lost and there was nothing Brian could do but close it up. These bees flew wildly, which I would soon see was not to be expected in a hive, intact and functioning.

When the next hive was opened I fulfilled my assignment. Very few bees flew up at all. Inside there were ten frames. Brian took his chisel and freed one. The frames are fixed with propolis—gum brought in by the bees from the neighboring trees. As he lifted it up I saw an incredible sight. On both sides of the frame thousands of bees huddled, producing embryos and laying down honey. I'm certain my eyes could not have been opened wider.

I began hearing a buzzing around my face mask.

"Does buzzing mean they're about to attack?"

"As a matter of fact," Brian assured me, "the bees are very docile today."

I watched as he checked the frames in this hive before closing it up again. I continued blowing the smoke. After all, I was protecting us while shivering in my boots.

The third hive's condition was similar, which pleased Brian. The fourth, while not overrun by robber bees, was not in the best condition. With the hives all closed we returned to the car, but Brian told me not to disrobe yet. Some bees had followed us.

"Now ... take the gown off and get into the car quickly."

"Quickly, are you kidding? I'm not called 'half a second Herbie' for nothing."

We met Pat and Barbara returning from their walk. Brian said sometimes roughly half the bees leave the hive as a swarm together with the old queen or a newly born one and search for a new site such as a tree limb. He said they can be retrieved by placing an empty hive under the limb, and giving it a swift shake so the bees fall into it.

"If the queen falls in," he said, "sometimes the entire hive will be restored."

Barbara assured him she wasn't going to be the one who shakes that limb.

Pat said swarming was very common and the law forbids doing any harm to a swarm of bees to get rid of them. One is required to contact a beekeeper to restore the bees in a hive. At the height of the summer each hive has approximately 60,000 bees.

With all my anxiety I was so pleased I hadn't passed up this opportunity. We drove back to their home and talked over tea and cookies. "Beehive Day" was a success.

Back home Barbara prepared a lovely dinner to end this wonderful day. There was one problem with it, however. She had purchased some anchovies in the market as a side dish to our meal. I was the first to bite into it and swallowed what I had bitten off.

"Oh, my God, this is awful! It's like a solid bar of salt. Don't eat it at all."

I got queasy and it was a while before I recovered. The remainder was discarded.

* * *

Paradou, near St. Rémy, south of Avignon, is not so small that one should have difficulty finding it. We were going to make our fourth attempt to have lunch there.

The first time we had planned to eat there was during our first visit to Provence years before. Not knowing our way around, we got lost. When I came upon a dingy place with a similar name I was certain I had stumbled into it. I told Barbara to wait in the car while I checked. As I opened the front door I found a very unpleasant-looking truckstop café. To be certain I went up to the sleazy-looking character at the bar.

"Is this Bistro du Paradou?" I asked in my best French.

In return I got a negative shrug and nothing else. I backed out of the café and waved to Barbara to stay in the car. We went on to a restaurant in Maussane-les-Alpilles.

On our second attempt, about five years ago, we found Le Bistro du Paradou and it was great. The third time, without a reservation with our friends, Judy, Seymour, Millie, and Oscar, we were turned away. We planned to try again after the market in St. Remy.

St. Remy is an hour from Entrechaux so we got an early start. The town was enchanting. After picking up a number of items we found ourselves at a stall of olives and dried fruits. We were stopping there for capers, added dates we hadn't planned on, vinegar-soured cherries we didn't need, and pistachios we would have been better off without. The owner was so charming and everything made our palates water.

In the corner of my eye I saw the same anchovies Barbara purchased the previous day, almost causing my demise. I explained to him we had bought some of them elsewhere yesterday. And they were so salty they made me sick.

He began to laugh while trying to control it, so as not to embarrass me.

"*Vous ne pouvez pas les manger. Ils sont conservés comme ça.*" Translation: They are being preserved like that and are not to be eaten.

"First you must soak them in water overnight. Then you drain them and soak them in olive oil. Then they can be eaten," he told me in French.

I joined in laughter about my faux pas. It reminded me of Gerald Ford in Texas eating tamales with the corn husks still on. I guess it helps to know the local customs.

This time we had a reservation at Bistro du Paradou. There is no menu. It's country style and delicious. The owner brought us a salad dressed with the local olive oil, which is much stronger than we usually experience. The flavor was exquisite.

The main course was a cassoulet of chicken, sausages, and white beans in a luscious sauce served in a large casserole dish, bubbling hot.

We ate it with delicious French bread followed by a selection of cheeses and dessert, all with a bottle of red wine.

* * *

The rain had been nonstop in December and January, and the sun was like that now. We took the outdoor furniture out of storage, hoping to have lunches under the sun.

It had been a wonderfully relaxing day in Provence. After dinner I was doing the dishes, listening to a CD of Michael Crawford singing "Love Changes Everything." Barbara came over and kissed me and we danced around the kitchen to the romantic background of that song. Being in love certainly makes a trip like this very special. I can understand it very well when Barbara tells every person to come to France with a person they love.

The next day brought another project. We had been unsuccessful in our search for curtains for our summer house and would try the Carpentras market. We also needed bubble wrap to pack the pottery purchased in France and Italy. After no success Barbara burst forth with enthusiasm. "I have an idea! Let's put together a picnic lunch, head for Avignon, find a spot to eat, go to a movie, and afterward try to find curtains in Avignon."

In Avignon the curtains would not be our only problem. Finding "a lovely spot" for a picnic was a challenge. I'm certain a local resident would know just where to go, but we didn't. We finally found park benches near the river.

After lunch we began asking for curtain shops in broken French. No matter where we went we got the same answer, *"Pas de rideau"*: No curtains.

After the movie we found the perfect shop and bought the curtains. Nevertheless, we did have a problem. We had gone to so many shops in Avignon, I was completely lost. I said to the saleswoman, *"J'ai besoin de trouver le parking pour le Palais du Pape."*

Outside I proudly asked Barbara if she heard me seek instructions. She said she had, but "who was Jay Beswan?" I fell into a fit of hysteria. After all these years of studying, that is what she made of my French. When I clarified that I had said, *"J'ai besoin ..."* (I need), she similarly became overwhelmed with laughter. But she protected her position as one who spoke French better than her husband with a counterattack.

"Herbie," she uttered in between her fits of laughter, "it's all your fault. Your pronunciation is atrocious." I guess she won another round.

Our attempts to find bubble wrap failed. We had great difficulty explaining what bubble wrap was. What in the world is the French word for "bubble wrap"? Even when understood it seemed impossible to find it in the south of France.

* * *

We had no television and that was just fine. The telephone rarely rang, eliminating long telephone conversations. But one part of our lives we had trouble giving up was the need to be a "news junkie." A reading, from cover to cover, of the *International Herald Tribune* met that need. Understanding that, you will understand how bad this day was.

Up early as usual, I drove to Vaison to pick up the paper and bread and get cash from the money machine. I came home with no bread and no cash and for good reason.

"*Madame, excusez-moi, où est le Herald?*": Where's the newspaper?

"*Le Herald Tribune n'est pas arrivé. Possible ... lundi*": The paper didn't come. Maybe it will on Monday.

"*Lundi? Lundi?*" I mumbled as I left the newsstand. Did she know what she was saying to me? I'd have no newspaper from Friday morning to Monday morning, seventy-two hours.

In a total state of depression I saw no need to get bread or the money. I might as well go home and go to sleep for two days.

When I returned Barbara gave me the news that brought me back to reality, "We've become the housekeepers for the foreseeable future. Our landlord's maid is not coming anymore due to a medical problem."

Our friends Buddy and Florence were coming to visit us. We'd have to clean the house before they arrived. I always believed that a prerequisite for being either a writer or a physician was knowing how to clean sinks and toilets. I tried to prove my mettle at both those two tasks, while Barbara prepared a lunch of a *pain bagnat*, a sandwich with tuna, anchovies, tapenade, cucumbers, tomato with oil and vinegar and garlic spread on the bread. You haven't lived until you've tasted it. As a side dish she made marinated roasted red peppers. For dessert we had *fromage blanc* with *crème fraîche*.

Consecutive days of warmth and sun didn't thrill us because we were planning to go skiing with the Kosts in just one week. It did not bode well for the snow conditions. I was hoping that our planned trip to Courchevel would not get canceled.

In the early afternoon we headed for the Sunday gathering of the

Beaumont English Language Library. They were having an author discuss his new book about Marcel Pagnol, the famous French writer and filmmaker. What a great treat! The speaker was Julian More, a writer of significant prestige. Among other things he wrote the play *Irma La Douce*. That afternoon he told enchanting stories about the life of Pagnol. The Stapletons have created quite a very wonderful institution in this library.

As we left we reminded Brian about dinner Thursday evening at our house.

"We'll be there if we don't forget," he quipped, making reference to his age.

Barbara thought he had said, "if we're not late," and responded, "It won't make any difference."

We all broke into laughter when Brian asked, "It won't make any difference if we don't come?"

* * *

Before going to Avignon to pick up our friends Buddy and Florence, I decided I would do something I had been planning to do for weeks. I went up to see the castle that sits high above our house. An old Roman ruin, it looked spectacular from where we lived. I began walking up a steep incline, steeper than I had expected. My normal pulse is very slow, in the range of 50 to 60. Getting it up to 100 during exercise can be difficult. I mention that because of the steepness of this hill. At one point I decided to stop and see what my pulse rate had reached. You can get some impression of the difficulty with the climb when I tell you my pulse rate had reached 135.

After walking halfway up I came to a road which continued the remainder of the way up to the château. It was the way to drive from the bottom without going through the walk I had just completed. How brilliant of me to have found the difficult route.

When I reached the top the château was gated and marked *"Privée."* So with that adventure yielding nothing, Barbara and I went to Avignon to get Florence and Buddy. All evening we reminisced about the incidents that occurred while we were in Turkey.

In the morning I dropped Barbara, Buddy, and Florence at the Tuesday Vaison market, while I took the car to the Renault dealer to have the last minor repairs done on the damage which had occurred to the back window several weeks previously. Back at the market I was confronted with the daunting task of finding them in a mass of humanity.

Fortunately, like myself, Buddy is quite tall. I looked high over the crowd and hoped that from my vantage point I'd see Buddy's head, and sure enough I spotted him. The next three hours of walking and shopping were hilarious. I couldn't figure out why Buddy would tell vendors to keep the change while Florence was negotiating lower prices.

Barbara and Florence had made a list, and after an hour Buddy and I were carrying a lot, but nothing from the list. The women had been infected with impulse buying.

Beyond a doubt the most successful vendor in the area was selling cashmere-and-silk sweaters for $25. The sign said cashmere and silk, but the label said "cashmere and silk and other fibres." I don't know what the proportions were, but I'd never seen cashmere sweaters selling for that little. It made me think of the description of a very dry martini, gin with a whiff of vermouth across the rim of the glass. Maybe these sweaters were allowed just a whiff of cashmere. Nevertheless, my companions bought four of them.

We ended the day in the pottery shop where some years ago Barbara and I had purchased a giant tortoise made in concrete with beautiful tiles over its back and a magnificent head coming out of the shell. Weighing hundreds of pounds, it finally arrived after a long ocean journey and sits proudly in front of our pool at home in Texas.

Subsequently, this wonderful potter, Alain Bertheas, made a spectacular iguana which sits on the roof of his shop just outside Vaison. For years I asked him to sell it to me, but he has always been unwilling to part with it. This time when he turned me down once again, I was at least able to tickle his funny bone. I asked him if he would leave it to me in his will. Unfortunately, I am about twenty years senior to him.

Barbara and Florence were organizing a menu for a dinner party. It seemed the plans changed every hour and we went from store to store looking for what was needed.

They jointly agreed to serve some wonderful *fromage* (cheese). We went into several *cremeries* asking if they had a cheese that was *fort* (strong). Finally we found the shopkeeper that had the answer. I assume this thought entered her mind.

"These crazy Americans want 'fort.' I'll give them 'fort.'"

She sold it to us with a warning. "Eat this last. It will drown out the other flavors."

We tried a small portion and my, was it ever *"fort."* It was made from *chèvre* (goat cheese), *roquefort*, and a great deal of pepper. Buddy took one try and said henceforth he would pass. Barbara and I both tried it, and believe me it was the strongest cheese I have ever tasted. It reminded me of mustard Barbara had discarded because it was so strong.

After tasting it I blurted out, "This makes the mustard taste like baby food."

Florence was the only one not to try it. "I'm saving myself," she demurred.

I told her that I could understand her terminology because eating this cheese was like losing one's virginity.

Last-minute changes to the menu occurred in the middle of the night when our two cooks, Florence and Barbara, recalled things that awakened them out of their sleep.

We took a break from cooking for lunch at St. Hubert, in Entrechaux. My friends chose the very inexpensive house rose wine. Barbara tasted it and responded first.

"Oh, this is atrocious!"

Buddy seemed to concur. Florence was slightly more generous. But they didn't send it back or order something else. Once the meal came a different chorus was heard.

"This wine's not so bad, once you are having food with it."

By the end of the meal the wine was "very good." My traveling partners do have a way of making everything turn out wonderfully. Once they've purchased it, it's theirs, so it can't be bad. Or is it that the three of them are cheap? Well maybe they're just frugal.

For the dinner we decided to use the giant table in the kitchen, but Barbara and Florence said the lighting was too bright. As a result two candlesticks from our bedroom became the centerpiece. The lighting was very romantic for dinner, semidark.

Barbara bought flowers at the supermarket, which were all dead, reminiscent of the flowers in Istanbul they had rejected. Florence would not be deterred by this setback and immediately went out into the street, taking flower cuttings to create an arrangement. I was a little concerned how the neighbors, if they were watching, might feel about that.

The dinner went well past midnight. The group had quite a bit in common.

The Kosts have a daughter-in-law from China, and Pat and Brian

Stapleton have spent much time there teaching. The mix of individuals turned out to be just right, and to me, at least, the evening appeared to be a complete success.

* * *

It was nearing the end of their stay and the Kosts wanted one last visit to the Carpentras market. It occupied a huge parking lot and all the streets that fed into it. After meandering for a while Barbara and Florence found an item that was quite interesting. Florence had lost her sunglasses and Barbara had broken hers. Both were looking for new ones when they came upon a booth selling sunglasses for 35 francs, about $5.75. The bargain price attracted them as they tried on all different styles, in general thrilled with what they had found. The glasses were purchased and we were on our way.

"I'm feeling nauseated."

"I'm feeling dizzy."

The two women simultaneously had multiple physical complaints. I asked Barbara for her glasses and looked through them. Although these glasses were supposed to have no correction, it was obvious to me that everything was distorted.

"It's no wonder you feel that way. In a few minutes you'll probably have a headache. What a steal! Too bad they don't work!"

Buddy and I were hysterical as the women were trying to justify their purchase.

"That's O.K. We'll get used to them."

The glasses would no doubt soon be put away in a drawer or found in the trash pail.

* * *

On our last day in Provence before leaving to ski we went to see two wonderful villages not listed in the our guidebooks. One was Malaucène, which is very close to Entrechaux. We had never ventured up into the old portion of that town.

After a climb up many steps, which is typical when visiting the old town portion of many of the villages in the south of France, we came to a lookout area. Down one side we could see miles of rolling hills. When we walked to the opposite side, imagine our surprise when we looked down on an ultramodern complex, including condominiums, a private club, swimming pools, and multiple tennis courts. The contrast was amazing.

Our second stop was in the town of Brantes, about halfway between St. Leger and Montbrun-les-Bains. We had been told to go there by several friends. Even after many visits to Provence, I had never heard that town mentioned, nor read about it or known anyone who had been there. From our location it took twenty minutes to get there. Like Rocamadour it sat on the side of a mountain. Brantes was very quiet and peaceful. Unlike Rocamadour there was almost nothing commercial in the entire town. We walked up the narrow cobblestone streets, higher and higher. The view from the top left us breathless.

On the way up we passed a pottery shop owned by two women with products different from anything we had seen elsewhere, such as ceramic chandeliers.

* * *

We arrived in Courchevel and checked into our accommodations, Hôtel des Trois Vallées. Then we had lunch before arranging for rental skis. The shop owner's description of the conditions on the mountain suggested that skiing was going to be a problem. Everything was not looking terribly bright, except for the sun, which couldn't have been brighter.

Our dinner at the restaurant of a hotel, called Cabichou, was exceptionally good. The next day we would test the mountain, or possibly the reverse.

Trying to start early in the morning in France wasn't possible. The mountain opened at 9:00 A.M., but the ticket booths opened only fifteen minutes earlier and shops not until 9:00. In the U.S. shops would open long before the mountain, but in France there's not the same push. In fact, except for restaurants, the shops all close for lunch.

The sun was bright and warmer than I ever remembered skiing in my life. The snow was like mush. We tried for preferable conditions on a north-facing ski run, but it was far from good. Besides that it was the height of the season and runs were packed with skiers. The poor conditions and crowds caused concerns about the risk of collisions.

It was so hot by lunchtime we had to go back to the hotel to remove our ski underwear and jackets. After lunch we made one last effort to find more skiable terrain. At the peak of the mountain we found a steep slope which was high enough to have not yet melted. But since there had been no snow, it was a sheet of ice. Buddy and Florence went first, and Barbara followed. I brought up the rear. Buddy, a fine skier, made it three quarters of the way down before falling and sliding the remainder of the way on this *piste* (ski run). Florence on the other hand had no such luck. She took a tumble near the top and slid head-first down the entire length of the run while Barbara watched from the top. Florence came to a stop at the very bottom and lay still with legs and skis twisted around.

Barbara, who had started down the hill, was fine until she saw Florence and went into a panic. Instead of continuing, she turned off the run and skied into an unmarked area of dense trees. I came down behind her, shocked by her decision. I immediately turned from where I was skiing and went into the treed area where she had gone. I told her to stand still while I scouted to see if there was a way down. I found myself at a steep ledge.

"Don't move!" I shouted. "I'm coming back to you!"

As I maneuvered my way back between the trees, I heard a small cry from where Barbara had been standing. Now she was on the ground and teary-eyed. She had tried to move out of the trees and fell. Major panic had set in for her. Before I could reach her, another skier came by, saw her crying, stepped into the woods, freed up her skis, which had become twisted, and left as I made my way to her. I was able to see down the hill and Florence was still on the ground with several people standing around her. I was certain she had a serious injury, but primarily I had to get Barbara down the mountain.

"I'll hold your skis. Stand up and walk, leaning toward the mountain, using your poles. Get over into the open area of the run and I'll bring your skis to you."

I had taken my skis off to be able to walk and carry her skis to her. Just as I approached her, she lost her balance and began sliding down the steep hill to about the midpoint. Now I had two sets of skis and my poles. Though I had the skills to ski down this run, I was certain I couldn't ski down this treacherous slope carrying a second pair of skis. I inched out onto the main run. Barbara was lying there, halfway down, in tears. She kept looking down at Florence, who was still on the ground at the bottom. Buddy was about fifty yards ahead of her, looking back and trying to figure out where everyone was.

I decided to try to slide down little by little until I could reach Barbara. No such luck. As soon as I began, I went sliding down past her.

Barbara, fearful that I would bang my brains in with the skis and poles I was carrying shouted, "Let go of the skis!"

Other skiers came by and picked up the skis and poles for us. We all persuaded a very anxious Barbara to allow herself to slide down and not try to put her skis back on. After some encouragement she agreed and came down to where I was lying.

By then Florence, who was not injured at all, was up and waiting with Buddy. Her problem at the bottom had been nothing more than an inability to get her skis untangled without assistance. Finally Barbara and I got our skis on and went down to them. Though harrowing, since no one was injured, we laughed about the incident in retrospect.

Barbara contemplated taking the gondola down instead of skiing, but that would necessitate an uphill walk to the lift. As a result she decided to ski down with the rest of us, but not before she gave us all cause for hearty laughter.

"I'll carry my own skis if I take the gondola down."

Buddy and Florence were completely broken up by the thought that she even considered it was possible I could ski all the way down carrying her skis.

After a thorough evaluation, including weather reports predicting warmer weather and no snow for at least another week, we decided there was no reason to remain. This was supposed to be pleasure, not work. We would leave in the morning.

Returning the skis presented no problem, though we felt sorry for the shopkeeper. The hotel was very understanding and charged only for the days we spent there. I was certain that no matter how bad the conditions, the ski passes would not be refunded, even though they had told us that conditions were excellent when we called.

I met Florence and Buddy at breakfast and told them it was unlikely we would be getting any refund on the lift tickets. But I had an idea.

"If the dumb American, who speaks such poor French, goes down and asks them for a refund, maybe they'll take pity."

What happened subsequently caused Buddy and me to laugh uncontrollably.

Florence, defending her husband, snarled at me, "Buddy speaks French fluently."

Somehow Florence had misunderstood what I meant, while Buddy understood completely that the "dumb American" I was referring to was me.

I tried with no success, and we were on our way, the temperature rising higher.

At home Buddy washed a white shirt of his which now contained thousands of fibers from the cheap 5 percent "cashmere" sweater he had purchased at the market the previous week. Buddy said his shirt, originally 60 percent cotton and 40 percent polyester, now had 2 percent cashmere.

"That means, of course, my sweater is now only 3 percent cashmere."

Four and a half weeks had now passed with no sign of precipitation.

Flashback

The weather in Provence is not always rain-free. I recall an incident that was quite different, which created an adventure. We had gone to Le Mesclun in Seguret for dinner.

On that night we had a table immediately adjacent to the window looking out over a beautiful valley. Seguret is a hill town with views that are very special. During dinner a phenomenal sound-and-light show was provided for us by nature with continuous bursts of lightning and thunder making the dinner very romantic in this dimly lit restaurant.

By the time we left the rain had stopped. But the sky was pitch black. We were staying in Gigondas, and as we drove into town there wasn't a light to be seen. Power had been completely knocked out. We drove up and allowed the car lights to shine into the courtyard, directly toward the front door, to see the keyholes. We began to search through the house for the candles and matches Barbara had remembered noticing previously.

"Try going a little to your left. Is the matchbox there?"

"I don't know. I can't feel it yet ... I've got it! I've got it!"

"O.K. Here's the candle ... *Voilà*, it's you."

If Barbara hadn't remembered an approximate location we would have been in terrible trouble because it was so dark you couldn't see your hand in front of your face.

We got into our night clothes and blew out the candles. Sometime during the middle of the night Barbara woke me out of a deep sleep.

"Herbie, could you please go around the house and turn off all the lights that came on when the power returned?"

Present

With skiing canceled we made new plans. In the morning we drove east to a town called Buis-les-Baronnies. Barbara and I had never seen it. Today was market day in Buis.

The town was very charming with lovely architecture. In the market Barbara spotted one other thing that drew her eye. It was a large bar of beige-colored soap.

"This soap is very special. It is made with honey, which makes it very soft," the vendor told her in French.

"I love the color," she whispered to me.

"It has propolis, which is an antibacterial, antifungicide," he continued.

"Isn't it beautiful," she murmured.

Pointing to my bald head he said in all seriousness, "My father, who is completely bald like you, uses it because it is so good for the skin."

"That will look perfect in the guest bathroom."

"It is also an anti-inflammatory and has been studied for all its advantages."

"I must have that bar of soap, Herbie. The color is perfect."

I bought it and the vendor was so pleased that we selected his soap. He felt certain the choice was made because the soap was of such great quality.

* * *

The drive eastward from Entrechaux was exquisite. The time of the year was certainly a factor. Everything was green with blossoms opening on all the trees. The restaurant where we had lunch the day before had beautiful fruit trees at its front entrance. We ate there a few days before skiing and the trees were just beginning to show their buds. Now they were in full bloom with gorgeous white blossoms. It was breathtaking.

As the evening approached, the combination of the sun shining and ominous clouds created a sky that was dazzling. Some mountains in the east had a red glow reflecting the setting western sun. We saw this show of nature from a distance as we returned through Vaison. The temperature was dropping and there was the feeling that rain might finally come this evening. It was a perfect night to stay home.

The rain never came and again the sun shone brightly. Coming to the end of their stay, Florence and Buddy wanted to take a long hike. The three-mile route wound through hills, vineyards, and groves of fruit trees. At one point, as we looked across the fields, we were at the same level as the chateau high above our house. In the distance we could see the top of Mont Ventoux, with the moon, seen in daylight, sitting above it. It's easy to understand why this area was a haven for the Impressionist painters. It's more beautiful than one can adequately describe. Only a painting can give it full meaning.

On Florence and Buddy's last day we walked through the Dentelles of Montmirail.

We stopped in a nearby town, Beaumes-de-Venise, and picked up food for a picnic lunch, which we ate at the mountain base. The baguettes, ham, and cheese tasted wonderful. We also had a delicious *citron* (lemon) *tartelette* and clementines (thin-skinned, delicious, seedless tangerine-type fruit from North Africa). The afternoon was wonderful.

On this final evening we went to Bartavelle for a farewell dinner. It was a long evening filled with laughter and friendship, and, of course, great food.

In the morning we took them to the train station. Of all the errors I have ever made with the French language, the one that always causes me to laugh the most, even when just thinking about it, relates to the train station.

In French the word for the station is *gare*. The "a" is soft, as in "far." Another word in French is *guerre*, which means "war." The "ue" is pronounced like our long "a," as in "fare." I frequently give *gare* the long "a" sound. The result is that I'm stopping people on the street and asking them politely in French, "Excuse me, where is the war?"

While in Avignon we were committed to resolving a problem. Over the past six weeks we had accumulated a lot of pottery. Much came from Viettri in Italy and more from Dieulefit, here in Provence. We had the challenge of how to get it back home.

In order to get the pottery back to the United States, unbroken, it would be necessary to find a great deal of packing material. We had contacted Buddy and Florence in Paris to ask them to find bubble wrap. In a big city like Paris they were bound to have better luck than we were having in the south of France. On arrival they told us it was only sold in very large quantities, so they decided not to buy it, leaving us still with a problem.

There was only one answer. We began searching the trash outside of business establishments, especially stores that might receive merchandise enclosed in bubble wrap. The four of us found a sufficient amount discarded to fill our packing needs.

In the morning before taking them to pick up a car in Avignon we stopped at a flea market. Both Buddy and I had had our fill of *brocantes*, so we sat in the car and read while Barbara and Florence went searching for something that would strike their fancy.

"Do they know we've got a time schedule we'll have to stick to?" I asked.

He told me to wait in the car while he checked to see what progress our spouses had made. Buddy soon came back with a report.

"The good news is that they understand the time schedule. The bad news is after I left them and walked a short distance I heard a crash. Florence apparently had purchased a plate and I heard her dropping it."

* * *

With our company gone and the weather still beautiful Barbara made a wonderful picnic basket and we drove to one of our favorite spots in all of Provence, Pont du Gard. Two million tourists annually visit this old Roman aqueduct across the Gard River, which provided water for the city of Nimes in the days of the Roman Empire. It was constructed in three levels extending high above the riverbed. At previous visits we've walked on the upper level. On this occasion, the first time we have been there in several years, only the lower level was open for pedestrians, because restoration is in progress to make certain that it remains intact, as their signs stated, "through a third millenium."

Sitting on a rockbed area on the side of the river under the Pont du Gard, we watched young boys jump off the rocky areas down into the water. Though the air was not very cold, probably in the high sixties, the water was much colder. Young lovers were kissing each other all along the beaches and rocks. If not in France, where would one expect to find young lovers? Dogs of all varieties walked with their masters along each side of the river and across the aqueduct. Children could be seen and heard wherever one looked or listened. The sounds were those of laughter and joy. We stayed for two hours.

We were near the end of our stay in the south of France. After three weeks in the United States we would return to Paris for the last six weeks of this extraordinary year in Europe. Looking forward to Paris in April and May is truly something special.

We had to decide which clothes to leave behind for Paris. There was also the job of cleaning up the house, for which we allotted two days. We wanted it to look fresh for the owner's return.

Barbara and I were making good progress in our preparations for leaving and decided to go to have pizza in Carpentras. We went to one of our favorite pizza restaurants, Chez Serge. There was always a very lively atmosphere there with a parrot that kept talking all night. I called Serge to our table as we arrived.

"I love your pizza, but for me, maybe not for others, there is too much cheese." I told him all that in French, which pleased me no end. "I would like to make up my own pizza. Is that possible?"

Serge, always the warmest of hosts said, *"Absolument!"*

"Great!" I then described a pizza with the basic tomato sauce they put on, the lightest sprinkling of cheese, and fresh tomatoes sliced on the top. It came out perfectly.

They had a list of at least twenty different kinds of pizza. Serge came to the table to inquire about our pizza. That is the custom at every restaurant in France. They always want to be certain the customer is pleased. I assured him I was, but added one comment.

"Next time I expect to see another item added to your menu, Pizza d'Herbie." I believe he had to think about that for a while.

Over dinner this evening Barbara and I did an assessment of our time in the south of France. I asked her if she had a word to describe our stay.

"The word to describe the French and their lifestyle, especially here, is civilized."

The idea that the French are not pleasant to Americans is the furthest thing from the truth. They have such wonderful manners and appear to teach them to their children. Every other word is "thank you" or "please." When a diner leaves a restaurant, he or she says "good evening" to the other customers in the restaurant, even the strangers.

At noon everyone closes up shop, even government offices, to go home to their families for lunch. As Barbara said, "They're civilized."

Like the rest of the world, this country is far from perfect. But I believe there are many things in France which would be nice to see back home.

We went to the Vaison market on our last Tuesday in Provence. Just as the vendors began closing their stands Barbara and I agreed we should take back something for our dear friends Judy and Seymour. It wasn't an easy decision, as they have been here many times. Suddenly Barbara had the perfect idea, beautiful French soaps. We found the stand selling them and a charming woman helped us select the nicest item. As she wrapped it Barbara bought a second package as another gift. Walking away from the table Barbara thought of two others. This time the woman gave her a discount. Once again Barbara remembered two others. The saleswoman was overjoyed at her good fortune. This time she even gave Barbara a little gift with the purchase. I'm certain she sold more to Barbara in the last minutes of the market than she had sold during the entire morning.

Then, as a favor to me, Barbara agreed to take the drive all the way up to the top of Mont Ventoux, the highest point in the area. I love going up there and we'd made the trip several times in the past, but never during this trip. Barbara is not fond of the journey because the peak is very cold and windy, which is what the name "Ventoux" means.

It involved a long, winding ride up the side of the mountain on a very good road. This was the coldest time of the year we had ever driven to the top. But we never made it. I was unaware that the peak is closed in the winter because of the ice and snow. The highest one can go in the winter is to the ski area, Mont Serein.

Due to the warm spell most of the snow was gone by now. This ski area had six short poma lifts leading to two chair lifts. It was a small ski area, just for local use.

When our packing was done we were horrified to see that our luggage and carry-ons plus the things to be left behind in Paris totaled eighteen pieces. There were six cartons being left in Paris with our landlord and twelve pieces we were bringing home with us. American Airlines was definitely going to go bonkers when we arrived.

Our drive to the airport brought the total mileage for this segment to 7,900 kilometers, 4,740 miles. Although the trip had been wonderful, this day was not perfect.

"You're putting eight bags on, and such big ones?"

"Well I thought we are such good customers you might allow it."

"I can't do that. I'm going to have to charge you an extra $220 for your baggage."

Simple mathematics made the picture crystal clear. All those wonderful bargains we found along the way now cost more than if we just purchased them back home.

The flight home was without flaw. Well ... almost without flaw. Barbara had a great idea when we packed up in Entrechaux.

"Let's not leave behind these super-delicious clementines to be thrown away. I'll take just four of them in my purse and we'll eat them on the plane."

On the flight we ate gloriously. So gloriously that neither of us ever thought about the clementines. When we arrived in Dallas it was necessary to retrieve the eight bags, plus the four carry-ons that we had. Lifting the huge bags off the moving carousel was back-breaking. I finally piled them up on two luggage carts and we headed for customs

"Is anybody bringing in any fruits or vegetables?"

Not only had we forgotten to eat the clementines, Barbara was carrying them. As proper citizens we notified customs about the clementines and were taken to a separate area where Barbara handed over the clementines in her purse. But that wasn't sufficient.

"Put all your luggage up on this table."

"Oh, my God," I thought. "I've got to lift all this luggage up on top of this table. It looks like it's ten feet high."

Piece by piece I lifted it all onto the table. I had already pushed the luggage for what seemed miles just getting to customs and now this. I was sweating profusely and was certain the agent would take my sweating for anxiety about something illegal I was carrying into the country. Actually I was nearly having a heart attack from the exertion, all because of those four clementines. They checked every bag and found nothing wrong. Then I was told to take them back off the table and pile them again on the carts and take them to the transfer point for our next flight. The water was actually pouring off my brow, and believe me I wasn't in the best mood when Barbara broke the camel's back.

I had taken my leather briefcase to Europe as a carry-on. Barbara had suggested next time I take a lighter, fabric briefcase, for traveling. But her timing was bad.

While I struggled with the sixty-pound bags, all because of clementines, she said, "You're going to have to bring a lighter briefcase next time." That was one for the book!

We arrived home safely and every piece of pottery we packed arrived unbroken, not one little chip. All the hard work at the airport was forgotten—well, almost forgotten!

When we return we shall be in wonderful Paris in the spring. April in Paris, what could be better?

Part Four
The Final Chapter

TWO DRIFTERS IN PARIS:
Conclusion of a Glorious Year

We took our last flight to Europe for this remarkable adventure in perfect weather. But we did become slightly concerned when we boarded the plane.

"Ladies and gentleman, I've got a little bad news for you," the steward announced over the aircraft speaker system, which uncharacteristically could be understood.

The speaker system was working, but the business-class galley was completely out of service. From their explanation the choice was either to cancel the flight or get everyone there with slower food service. It turned out not to be a problem at all.

However, one thing did go awry about halfway into the flight. Barbara made a sudden turn in her seat.

"Yikes!" I shrieked as she accidentally knocked a full glass of water directly into my lap. I was soaked clear through. But it was an accident, and no amount of fussing would make me any drier. By the end of the flight I was completely dry—well, almost dry.

As we approached our Paris apartment in a taxi, we found ourselves in the middle of a demonstration. Interns from hospitals were marching against the government's new health-care policy. The gendarmerie came with paddy wagons and took them away. As a physician I felt some pride in the initiative the students were taking. I'm not certain their parents were feeling the same way, but the crowds were cheering for the interns.

Once settled, we contacted Hugh and Sylvia, friends vacationing in Paris. They could accurately be called Parisophiles. They adore this city. But who doesn't? We had dinner together at an Alsatian restaurant and gossiped about things happening back home.

The evening had been wonderful until we received a phone call at midnight. It came from a close friend, Oscar, and the news was frightening. Our dear friend Seymour had had a heart attack. Now we waited anxiously to hear about his progress. Seymour is someone special, so all day long we were thinking about him. Finally by the afternoon we got further news. He was progressing marvelously, and we couldn't have been happier.

* * *

I had read that Daniel Barenboim was conducting *Lohengrin* to glowing reviews. This was the final performance. At the box office they said, "It's all sold out. But people will be selling tickets in front of the theatre before the performance begins at 6:30 P.M."

Barbara and I formulated a plan. Since we were uncertain if there would be tickets available at all, there was no reason for both of us to go to the theatre. I told her to wait in the apartment. If I got tickets, I'd call for her to come. When I arrived at the theatre at 5:30 P.M., scalpers were already selling poor seats at inflated prices. I decided to wait and see.

The head scalper, spotting me as a buyer, approached and with great authority said, "You sit down over there. I'll find the seats you want and bring them to you."

I caught on quite quickly, considering I'm not a scalper. He didn't want me buying tickets on my own. Their technique is to buy tickets from those with extra seats at bargain prices and sell them to suckers like me at a markedly elevated price. Buy low and sell high. Barbara and I are considered experts at buying high and selling low in the stock market. But I do know how the other system works, so I followed them around until they came across a man who had one extra very good seat. They offered him a low-ball price. He countered with a price still under the face value, but not as low as they would like.

I jumped in. "I'll take it."

The scalpers were flabbergasted. Who was this person cutting in on their territory?

By then it was obvious the two seats I'd get would be separate. I obtained another single ticket, and though the public telephones were crowded, finally I reached Barbara.

"Rush over here right now."

I hung up the phone and waited anxiously. At 6:25 my darling arrived.

Flashback

This was not the first time we had an unusual ticket experience in Paris. Once we ordered opera tickets in advance for the new Bastille Opera House. After waiting for one hour, I was told, "I'm sorry, there's no record of a reservation and no tickets are available."

Disappointed and empty-handed, I dashed off to see if I could get tickets for the symphony. By then that box office had closed and I was without tickets again. But a large poster indicated there would be a concert elsewhere that night with Barbara Hendricks, the famous American opera singer. It was already 6:00 P.M. so I'd have to rush back to see if Barbara wanted to try, knowing they might very well be sold out as well.

When I returned she said, "Let's go for it."

We dressed and were on our way, only to find the remaining tickets were standing room above six rings of seats. We were about to leave when a young man approached.

"I've got two tickets I can't use. Would you like to buy them?"

We sat in the second row of the orchestra that night.

The Present

After *Lohengrin* we returned to our neighborhood, and dined until 1:00 A.M. at Le Procope, the oldest café in Paris. A message on our answering machine provided good news. Seymour, after his quintuple bypass, was watching a ball game. We'd sleep much better that night.

Sundays are special days for us in Paris at this time of the year. Concerts are held every Sunday morning from September until the first week in May at the Théâtre des Champs-Élysées, on Avenue de Montaigne, a beautiful street lined with famous couturiers. Fortunately, on Sunday they're all closed, so we couldn't be enticed to buy.

The series presents famous chamber groups and individuals. Open seating at 100 francs per person (about $17) is a wonderful bargain. That Sunday a chamber group from Germany played Beethoven to the great pleasure of everyone in the theatre.

After the concert we met Sylvia and Hugh for lunch at Brasserie Balzar on the Left Bank. Then we took them over to see our apartment, which was the pied à terre in Paris for a couple who live in Nice. They are friends of the family who were our landlords in Entrechaux. Though only 440 square feet, the apartment was remarkably efficient, with a generous living room, a small office, a bedroom, a modern bathroom with a tub/shower combo, and a fully equipped kitchen with refrigerator, stove, oven, microwave, and dishwasher.

Close by were three markets on rue de la Seine, rue Buci and the St. Germain market. Having made the decision to eat one meal each day at home, lunch or dinner, we went browsing through the shops selling take out food. There were at least a dozen different meals we found we could put together. We picked up a few wonderful things and returned to the apartment for dinner, with wine and a new cheese for us, *époisses*.

* * *

Another day we went with Hugh and Sylvia to the Musée de l'Orangerie to see the collection of impressionist art, especially Monet's paintings of the water lilies. But after lunch there was no meeting of the minds as to where we would spend our afternoon. Barbara and Sylvia said they were going shopping on rue Faubourg St. Honoré. Not finding that exciting, Hugh responded, "I'm going to the Madeleine, which has always been under restoration when I'm here. I'm going to get to see it this time."

I decided to do neither and just walked up the Champs-Élysées to the Arc de Triomphe and then back down beautiful Haussmann Boulevard to meet Hugh two hours later at the Opera Plaza. This city is the most wonderful place to walk. The Champs-Élysées was a feast of flowers at the Place de la Concorde. As I approached the arch I was swallowed up by masses of tourists and shops. What fun it was to be strolling there!

When Hugh and I met in the plaza I took him to a money-exchange shop on rue de Scribe where I had found the best rates in Paris. He was thrilled with his financial coup.

Later Barbara and I decided to go for dinner to Le Petit Zinc. Decorated in old zinc, it's very charming. We sat at the end of a row of four tables. Next to us was a lovely Dutch couple, speaking to a Danish man seated opposite them. We all joined together in conversation. Dutch, Danish, and American, we were all speaking English. At the other end of the table another couple joined in the conversation. They were from Germany. The conversation progressed through the rest of the evening with everyone speaking English. By the time the meal ended, hours later, we found that the German couple now lived in California. They were friends of many of Barbara's closest childhood friends there and lived only minutes from one of our children. The Danish gentleman couldn't believe it.

"Two hundred and eighty million there and you both know the same people!"

The couple from Holland were especially interesting. They had lost a child who was handicapped. Previously a successful businessman, he had given up his career and was starting a new one in France providing services for the handicapped.

In the morning I told Hugh and Sylvia we would take them to a new place to have lunch, recommended by our dinner companions the night before, called L'Espace Cardin.

On arrival we found the restaurant no longer existed. Then I recalled another suggested by friends, Jack and Belinda Frishman, and did I get brownie points for that.

Le Grand Colbert was packed, but we got the last table. Each of us ordered wonderful dishes. Barbara had a salmon terrine and grilled tongue. Sylvia and I both had the *soupe de poisson* (fish soup) with *rouille*, garlic, and cheese. I added a salad of goat cheese and tomatoes in olive oil and Hugh ordered curried lamb and a salad. Meanwhile Hugh regaled us with wonderful stories about his family's origins in Iowa, where Sylvia and Hugh were both born. We didn't leave Le Grand Colbert until two and a half hours later. The meal was completed with one delicious *baba au rhum* that we all shared.

We walked through Place Victoire to Dehillerin, a shop established in 1820 which sells everything one could crave for the kitchen. Barbara never leaves there without some purchases, at times, unwittingly, the same item we bought on a previous visit.

It was reminiscent of a story Sylvia told about bringing back a piece of Limoges from Paris for one of her children, only to find that she had brought the same gift the year before. If you loved it when you saw it the first time, why wouldn't you love it again?

Our stroll led us to the Palais Royale gardens. Parisian gardens are beyond description, and the Palais Royale is one of the loveliest. Rows of trees, each manicured, line both sides of the grounds. It is surrounded by a palace occupying a square block encompassing the gardens. Inside the lines of trees are beds of flowers, including tulips in an assortment of colors. There are fountains and a sandy area where children play. Within this serene space people sit, read, eat treats like ice cream, embrace, or just contemplate the beauty of the surroundings. One could sit there for hours ... and many do.

When we finally left, we were in front of the Louvre, my favorite museum in the world. Even without entering, just walking through its grounds catches my heart.

To quote *Paris Access*, "It is the single largest building in Paris, the largest palace in Europe, the largest museum in the Western world ... It has 224 halls and its Grande Galerie is longer than three football fields. It took seven centuries to build, spanning the lives of seventeen monarchs and countless architects."

The museum is closed on Tuesdays but the grounds are open to walk through. When it was the royal palace, it's easy to imagine how a family could occupy it and believe they were the most important people alive. Certainly they considered themselves omnipotent enough to say of their starving subjects, "Let them eat cake."

Walking through the grounds, crowded even when the museum is closed, one sees the pyramidal structures created by I. M. Pei in 1989 to help the flow of visitors to the museum. We exited on the side facing the Seine, and crossed one of the many bridges, Pont des Arts. The *bateau mouche*, sightseeing boat, passed beneath us. Along the quai were exquisite buildings. To the east was the island of Cité, in the middle of the Seine, and the spires of Notre Dame. We were then on the Left Bank with its boutique-lined streets, and walked joyously home. The following day was to be spent with our friend Bruno, who would take us, in the afternoon, to a place he promised we had never seen.

Flashback

Bruno has been a wonderful friend ever since our first meeting. We were thrilled to have him return to our house in San Antonio on several occasions while doing research for a book. He was always more than generous to us, offering his homes in France for us to use when we came there. One of those times was almost five years previously.

Arrangements had been made for us to stay at his apartment in Paris, after three weeks of traveling around France. Bruno was not going to be in Paris when we arrived at 6:00 in the evening. That was fine, as we had a previously scheduled dinner engagement.

"I'm jumping into the shower right now," Barbara advised me.

"Herb, how do I get this hot water to work?" Barbara asked standing at one end of the tub in her birthday suit.

I wasn't concerned. It wasn't the first time the request had been made of me to figure out how to operate a new shower. I'd have it solved in a minute. Well, maybe it would take two minutes. Well ... maybe there wasn't any hot water.

"Aha!" I said. "If you wanted hot water you should have stayed in a hotel."

At a loss about what to do, I called Bruno's daughter Florence, who also lived in the building. Like myself, Florence had no explanation and called Bruno's brother, who lived there as well. Unfortunately, he was a violinist, not a plumber, and had not a clue. With everyone wandering in and out, Barbara had put some of her clothes back on. But her being half naked didn't seem to bother them. Remember, they are French.

Finally Florence called Bruno and the decision was made. The next day Florence would go with me to the plumber, bring him back, and try to resolve the problem.

So Barbara and I, unbathed, went to dinner with our friends Pat and Sheldon Goldberg. For us it was a lovely evening. Unfortunately, the same could not be said for Florence. She went to the movies with friends quite far from home. Sometime after 1:00 in the morning, when they were ready to return home, the subways had stopped and they didn't have enough money for a taxi. Walking home, she arrived well into the morning. You can imagine how thrilled she was when I knocked on her door at the previously arranged time of 8:30 A.M. to go find the plumber. She went with a smile, nevertheless.

At the shop I didn't like the sound of the conversation. Too many words went back and forth between Florence and a young man dressed too nicely to be the plumber. I didn't understand any of those words except *"Non,"* and didn't think that was good to hear.

Florence told me the plumber was off to school for three months, but the young man gave us two others to try. Florence's feet were killing her from the walk the night before, but we kept on walking. Florence stopped in a bar to ask directions of a man draped over the bar counter. I don't know why she had no fear about being in that rundown bar or how she was able to breathe over the stench of alcohol, which was so strong. But, even with new directions, we still had difficulty finding the location we sought.

Bruno's perception of his daughter, like most parents, was that she was not mature enough to see a problem and solve it. Like the rest of us, he was wrong. Florence took the bull by the horns. She saw a plumber's truck stopped in a line of cars at a red light. She went into the street and began talking to the driver. By an amazing coincidence, he was one of the plumbers recommended. Mind you, this occurred in the midst of heavy traffic.

I heard Florence say the word that buoyed my confidence, *"Voilà!"* We were approaching a holiday weekend and I dreaded the thought of three days with no hot water.

He told Florence to return to the apartment and he would meet us there in fifteen minutes. True to his word, he arrived on time. Searching for the water heater, he found that during a previous renovation, workmen plastered over it completely, allowing no access. To my amazement, he took the wall apart, found the heater, jiggled some screws, and said the problem was solved. It would be an hour before we had hot water. But he was leaving. I felt a sense of panic. If there wasn't hot water in one hour, we were stuck.

Barbara and I went out for coffee and pastries, returning in about one hour to find the hot water flowing freely. The apartment was wonderful and dear sweet Florence had saved the day. If she wasn't outgoing, aggressive, and dynamic, I didn't know who was.

Present

Bruno took us to the largest park in Paris, the Bois de Bologne. We had been to the famous forest many times in the past, because that is where the French tennis championships are held at Roland Garros. But Bagatelle Gardens was a place we had never seen.

The gardens were absolutely beautiful. Some portions were quite formal while others were in a very natural setting. The flowers and their colors were breathtaking.

After a while we went to Bruno's apartment for the dinner he had prepared.

Flashback

Having dinner with Bruno reminded me of an evening we spent with his daughter Florence. We had invited her to join us at one of our favorite *brasseries*, Vaudeville. Barbara knows French better than I, but doesn't have the nerve to speak it as often as I try. Maybe the proper word is not "nerve," but rather *gall*, or *stupidity*.

Nevertheless, Florence and I made a pact. She would speak only English, and I only French. It was a good deal because my biggest problem was being able to understand the spoken word. I can read and speak a lot better than I can hear the language. It was a riotous evening. We laughed so hard the other customers couldn't stop staring. I'm not certain what they were saying about "those silly people," but we were having great fun.

After the meal, lasting four hours, I remember asking Florence about my language ability and recall very well her response.

"Your Français ees wonderfool. Bot, eet ees not fentestic!"

Present

With the papers reporting a drought from six straight weeks of sunny, rain-free weather, Barbara went window-shopping and arranged to meet me in front of St. Sulpice.

St. Sulpice is quite a church. Originally constructed in the sixth century and rebuilt a number of times, it was gradually enlarged to its present immense stature. Of particular interest, sunlight shines through a hole in a window, casting a light on an obelisk marked for noon at different times of the year, giving the church its own sundial.

The front courtyard was surrounded by blossoming trees and a spectacular fountain spraying from gargoyles.

I stopped a few French men and women and asked, *"Excusez-moi, qu'est-ce que c'est le nom de ces arbres?"*: What are these trees called?

Each person gave a negative shrug, except for a group of teenagers who just giggled at the question. Then I stopped two charming, well-dressed women and put the same question to them. *Voilà!* I hit the jackpot.

"*Ils sont marronniers*": They are chestnut trees.

She told me they were all chestnuts even though some had red blossoms and some white. She also made it clear they weren't edible, to avoid having me do something crazy. The search for the information and the discovery, accomplished in French, was great fun.

It was then that a marvelous thought occurred to me. While walking the streets of Paris, I had sung to myself, numerous times, "April in Paris." It begins with the line, "April in Paris, Chestnuts in blossom." Here I was, and it was not just a lyric. It was happening. Just as the song says, the chestnuts were in blossom, and they were beautiful.

Barbara appeared on the scene, to keep me out of trouble with Frenchwomen. We went for a simple lunch at Chez Paul on the Cité and then walked, more than a mile, to the d'Orsay Museum. It's a jewel worth visiting just to see the architecture of this restored train station. The Impressionist collection is superb.

* * *

For the first time in three months it rained. But we wouldn't allow a little something like that to hold us back. We had plans and we were going to stick to them. After a marvelous lunch at Ferme St. Simon we went to the Marmottan. It's the site of a great number of Monet paintings, probably the largest collection outside Giverny, his home. But something was even more interesting. On a wall of the museum there was a description of Monet's family genealogy. His first wife died shortly after having their second child. Some years later he married a widow with six grown children. As I followed the history down the generations there was a very interesting connection. One of Monet's sons, from his first marriage, married a daughter of his second wife.

By evening it was time for a necessary chore, the laundry. When I went to the laundromat I found the instructions difficult to understand. Fortunately there was a woman there who spoke English and explained the process to me. I loaded everything in the machines and sat down to do some work while I was waiting.

About five minutes later a young American woman, about twenty-five, came in and approached me.

"Can you speak English?"

"Yes, but with difficulty," I responded.

She laughed and asked if I knew how the machines worked. By this time I was an expert and taught her the process. It reminded me of an old story that has been told about medicine for years. Once you enter your training, there is a three-part process. With each new procedure, first you see it done once, then you do it once, then you can teach it. It sounds a little scary, but it seemed to work fine with washing machines.

My expertise soon deserted me. The dials on the dryers were broken, and the machines were set to maximum heat. Unaware, I placed a load of cotton underwear in the dryer for seven minutes. When the time had expired the clothes were still slightly damp. So I added more coins for an additional seven minutes. That was a bad move.

When the dryer stopped I tried to remove the clothes and burned my hands, but not on the dryer. The cotton was burning hot. So quickly I threw the clothes into a plastic bag I had brought to carry them. Before I knew it the bag melted onto my underwear. I could hardly believe my eyes. The next half-hour was spent peeling as much plastic off the shorts and tops as I could manage. I hope I'm a better doctor than a launderer.

* * *

Wonderful classical music is easily found in Paris. After lunch we went to the Théâtre des Champs-Élysées to hear Riccardo Muti conduct the National Symphony of France and the choir performing "Stabat Mater" by Rossini. The applause was incessant, only ending when Muti asked for the house lights to be raised.

* * *

Shopping in Paris bakeries took great will power to avoid buying everything in sight. The pastries are so beautiful. In the south of France there were multiple patisseries (pastry shops) in every town. Though these shops made lovely pastries, they couldn't compare with the Parisian shops. Looking in the windows was like walking past a series of art galleries. The nicest one in our neighborhood was one of the best I'd ever seen. It's called Gerard Mulot, and there were always large crowds waiting in line to be served.

* * *

After breakfast Barbara and I returned to the Théâtre des Champs-Élysées for our second concert of the weekend. This was to be the next to the last Sunday-morning concert of the season. A German ensemble orchestra played all Bach.

For years I had taken my children to children's classical concerts in New York. They were presented at a child's level with the conductor explaining different aspects of the music to them. As might be expected with small children, there was always a hum of conversation in the audience. Some seemed to be interested, while others were bored.

The Sunday-morning concerts in Paris are free to children under the age of nine with a large group attending. But the selections were for rather sophisticated adults. Amazingly, during the entire concert, an hour and a half, not one peep could be heard from a child. It was astounding.

Every country has its own wonderful culture. In an article I read about France the writer put it quite succinctly. "The people of the United States and France are distinctly different culturally. The French are not just Americans who speak a different language."

After the concert we met Sylvia and Hugh for lunch in a little brasserie on the Île St. Louis, not surprisingly called Brasserie Île St. Louis. Packed in like sardines, we had the best time. All four of us ordered a special French dish, cassoulet, a casserole of beans, beef, and sausages. It may not be the healthiest dish in the world, but I loved it.

Then we walked to Notre Dame, where crowds milled around an outdoor fair with farm animals, cows, pigs, and goats, in pens in the middle of the street—what a sight.

When we entered Notre Dame a mass was in progress and there were several thousand people present as the priests in their resplendent robes performed the service with a choir and a female soloist. The voices echoed through the separate chambers surrounding the central transept. The entire experience was very moving.

* * *

Each day in Paris was wonderful. We lunched at Epi Dupin, a restaurant so small and so popular that we had had difficulty obtaining a reservation there in the past. Then it was off to the Picasso Museum, the best of the many Picasso Museums I've seen around the world. I do not consider myself an art connoisseur, but I do love that museum.

The range of Picasso's work is astounding. He worked in every art form from prints to painting to sculpture. His work spans the range from representational to cubism and way beyond my tastes.

The museum chronicles Picasso in relation to the many women in his life. One section always brings a smile to my face. It's the portion covering the period of 1930–35, when he was using, as a model, a young, teenage secret mistress. I have had some minimal training in art, including drawing from nude models, so I can understand the value of having such models. But Picasso's pictures from that period are of massively distorted bodies. In some cases they seem to be dismembered, and in others with anatomical parts in all nonanatomical positions. I am not offended by his wild distortions of the human body, but I find it so humorous to think that it would be necessary to have a human model to paint those pictures that have absolutely no resemblance to anything in real life.

In the evening we went to our third concert of the weekend. This time it was Sir George Solti conducting the London Philharmonic. The evening left us with a feeling of ultimate pleasure and thankfulness at our good fortune. It turned out to be the last chance we would ever have to listen to Solti conduct, as shortly afterward he passed away.

In the morning we shopped to take advantage of saving the value-added tax if purchases totaling $200 were made in one store. I wanted just one item. During our last stay in Paris I had bought merino wool turtleneck sweaters at Printemps that fit perfectly.

We went to that department and found just what I wanted and asked for an extra-large. Understanding what happened subsequently requires the knowledge that the French prefer their clothes to be more tight-fitting than Americans do.

Trying on a blouse earlier in the week Barbara commented to a saleswoman, "These tops are all so tight-fitting."

"Wait for another year or two and Frenchwomen will all be in corsets to give them an even smaller hourglass figure," the woman responded.

She ended the conversation by saying that the same thing would happen in the U.S. But it would take a few years for us to catch up to the French. It's probably true.

Back to my turtlenecks, my saleswoman went into a complete dither. She refused to allow me to purchase the extra-large. She was certain that in an extra-large I would float away. It was impossible to dissuade her. So we purchased the large, hoping she was right.

* * *

Another morning we took the Métro to the eighth arrondisement. Paris is divided into twenty zones called *arrondisements*. Knowing which arrondisement a destination falls within makes it much simpler to find. The eighth arrondisement is in north central Paris.

We started the day at the Musée Nissim-de-Camondo, a grand townhouse which had been used for the filming of *Valmont*. The home was owned by the Camondo family. After Moise Camondo's son Nissim was killed as a pilot during World War I, Moise donated the house and the collection of art and eighteenth-century furnishings to the city of Paris in memory of his son. But the saddest part of the story is that Moise's daughter, son-in-law, and grandchildren all died at Auschwitz during World War II.

From there we walked a few blocks to Parc Monceau, another of the absolutely exquisite parks in Paris. The flowers were indescribable. There were trees, ponds, grottoes, small bridges, and children playing wherever you looked. No one should come to Paris and not see the parks. I regretted that it was our first time in Monceau.

Much more physical beauty is maintained in Paris in comparison to other cities we have seen. It certainly isn't because they have excess funds, as the newspapers daily report their economic problems. It has to be related to their priorities. In the French culture the need to enrich the soul seems a little more important than in some others.

We walked to the Madeleine and had lunch for the first time at Fauchon. Some French travelers might be surprised we hadn't ever dined there previously, as it is a gastronomic center in Paris with separate shops of wine, pastries, candy, produce, prepared delicacies, and general gourmet treats. We ate a reasonably priced lunch in their cafeteria. A restaurant and a bistro there charged significantly higher prices.

For dessert we shared a lemon tart with a paper-thin edible slice of lemon on top. It was, by joint agreement, the most luscious lemon tart we had ever tasted.

* * *

On France's Labor Day, with no museums open and great weather, we went to the most famous cemetery in Paris, Père Lachaise, the burial site of French and non-French stalwarts of the arts, medicine, and industry. This huge cemetery contains thousands of tombs, some massive beyond belief. With a map we found the gravesites of Mozart, Piaf, Yves Montand, and Simone Signoret. There were also those of Delacroix, Max Ernst, Gertrude Stein, and Alice B. Toklas. But none drew the crowds and the police protection of one other gravesite, the resting place of Jim Morrison, the rock star. His gravestone was covered with graffitti, probably explaining why the police were guarding it.

After dinner we walked past the Louvre, over the Seine to home at midnight.

* * *

In a phone conversation with our friend Judy, Barbara complained about the difficulty in buying clothing because everything was cut for the tall, slender Parisians.

"Oh, you mean the giraffes," Judy responded.

After that, whenever we walked down the streets of Paris, Barbara kept identifying the passing "giraffes." They certainly were quite lovely.

Then one day, instead of mixing her metaphors, Barbara mixed her animals.

"Look, over there, another kangaroo."

"A what?" I asked.

"Sorry, I meant giraffe, but she is sort of hopping around."

But walking down the street one was confronted by one of the worst things in Paris, the ubiquitous nature of dog manure. Avoiding it became a major preoccupation. Though the streets were constantly being cleaned, the dogs produced manure faster. There appeared to be no laws there that required dog owners to clean up their dogs' mess.

A second ever-present sight was the beggars. They were very polite, never pushy or aggressive, just standing with their hands out waiting for someone to give them money.

With unemployment at an all-time high, others who were not beggars provided some sort of service, generally musical, hoping to get donations for their performances. Though the economic difficulty for these individuals was anything but funny, some incidents were interesting and somewhat humorous.

Planning to go to a movie I looked up the information in the weekly guide. There was a sentence I couldn't translate. The movies, like the museums, all have different policies. Some give reduced rates for children, some for seniors, but one theatre listed a third category with a French word I had never seen before. I looked it up in the dictionary and found that it meant "unemployed." The government in France provides many social services, but it was the first time I had seen services provided by a private business.

Then, at a Métro station, another strange thing occurred. Entrance was made by inserting a ticket into a slot in front of a swinging door. As I inserted my ticket I heard Barbara say something, and I turned to see if she was having a problem. She quickly resolved it, but now I had a problem. I had inserted my ticket. The door opened, and while I looked at Barbara, my door had closed. Now my ticket was gone and I was still on the outside. There appeared no way for me to pass through without using another ticket.

I stood there confused when suddenly I was confronted by a beggar who had been standing at the entrance. He reassured me not to worry. With a rapid set of arm motions waved in front of a hidden electric beam, he got the door to swing open and told me to pass through. As I did, he asked much more firmly than any previous beggar for reimbursement for his services, which of course I could hardly deny.

A third phenomenon, apparent all over Paris, was the multitude of people in every situation using cell phones. One day I saw how it was affecting their society, especially the children. While we were walking, a child about seven came toward us on her roller skates. One arm was swinging in the rhythm of skating. In her other hand there was a toy phone held up to her ear, while she spoke to an imaginary person, a sign of the times.

*　*　*

It was a perfect museum day. Raining at last, we started at the Paris City Hall, known as the Hôtel de Ville. The show was about postwar Paris in the '50s. The exhibit showed common everyday items of that time, including furnishings, advertising, radios, kitchen equipment, and photographs of the period, including the new Métro system.

From there we went to a wing of the Louvre called the Musée des Arts de la Mode (Museum of Fashion), which presents apparel from over the centuries. But it was closed on Mondays. Not allowing that to get us down, we walked to the famous tearoom Angelina's. There we would have their famous hot chocolate called L'Africaine, so rich and thick you have to eat it with a fork. Guess what! It was closed just for one day for renovations, and this was the day. But neither rain nor closings could discourage us. We decided to put them off for another day.

It rained again the following day and Barbara sent me to the market to get a few items for the dinner she was preparing at home. Among other things, I was instructed to return with one head of garlic, *"ail"* in French. At the green grocer I looked all around and couldn't find any garlic. I asked, *"Avez-vous ail?"*: Do you have any garlic?

A finger in the direction of the corner of the store sent me to the garlic. But where was it? I felt like a fool, and returned to the same shopkeeper.

"Excusez-moi, où est l'ail?": Pardon me. Where is the garlic?

Totally frustrated, she came back with me and pointed to a huge bin filled with something I had never seen. They were very white with long stems on the bottom. When I took them home, Barbara was ecstatic.

"These are spectacular. They're so young and fresh. I can't get these at home."

Sometimes it's so easy to be a hero, but only sometimes.

An Aside

We noticed that cigarette smoking in Parisian restaurants had tapered off from our experiences in earlier trips. Some restaurants had non-smoking and smoking areas. It took them a lot longer to know how detrimental cigarettes are, but they seem to be catching on.

During lunch one day we sat opposite three very elegant French people. The level of affluence could hardly have been more obvious from the manner of their dress and apparently very expensive jewelry. After a while two of them began smoking.

I turned to Barbara and said, "They're good-looking, and rich, but not smart."

Barbara, who definitely is less tolerant of smokers than I, changed her approach suddenly with, "I agree, but something else occurs to me. It must be very relaxing for them to light up a cigarette after a wonderful meal, or maybe even after making love."

You can tell she understands the French when she senses that it's a tossup for them between eating a great meal and making love.

I thought about it for a moment and partially agreed. "Lighting up a cigarette is a source of oral gratification. And we know that's very relaxing to human beings and gives me a great idea. I'm wondering if it will go over in these wonderful French restaurants."

Barbara listened intently to hear what I was going to suggest.

"We both know that smoking is something we absolutely won't do. Right?"

"Right!"

"So what if, after a lovely meal in a French restaurant, we take out baby pacifiers and sit sucking on them as our oral gratification without the nicotine and tar."

Barbara gave me that typical look that can only be translated as, "That's what I really call a dumb joke."

Barbara seems to have the instincts to be a teacher. She's always grading my humor, and, more frequently than not, I feel as if I'm going to flunk out.

Present

We decided to go to a series of museums which would all be first-time visits for us. We started with a second attempt at the Louvre's Museum of Fashion. It was worth the wait. Then it was off to a museum called Carnavalet. Our friend Hugh had suggested it. It's also called the Museum of the City of Paris. Though small, it presented a picture of Paris through the centuries. There were beautiful furnishings and many wonderful paintings. I wondered how an inconspicuous place like this could have all these paintings in a city with so many important museums. It didn't take long to figure out the answer. Almost every painting was attributed to no one, only a place and time. Some were from France, some were Flemish, but with no identifiable artist.

Most of the paintings were portraits of famous individuals in French history. And, although the artists were not identified, there was much information about the subjects in the painting. Many of them had been assassinated or beheaded. In one case it said the subject, Henri de Lorraine, was murdered in Blois, the town in which Barbara panicked when a maid barged in on us while we were making love.

I said to Barbara, "You thought you'd almost die in Blois, but he really did."

Then there was Marie de Miraille. She was something special. She was about to be married when it was discovered she had strangled her expectant husband's wife. Instead of a wedding ceremony, she was hanged.

The building that houses the museum was the residence of Madame de Sévigné. During our time in the south of France we had gone to Grignan on several occasions. It was there that the daughter of Madame de Sévigné lived. The Madame, who was a great letter writer, and outspoken, became a friend of the French royalty. On six occasions she was Louis XIV's guest at Versailles. The letters to her daughter are famous, and in Paris a street and numerous other places are named after her. A section of the museum is a reproduction of her salon. A guide told us about Madame de Sévigné's history and the recent 300th anniversary of her death, which was celebrated in January. Among other things the postal system made first-day covers in cards, envelopes, and stamps in her honor.

From there we went to another restaurant in the Marais for the first time. The food was quite good and extremely inexpensive. The establishment has two names, L'Impasse or Chez Robert.

At an adjacent table sat four American women, having a grand time. They had just arrived in Paris for their first visit. Hearing us speak English they began asking for advice, which we gave, probably excessively. But they seemed very appreciative.

I told them the wine here was not like in the United States, where wine can be good or bad. I advised them not to waste their money on expensive wines because they were all so good. They could even order it, with confidence, by the glass or carafe.

Then one of them scowled, saying she didn't like the wine she had. Oh, well!

To end the day we went to the Musée des Arts et Métiers. The museum has inventions from the fifth century on, which seemed enticing to us. Alas, it was closed for renovations. We'll see it on a return visit, and it will only be even better.

* * *

The following day we went to visit Bruno and Hélène Verlet at their lovely home in Vulaines. It was raining and they were concerned it would ruin our day.

The train ride to Fontainebleau took only thirty-five minutes. Bruno picked us up and took us to the house, where Hélène was preparing lunch. During lunch it never stopped raining. But the moment we left to visit a place they wanted us to see, the rain stopped.

The spot they had chosen, called Courance, was twenty miles from Fontainebleau. It is an old estate with a chateau surrounded by an immaculately cared-for park and gardens, with ponds throughout. We walked the grounds and then returned to the chateau for a guided tour. The rooms were furnished in great taste with lovely art. The chateau is still occupied by the family, but they allow it to be shown as a national treasure on weekends and holidays with fees collected to maintain the grounds.

We were very impressed until ... and then it happened. The guide took us into the game room. There the owners had commissioned a mural which occupies an entire wall. It is a picture of the five brothers who presently are the owners. It looks like a great big billboard ad sitting in the middle of everything that was hundreds of years old.

I told Bruno and Hélène I loved the park and chateau, but I thought the picture was really tacky. I believe they weren't too fond of it either.

They are such dear people that the day spent with them was delightful for us. After lunch Hélène showed us pictures of her family, which she documents through eight generations. The furthest back are, of course, in paintings. Her grandfather was a major force in the Protestant Church and a member of the Académie Française. There were even pictures of him with Charles de Gaulle. With knowledge of only two older generations in my family, I was immensely impressed. We took the 6:00 train back and had dinner at La Bastide Odéon, in our neighborhood.

There was one other thing that happened which was quite strange. After we got off the train from Fontainebleau we went downstairs in the station to catch the Métro. Only a minute or two had passed before the train entered the station. As it pulled in front of us the train looked very different and I began to get nervous that somehow we had gone to the wrong place to catch it. But I had no time to think as the doors opened and we all entered. We had been on the Métro every day without fail, most days four or more times, and these seats were different. The handles were different. And, then, I could hardly believe my eyes. I could see people all the way through the train to the very back, about six or seven cars, extending to the end of the station. There was no break at all.

A man standing next to me sensed my confusion from the expression on my face.

In English he said, "This is the new car that just started this week. They are adding them on little by little."

It was beautiful and totally different from anything I've ever seen in a subway or a train. You can't imagine what it's like, from inside the train, to see a single car the length of the train. Corrogations in the frame of the train allow it to bend at curves. It is the same feeling as looking down the length of an airplane, but with more room. It will probably take a long time before all the cars are replaced by these ultra-modern new ones.

* * *

Only on weekdays can one eat lunch at any of the very fancy restaurants in Paris. They all close for Saturday lunch and all day Sunday. As inexpensive as many of the Paris restaurants are, the multiple Michelin starred ones are extremely expensive. It is not uncommon to see dinner menus running from 800 to 1,000 francs per person. That's about $140 to $175 without wine. And the wines correspond in price. As a result a dinner for two could easily be between $350 and $450. It was not within our budget.

But all the finest restaurants usually have a much lower priced luncheon menu. The average luncheon price of those restaurants appeared to be between 350 and 500 francs per person, bringing the tab down a little to $60 to $85 per person without wine.

It was time to do some research. After many calls to the finest-rated places I came upon Amphycles. The price-fixed menu there was 260 francs per person. Our decision was made. We would celebrate Mother's Day there, two days early.

As in the other starred restaurants there was something extra, not on the menu, to start the meal, usually very small hors d'oeuvres. They brought fresh mushrooms, over which they poured mushroom soup. Every dish was served by several waiters.

The next course was a fish appetizer. The fish were whole boned rougets, stuffed with anchovies. On occasion I have seen the French eat parts of a food I would never consume, such as large portions of solid fat on the edges of meat that I would always cut away. When we were through I asked the chief waiter for our table whether the French consume the fish heads we left behind. He assured me they would not.

Barbara and I opted for fish as our main course as well. We were told that the special dish, being prepared for today, was St. Peter with tomato and olive sauce. We asked if it was on the price-fixed lunch and were told it was only served on the à la carte menu, and considerably more expensive. As a result we ordered something else. Then the waiter returned and said it would be fine to have the special dish on the price-fixed menu. It sounded so lovely that we concurred. They probably found they had more fish than they were going to be able to use. Whatever the reason, once we tasted it, we were thrilled.

It was covered with thin slices of cherry tomatoes. Each thin slice had a separate slice of an olive on it, and it was bathed in an olive oil sauce. Oh, my, was it delicious!

The next course, the fourth, was dessert. There was no choice. A cannelle had been carmelized and filled with rhubarb. Alongside were fresh strawberries and raspberries in a red sauce. It was mouth-watering. But there was more. They then brought out a plate with a multitude of sweet delicacies. There were all different types of little cakes and cookies. That was followed by coffee with small chocolate candies.

What a meal! We ordered a delicious red wine which was priced at 100 francs for a half-bottle. That is all we normally consume at a meal. The total bill for everything for the two of us was 620 francs, less than $110 including tax and tip.

The service was so attentive, when Barbara went to the restroom, one of the lesser waiters accompanied her to be certain she found her way. It made her a little nervous about how far he was going. But to her great satisfaction, he didn't enter the restroom.

As the meal ended, the chef came out to greet all of his customers. He came to our table first, probably because we were the only people he didn't know. When he approached the other tables he gave them warm personal greetings and kisses.

Our Mother's Day luncheon celebration lasted more than two hours. We planned to go to two museums in the area and then to find a special Mother's Day gift for Barbara. With our track record you won't be surprised to know the restaurant was the most successful part of the day. Both museums were located in the Palais de Chaillot. One was closed for renovations. It dealt with the architecture of Paris. We'll see it the next time we're in Paris. The second was a French museum of film, offered in a guided tour only in French. We decided to pass on that. Our Mother's Day window-shopping fell flat as well.

* * *

Bon Marché's food wing is more like a museum than a market, with exquisite displays. As we walked there I asked Barbara, "Would you like to see my private club?"

"Private club? What are you talking about?"

"There it is across the street. If you're really nice I'll get you an invitation."

I had been given the responsibility of doing the laundry in Paris, and the name of the laundromat was "Club Lav." When Barbara saw what I was referring to, she declined the invitation. But at least this time she did laugh at my attempt at humor.

After meandering through Bon Marché we had a lovely lunch down the block at Le Bistrot d'Opio on rue Guisarde, then spent the day shopping. We found a Mother's Day present and ended the day at our favorite local pizzeria, Mama's, before returning home.

There's something special about staying in one location for an extended period of time. It got to feel like home, getting to know the local merchants. My corner newspaper man at the kiosk gave me a big greeting every morning. The baker expected me to stop by. And the local pizzeria always found a table for us somewhere. Waiters would greet us with a cheery *"Bonsoir."* It was all warm and friendly. It was Paris in the springtime.

* * *

A great many restaurants in Paris serve oysters. I'm not an oyster eater, but Barbara loves them. In our neighborhood there were fish markets on rue de Seine and rue Buci. I had promised Barbara we would buy oysters and take them back to the apartment for her. After a while I began feeling bad that so far we hadn't done it even once.

On Saturday night before Mother's Day we went to the fish market, but arrived late. The owner would sell us oysters, but had no time to open them. Uncertain if we might have difficulty doing that ourselves, we planned to buy them the next day for lunch, not knowing that they closed early on Sunday.

I screwed up once again. Arriving after all the fish had been put away, I was feeling extremely guilty. It was Mother's Day, the holiday founded on guilt. So instead we went to a brasserie in our neighborhood specializing in oysters and Barbara got her fill. She said they were great, and I felt some of the weight of the world off my shoulders.

* * *

The public sale for French Open tennis tickets was announced. Bright and early I took the Métro to get my place in line. It was already about one hundred deep when I arrived. Three hours later, having read every word in the *Herald Tribune* standing up, I was lucky enough to get tickets. People near me identified scalpers they recognized from year to year. One even tried to sneak in line, and a policeman forcibly removed him. I wish I could have found a policeman so easily in earlier confrontations with pickpockets.

Barbara had been waiting so long at the apartment she was certain I was dead, lying in a gutter in France. When the doorbell rang she had no doubt it was the gendarmes wanting her to claim my body. Actually, it was me, alive and with tickets.

We decided that day to be typical tourists and went up the Eiffel Tower for the great views of Paris in its glorious splendor of flowers and trees in full bloom.

* * *

A few days later we made a second try for the hot chocolate at Angelina's tea room, which was like drinking a thick chocolate bar. Then we walked down the rue de Rivoli toward the elegant Place de la Concorde, stopping in a few stores along the way.

"Oh, my God! I've lost my Mother's Day present," Barbara blurted out in panic. It was a pin we had purchased two days previously which she loved. I thought for a moment she was going to be in tears and felt so bad for her. We recalled seeing the pin on her jacket earlier, while stopping in a store to look at a piece of costume jewelry. We knew she had it then, because she had held the costume jewelry up against her jacket.

We rapidly retraced our steps on the rue de Rivoli, our eyes pinned to the sidewalk, checking each store where we had stopped until we got back to the costume jewelry shop. Unfortunately, we found nothing, and Barbara's depression was obvious. She was about to cry when she put her hand up to her shoulder and across the pocket below on her chest. Feeling something, she suddenly threw her fingers into the pocket, and there it was. Her pin had fallen off her jacket right into her pocket. The look of joy on her face was radiant. Her disconsolate feeling had been as much due to her guilt about losing a gift she had just received from me as it had been the loss itself.

We retraced our steps to the most lovely street in the world, the Champs-Élysées. Heading toward the Arc de Triomphe, we passed the President's Palace with beautiful flower gardens and Georges Pompidou's statue. Huge trees lined the length of the street.

On the left was the Grand Palais art museum, before Boulevard Franklin Roosevelt and Avenue Montaigne cross the Champs. A circle there, Rond-Point des Champs-Élysées, has six grand fountains surrounded by flower beds in the shape of four-leaf clovers.

Recently the city eliminated side roadways, creating sidewalks where cars used to drive. Now vehicles come down the center of the street with spacious sidewalks. There are walking paths, trees, flowers, and always an empty bench on which to sit.

An Aside

The city has no shortage of tourists, but in June and July they pour in like a river that has overflown its banks. We've had the luxury of avoiding Paris when the largest crowds are there. Though we've never been there in August, it is almost like a national holiday. Many business establishments close for the month. In restaurant guides it is common to see the following, "closed Saturday lunch, all day Sunday and August."

In August the Parisians go to the beaches. They're less concerned about a loss of income than a style of life. Tourists who have been there then tell me they love Paris in August. There are enough establishments open to fill their needs and the city is empty.

Present

Paris was having its major antique show of the year. Vendors come from all over Europe to this fair, held on both sides of the Seine near the

Bastille. Barbara decided there were gifts we still had to buy, to say nothing of more "things" for our home. What will happen to those "things" when we're gone? The family will probably have a yard sale, and all that junk will find its way back to the Paris fair to keep the economy growing.

We remained in the vicinity and went to the Musée Cognacq-Jay. This private collection of art and furnishings was accumulated by the family who owned one of Paris's major department stores. To have been collected by one couple, it was quite impressive.

Staying in Paris for so long allowed us to be half tourists, half locals. Cooking in on occasion, getting to know local merchants, going to the movies, or just sitting in the parks made us feel like residents of Paris. But that didn't stop us from going up on the Eiffel Tower and walking the Champs-Élysées like the tourists. Then one evening, when night was falling, we took part in the ultimate tourist attraction. We went to the Seine and took the hour ride on the river with the city lit up. It was touristy, but beautiful.

The boat, one of many passing each other on the Seine, was full. We were seated next to two young girls from New Orleans, having the time of their lives. It was spring in Paris and they were on the boat in shorts, bare-legged, on a cold night. Barbara and I were bundled up, but nothing bothered these girls. Their adrenaline was keeping them warm.

We eavesdropped, one of the drifters' favorite pastimes, and smiled when one turned to the other and said in all seriousness, "This reminds me of New Orleans."

Nothing was probably more striking than passing under the Eiffel Tower fully lit.

* * *

Paris has two subway systems. Everyone uses the Métro, with so many lines that one can get anywhere in the city by connecting two of them. But there is a second subway system, which we had never used. It's newer than the Métro and is quite different. There are four lines, with spurs that go off from them. Each line travels out to suburban areas with widely spaced stops that interconnect with the Métro system. Travelers to suburban areas can take a Métro to an interconnection and switch to their suburban train.

We were living only a very short walk from a connecting station for the other line, the RER, so we decided to try it. The trains are more modern and look like real railway trains. In just three stops we covered a significant distance in a very short time.

An Aside

Having told you about a different form of transportation in Paris, I feel compelled to say something about driving in Paris. I've driven there many times without difficulty, but there is a fable that if you drive up the Champs-Élysées and get into the traffic circle around the Arc de Triomphe, chances are you will drive around the circle, unable to get out, and never be heard from again. Actually it isn't that bad. Cars move rather rapidly, but they do drive on the right side of the street, as in the U.S. That's a big help!

Parking there is the funniest thing. It's so difficult, people leave their cars on the sidewalk. To counteract that, Paris has many streets where the city has placed three-foot-high metal stantions on the street side of the sidewalk along the curb. They're about six feet apart so no one can drive up on to the sidewalk. It was the only way to stop cars from parking there. The stantions aren't found on the corner where pedestrians are crossing, and I've seen cars driven up on the sidewalk at the corner and left there, blocking all pedestrian traffic. When it comes to parking, this wonderful city is definitely a little crazy.

Present

The RER took us to a recommended restaurant, Au Bon Accueil, which was packed with French professionals, all very well dressed. Some sitting near us were Americans working in Paris. One was with the American Embassy.

Eavesdropping again? I frequently wonder, are we the only ones eavesdropping on restaurant conversation? If that seems rude, the people at the neighboring tables at times speak so loudly, they obviously don't mind. It's impossible not to hear the conversation, especially if you lean and turn your ear in their direction. At times it's awfully interesting.

After lunch it was off to Les Invalides, a grand building we've seen from the Place de la Concorde a number of times, but had never entered. It is the museum of French military history, including detailed information about World Wars I and II.

Then we walked to the Rodin, where one can see five hundred sculptures by this phenomenal man. Overwhelming does not adequately describe that sanctuary.

After dinner we went to the best deal in town. Concerts sponsored by Radio France at the Théâtre des Champs-Élysées provide unsold tickets one hour before the concert to students and senior citizens for 50 francs, $8.75. Barbara and I got two of the top-priced seats, even though the place was almost completely full. It was an all-Brahms concert with the National Symphony of France and Joshua Bell as the violin soloist.

* * *

The world was not created so that every day would be perfect. We were about to have a day much less than perfect. Barbara had an appointment to have her hair cut by a hairdresser she had known from the past. But the shop was quite far from our apartment.

Our arrangement was to meet at the hairdresser's later in the morning. Now, Barbara's sense of direction isn't spectacular. Worse than that, in the directions I had provided, the name of one of the streets was misspelled. When she left the Métro she got lost and found it necessary to use her quite good French language skills.

"How do I get to . . . ?" she asked in French of two teenagers.

They led her to her destination where, by then, she was already a half-hour late. But she did get a great haircut.

Meanwhile at the apartment I was in trouble as well. Assigned to do the laundry, everything white I removed from the washing machine, my underwear and the white towels, had turned a beautiful shade of Monet yellow. All subsequent attempts to take the color out with bleach failed. Barbara said it would be no problem.

"Just tell everyone that yellow underwear is the rage in Paris."

Finally the restaurant we had selected for lunch was closed. It had gone out of business. So we folded our tents and went home because every day isn't perfect.

But I had assumed when we went to sleep that the worst was over. We would awaken to a new day. If a day is going to go sour, though, you've got to allow it the full day.

We went to sleep surrounded by our quiet courtyard. In possibly an hour or so, a storm began that could wake the dead. The thunder sounded as if it was striking in our very bedroom, with one clash after another, seconds apart. It continued for about half an hour before suddenly ending. Obviously we were unable to sleep during that show of nature. Finally, we dozed off, when suddenly at about 4:00 in the morning a new problem arose. Someone in another apartment on the courtyard turned up a boom box to its full power with rock-and-roll. It was a Friday night, and the possibility that a neighbor was mildly inebriated was not out of the question. Within minutes another Frenchman was screaming, at the top of his lungs, for the music to be turned off. He was successful in his efforts. Nevertheless the blast of music and the shouting awakened us once again. This time it took a little while before we could get back to sleep and finally end the day.

* * *

Barbara had made her final purchases, including more of the wonderful chiffon scarfs. She had accumulated a number of them to bring back as gifts. During previous trips to France, Printemps would take all the charge slips and if they totaled over 1,200 francs, about $200, the tax would be rebated. We were well in excess of that.

Since we were last in France, the law had changed. The purchases in excess of 1,200 francs all had to be made on the same day. Unfortunately we had divided up our purchases on different days. On two separate days we had purchased about 1,100 francs' worth of items each time. Wasn't that brilliant? For each of those days we received no rebate. The woman at the desk felt so bad for us, she asked if the store could give Barbara a gift. Guess what it was, a scarf! It was just what we needed, another scarf.

In the evening we had dinner in a restaurant with tables packed together. A couple from Ireland, seated next to us, gave us a history lesson about Ireland and England. On the opposite side was a couple from Spain. When we told them we were from San Antonio, where the majority of the population is Hispanic, they described how the United States had taken Texas away from the Spaniards in Mexico. We felt a little guilt, but not enough to dampen the fun as we talked to our interesting dinner companions.

Barbara completely confused the waitress with our fractured French. "Je voudrais de foie de vieux." Translation: I would like some old liver. She meant to request *foie de veau*, veal liver.

The waitress didn't think that was available, but realizing what Barbara was trying to order, broke into laughter.

It was reminiscent of a time I was requesting a restaurant reservation by phone. I was supposed to be asking the gentleman at what hour they closed. It should have been "À *quelle heure êtes-vous fermé?*" The phonetics of that would be "a kel err et-vu fermay."

Instead of that I said, "*A kel air et-vu ferm?*" The closest translation of that, since it actually makes no grammatical sense, is "In what parking lot do you farm?"

It is not difficult to understand that there was no response at the other end of the line. After a while the owner figured out what this crazy American was asking.

* * *

Earlier in the book I described a couple we met in the military cemetery in Gallipoli. We talked for five minutes, made friends, and planned to see them in London. They were arranging for us to go to the theatre several times during our stay there.

We arrived early for the Eurostar "Chunnel" train, due to the requirement, no one can board later than twenty minutes before departure time. Like the military, they ask you to rush and wait. Boarding didn't begin until ten minutes before departure. The train was empty, but wonderful. I believe their economic philosophy is faulty. If a business's volume is insufficient, prices should be lowered. They believe in raising prices to make up the loss. Ultimately, that results in bigger losses and even threatens its existence.

An unusual breakfast of a terrine of meat and a Greek salad was served. It was quite good, if strange for that time of the day. The time under the Channel itself is very brief, only nineteen minutes. Barbara had thought it would make her nervous, but it is no different than being in the Métro. She read her book as if nothing at all was going on. The entire trip was less than three hours. However, the speed is to the credit of the French. On the French side the train runs at about 180 miles per hour, twice as fast as on the English side. England has still not upgraded its rail system to allow for that high a rate of speed.

On arrival we checked into our hotel, The Claverly, and went to lunch at Clarke's, a highly recommended London restaurant. The prices were much higher than in France.

As I meandered through the streets of London, there was one thing I wasn't going to miss from Paris, the constant presence of doggy-do. The reason became obvious after a short while. Posted on a sidewalk pole was a local ordinance. "Anyone allowing a dog to foul the footpath will be subject to prosecution." The language was clear and British.

Being in London, we wanted to take advantage of what was offered. A very special thing we can't share in France is the theatre.

We met Jan and Tony, our Gallipoli friends, in the West End and saw *The Herbal Bed*, a play about William Shakespeare's daughter. Then we walked to a restaurant and had an evening filled with reminiscing about Turkey. It was great, except for ...

It was well past midnight when we arrived back at our hotel. We had exited the restaurant rather quickly, realizing how late the hour was and that Tony and Jan had a full day's work ahead of them. The restaurant's exit area was very dark. We jumped into the taxi and were whisked back to our Knightbridge address.

Back home my first words to Barbara were, "These are not our umbrellas." It was almost 1:00 in the morning. At that hour there was nothing to do. The next day I called but no one else was asking for their umbrellas.

After a very tasty full English breakfast including kippers and eggs, Barbara and I were off to see London. The Victoria and Albert Museum had a show of English fashions from 1947 to 1997. We spent two and a half hours there, mostly at the special exposition. The museum, constructed under the supervision of Victoria's beloved Prince Albert, is huge. We covered 10 percent of the museum in that two and a half hours, giving some indication of its vastness. We had lunch nearby at Gilbert's and made the mandatory visit to the most wonderful department store in the world, Harrod's. That store has always emphasized service when most of consumer sales are geared to discounts and no service. We passed through their food halls and into the fashion jewelry department, where we did spot a lovely pin, but didn't purchase it.

On our second night in London our gracious hosts got tickets for *Martin Guerre*, written by the creators of *Les Misérables*. Though quite good, the show was not up to the standards of *Les Misérables*. But we were anxious to see it, as one of Jan's clients had a leading role. The first number went without a hitch when suddenly the curtain came down and the house lights up. We couldn't imagine what was happening. Then ...

"Mr. ———," fortunately not Jan's client, "playing the role of ———, has fallen backstage and injured himself. He will not be able to perform this evening. The role will be played by his understudy, Mr. ———. The performance will resume in five minutes."

In all the performances we had seen in the past, we'd never experienced that. The remainder of the show was uneventful. Afterward they took us to The Ivy restaurant, filled with theatrical personalities whom Jan knew. At midnight we said our final goodbyes to Jan and Tony, thanking them for their excessive kindness while we were in London.

On our last short day in London I needed to get an early start because I had two chores to accomplish before lunch and a theatre matinee. We had a gift for Jan and Tony from Fauchon's in Paris and had forgotten to bring it to the theatre the night before.

To reach their office I needed to take two trains on the Underground, the first for just one stop and the second a long ride to a location in London I had never seen. We hadn't been moving for more than a minute when we stopped in the tunnel for half an hour. Now I was behind schedule. When the second train arrived at its stop I had no idea where their office was located. After a while, I could tell by the building numbers I was going in the opposite direction of my destination. I was almost an hour behind schedule.

I dropped off the package and returned to the Underground, but found the signs difficult to follow. The map indicated I was going in the right direction. I had a copy of the *Herald Tribune* and began reading. The next time I looked up and saw the name of a station, it was totally foreign to me. A fast glance at the map in the railway car revealed the train I was on went off on a spur in a totally different direction. My God, what a mess I was in! I got off at the next stop and crossed to the opposite side of the tracks to return.

Through all these changes I found myself in an industrial area of the city. I rushed to get a train to take me back to where I belonged, but found I had gone so far out of the range of my ticket, it was no longer acceptable. Fortunately, a guard was there, and when I explained my plight to him I was allowed to go through the turnstile without a ticket. I was lucky to be able to describe my misfortune in English. Of course, in Paris, the system is so simple I had never found myself in such a jam. There's not the slightest question in my mind that the Paris Métro system is far superior to London's or New York's.

When I got off the train, I was an hour and a half late. I knew Barbara would be in a panic, calling the police and all the hospitals to find out where my body could be found. I had called the hotel, but she was out of the room. So I left a message.

As late as it was, I was committed to stopping in Harrod's to pick up the lovely pin we had seen the day before as a gift for her. The purchase was completed quickly and I returned to find her in a semipanic in the lobby. I got a hug and kiss, just for being alive.

She told me, as per our understanding, she was not at the hotel when I called because she had gone to Harrod's to pick up a needlepoint project to work on this summer. But the pattern she wanted was not in stock, so she was going to wait and buy it at home.

"But don't worry. As a consolation to myself when I couldn't get it, I went to the jewelry department and bought the moon pin for myself."

"You bought the moon pin ... the moon pin?"

I pulled the bag out of my pocket.

"I bought the moon pin as a gift for you. I guess they had more than one."

We dashed back to Harrods and returned one before going to lunch. It certainly can be difficult buying gifts for some people!

Our stay in London ended wonderfully with lunch at the Oak Room, our best meal in London. Then we were off to the theatre to see *The Goodbye Girl*. It was a wild day.

After carrying our suitcases from hotel to restaurant to theatre, the Underground took us to Waterloo Station to get the Eurostar train back through the Chunnel and home.

It was a wonderful three-day trip. London and Paris are grand, but so different. London is truly alive. Though very crowded, it's clean as can be. The people were warm and friendly and it's a big plus that they speak English. London's buildings are marvelous, but with an austere feeling which, for me, is surpassed by the romantic beauty of Paris.

There is no comparison in the food. The French have it over everyone.

* * *

Back in Paris, on my last trip to the laundromat, I saw two young American women come in. They were in a state of complete confusion. Sympathetically I began to tell them how to use all the equipment step by step. I showed them how to obtain soap, start the machines, and set the temperature, and how the dryers were to be operated.

"I have the feeling your laundry has been done by your mothers in the past."

They agreed and added, "You've been so sweet to us. How long have you been working here?"

Well, then I knew where my next employment was going to be.

* * *

We had planned this day for a long time, but were ecstatic with our good fortune of perfect weather for a trip to Claude Monet's home, studio, lily pond, and gardens. We took the train from St. Lazare Station to Vernon, and then taxied to Giverny.

Monet's residence for more than the last forty years of his life was wonderful to behold. It was an absolute explosion of color, even though this early in the season many flowers had not yet opened their blossoms. The roses and most of the geraniums were still closed at this time of the year. In the house, Barbara and I loved the kitchen and dining room, colored in very gorgeous blues and yellows. We won't soon forget that day.

While wandering through the area someone called out, "Herb." It was Joanne and "Wig" Wigodsky from back home. Here we were in Giverny, and two couples from San Antonio bumped into each other accidentally. After seeing Monet's beautiful setting, we joined them at a new local museum, the Museum of American Impressionists in Giverny.

* * *

It was evening by the time we returned to Paris, and time to pack again. We were on the move. the next morning we were heading for Brussels to meet our friends Louise and Mike Beldon, who had come to Europe to visit their son and daughter-in-law. They had friends in Brussels and were going there with their children for the weekend. We were game for everything this year. It would be my first time in Brussels or anywhere in Belgium. Barbara had been there briefly many years before.

We arrived by TGV train in Brussels in two hours. Seated next to us was a very nice young German student who had been in France visiting his girlfriend. He was starting a thirteen-month obligation to civil service. Compulsory service in Germany requires either ten months in the military or thirteen months of nonmilitary service. He said he would drive a school bus mornings and care for church lawns in the afternoon.

Louise and Mike Beldon's friend's brother, Nicholas Blake, picked us up at the train station and took us to our hotel. Of course it was necessary to first find him at the train station. As soon as we walked into the main hall of the station someone said, "Keysers?" Nicholas was obviously advised that I look like Yul Brynner and immediately spotted us. Total baldness has its advantages.

The four Beldons joined us for lunch without our local hosts. We chose a restaurant suggested by the concierge at a downtown hotel. I like to ask the advice of a local. We thought the meal was acceptable.

The city has a large central plaza with crowds of tourists milling through the small streets surrounding the square called the Grande Place. In that square there is a church with spectacular architecture, constructed over a period of hundreds of years. Our hosts, guiding us in the afternoon, noted the building had many strange errors. The entrance was way off center and the surrounding architectural forms were all askew. In one portion the windows had squared-off tops instead of the arches, as in the others. The Bakers explained that multiple architects had supervised the construction over the centuries. One even committed suicide. I guess some of the errors got to him.

There were a number of very old buildings in the beautiful square. Each one had architecture and carvings representing different guilds or trade unions.

I asked about the history of Belgium and was told it became the country it is today in 1830.

"What was it before that?" we asked.

"Everybody came in to conquer us. They made us a part of France and Germany and England and. ... About twice a year somebody else wanted this country."

Our day culminated with Francis and Dominique Blake, our hosts, taking us to a wonderful dinner at La Taverne du Passage, a restaurant catering primarily to locals.

"Where did you have lunch?" Francis inquired.

"At a small restaurant on the Grande Place."

"And what did you eat?"

"A dish called *schleump*."

... Off to See the World · 191

"*Schleump?* No, you didn't eat that vile food they just feed to soldiers, did you?"

We cowered in our seats, ashamed of our ignorance. *Schleump* is like shepherd's pie. It's mashed potatoes mixed with vegetables. We all thought it was quite tasty.

In the morning we took a train to Brugge. The city is old and hasn't changed a great deal. The map recommended a walking tour and a boat ride through the canals. Both sounded fine. But first we stopped at an outdoor tourist restaurant for lunch. Louise, Maria, and I had standard fare. Barbara, Jonathan, and Mike consumed enough mussels to feed an army. Thank God none of them were on a diet.

Stopping in shops on our walk, Barbara won the award for the most purchases. Then we took the boat trip down the canals past the old homes and public buildings.

After walking for several hours, we were no longer near the point where we had started, having taken a bus from the station into the center of town. Fatigue was beginning to set in. A quick stop at a bakery, requesting information from the proprietor, revealed that our walking had brought us nearer the train station. So we could skip the return bus ride.

Though that might not appear to be significant, it was an extremely important revelation. It resulted in a sigh of relief and a moment of excitement. The sigh of relief was because we had spent, in bits and pieces, all the Belgian cash in our possession. We had some concerns about whether there would be enough money for the bus. The excitement was because the little cash we had left was now free for use.

Louise immediately said, "Let's buy a loaf of bread. I'm starving and I'm not certain when we'll get dinner."

It wasn't surprising this group would think of food as soon as coins jingled in their pockets. But in all fairness, Louise, Mike, Jonathan, and Maria were going by car directly from Brussels to Germany after the train ride back from Brugge, while we were on our way to Paris. Missing dinner for them was a definite possibility. We got a loaf and ate it on the street as we walked toward the train station.

Jonathan reminded us of another dumb thing we had done by buying the bread. Their car was parked in a lot in Brussels and they had no cash left to get it out.

Mike reassured him there would be no problem. Once they got back to the station, there would be an ATM to get a fresh feed of Belgian money. On arrival at the Brussels train station Barbara wanted to use the restroom, which required 10 francs in exact coins. I had 100 francs, about $3, left, but no coins. Then I remembered I had to retrieve the luggage we had stored at the station in Brugge and I got change in coins. We got the luggage, used the restroom, and still had a few Belgian francs left. Finally, trying to get rid of the last bits of local currency, we searched for something inexpensive and bought a candy bar with the last few francs. So a wonderful day with the very sweet Beldon family ended with a sweet Belgian chocolate candy bar on the train.

* * *

We made a decision not to spend our last few days in Paris indoors. There'd be no museums these last three days. We couldn't go to the Louvre anyway, as they were in the middle of a strike. Someone's always on strike. The short-term visitors were extremely disappointed with the Louvre closure. But I guess that was why they chose to strike.

While walking we stopped in a Louis Vuitton shop, trying to replace a wallet stolen from Barbara a year ago. The prices were much better than in the United States, but the product line was completely different, so Barbara didn't find what she wanted. However, we had a wonderful conversation with a saleswoman working there. She had completed seven years of college education, but was unable to find work in her field. Unemployment in France was extremely high and very depressing for the local residents.

We chose L' Epi Dupin for lunch and then continued walking down the Seine, and across one of the bridges for the breathtaking view. On the right bank, as one of our last purchases, we bought a toaster as a gift to our landlords to replace one that had broken.

* * *

This was the one day we were going to the French Open tennis matches at Roland Garros. Up early, we did some chores before leaving. Medications were so much cheaper in France than back home that we decided to buy some of the most expensive ones before we left. The main one was a preparation I had written about earlier in this book, gingko biloba, which Barbara takes once a day to improve memory.

She decided against buying the French version because they were to be taken three times daily.

"Barbara, you're right about the French pills being a nuisance because they have to be taken more often, but do you realize yours are supposed to be taken twice daily?"

She shook her head with self-annoyance and said, "I know. But I always forget!"

The gingko's really doing a great job.

The major excitement of the day occurred between the matches. Barbara and I had gone out into the open grounds of Roland Garros, where the crowds, the food services, and the booths selling everything are located. It was like a glorious, giant circus.

I was carrying a string bag with our sweaters, hats, books about the matches, etc. A middle-aged Oriental man, about forty-five years old, came past me holding a tennis bag that had a zipper. As he swung his bag past mine, a very unusual thing happened. The zipper on his tennis bag caught on a string of my bag. We were attached. We both began laughing as we manipulated the strings and the zipper to detach them.

In the process of separating them a group of about six girls began screaming and three of them chased the Oriental man as he walked away from me. With pens and programs in their hands, they shouted at him.

I immediately asked the girls, "Who is he that makes you so anxious to get his autograph?"

"Michael Chang!" they shouted.

I assured them that the gentleman they were chasing was not Michael Chang and was at least twice his age.

"He isn't? Oooohhhhh!"

* * *

The last full day had a sad note to it. The year had been so wonderful, and suddenly all these experiences were about to end. There was a lot of packing to be accomplished, without choices. Everything was leaving on this final leg. Everything, that is, except for items we inadvertently left behind. The apartment, though lovely, was quite small. You'd think that it would be impossible to leave something behind, but we did.

We couldn't bear to miss one of our favorite restaurants, Le Maraicher, on this last day. An amazing thing happened there. It had been our custom to bring a menu book with translations whenever we went out to eat. Somewhere along the way we lost our book and had to buy another.

When we entered Le Maraicher the owner said, "I think you left this here last time."

It was our original menu book. Now we have two.

After packing we went to Procope for one last chance at Barbara's favorite oysters. They had gotten to know us so well, a big greeting was forthcoming on our arrival.

I doubt that we will ever take a trip this long in the future, but I wouldn't have passed it up for anything. We had the time of our lives, met so many people, tried new and exciting experiences, and became part of a community instead of just tourists.

All of the friends who joined us were significantly responsible for how great this experience turned out to be. We can never thank them enough.

People all over the world are pretty much the same. Given a chance, they're great. We adore traveling and enjoyed all the countries we visited, but most of all France. And to Paris . . . the two drifters love each other a lot, but they are madly in love with you.